KNIFE, LIFE AND BRONZES

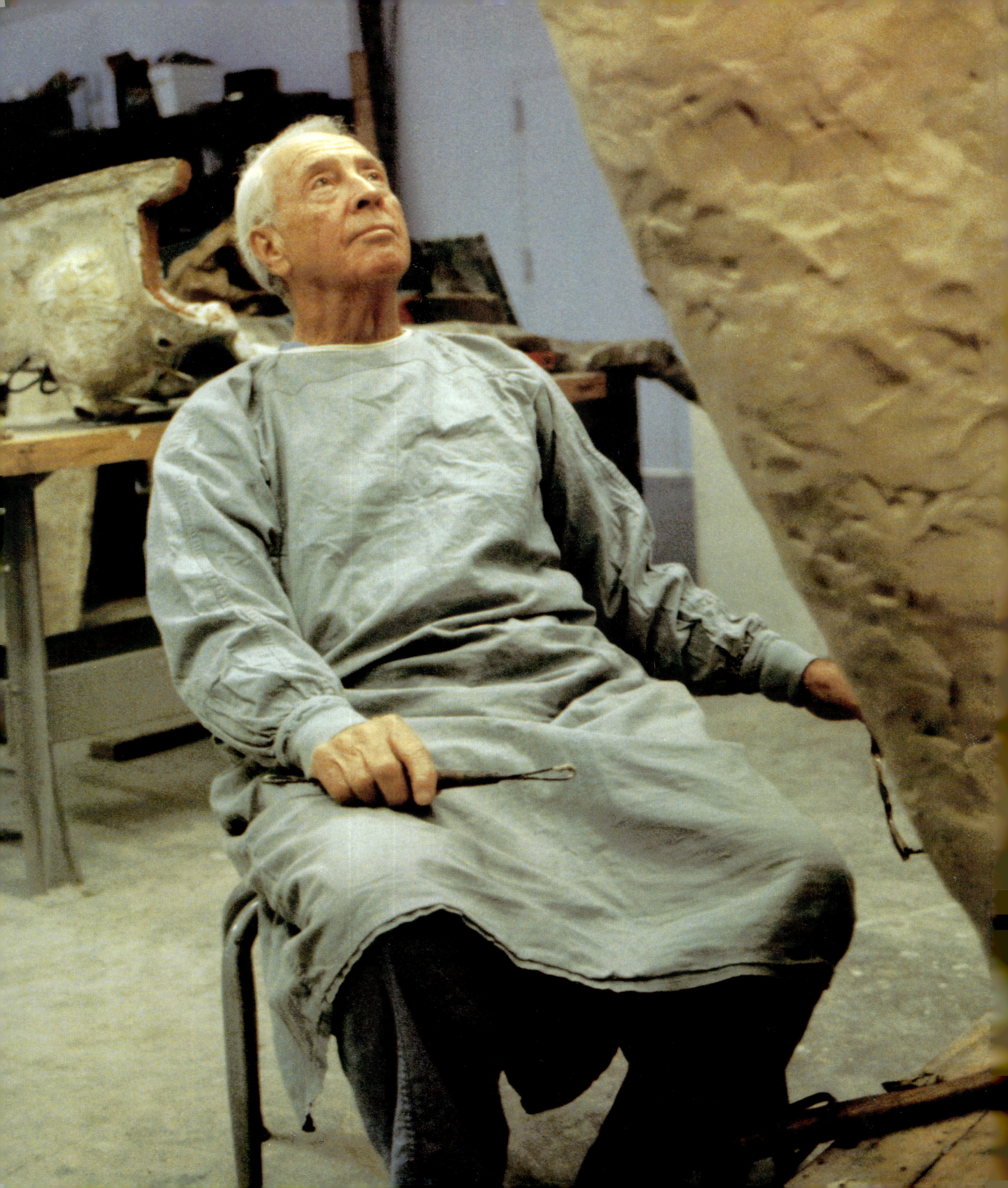

KNIFE, LIFE AND BRONZES

Sculpture and Vignettes

by KAARE NYGAARD

NYGAARART LTD., *Scarsdale, New York 1986*

Distributed by Pace University Press, New York

Also by Kaare K. Nygaard, M.D.

Hemorrhagic Diseases:
Photo-Electric Study of Blood Coagulability
Mosby, 1941

The Spirit of Man:
The Sculpture of Kaare Nygaard
1983

Book design by Philip Grushkin

Text edited by Nora Beeson

Published by Nygaarart Ltd.
Scarsdale, New York 10583

Distributed by Pace University Press
Pace Plaza, New York, N.Y. 10038

Printed and bound in Japan

Library of Congress Catalog Card Number: 86–90671

Contents

TO *Martha Graham*

IN AWE OF THE PAST

IN LOVE OF THE PRESENT

IN GRATITUDE FOR INSPIRATION

FROM AN ALWAYS CREATING SPIRIT.

I AM A DANCER

"I am a dancer. I believe we learn by practice. Whether it means to learn to dance by practicing dancing or to learn to live by practicing living, the principles are the same. In each it is the performance of a dedicated, precise set of acts, physical or intellectual, from which comes the shape of achievement, a sense of one's being, a satisfaction of spirit. One becomes in some area an athlete of God. Practice means to perform, over and over again in the face of all obstacles, some act of vision, of faith, of desires. Practice is a means of inviting the perfection desired.

Even as I write time has begun to make today yesterday—the past. Even the most brilliant scientific discoveries will in time change and perhaps grow obsolete, as new scientific manifestations emerge.

But art is eternal; for it reveals the inner landscape which is the soul of man"

MARTHA GRAHAM, *1950*
"I am a dancer"

WHAT IS GREAT ART?

No work of art is Great Art till it has passed the final test of fire. That sizzling heat can free the abilities, the emotions, the associations of the viewer and the listener. It allows him an entry into that mysterious process so hopefully begun by the artist and sometimes successfully completed by the sensitive audience. It finalizes in one fortunate second new knowledge, new experience, fresh views and vistas, something much worthwhile, intangible, while still imperceptibly filled with life-awareness.

Great Art does this—that is its justification, its challenge.

Great Art is aggressive. At times it kills. It never annihilates. It never evaporates. It creates always new problems and new miseries and new meaningful beauties.

Great Art comes *from* humans.

Great Art is *directed* at humans.

It is generously offered to humans with the willing gift to perceive and with the urgency to involve themselves in the eternal, life-blessed creations of all nature, including us.

Great Art and life are symbiotic. They are one and like us great art never remains. It is eternally changing.

KAARE NYGAARD, *1986*

WHAT ARTISTIC AND SCIENTIFIC EXPERIENCE HAVE IN COMMON

"Where the world ceases to be the scene of our personal hopes and wishes, where we face it as free beings admiring, asking and observing, there we enter the realm of Art and Science. If what is seen and experienced is portrayed in the language of logic, we are engaged in science; if it is communicated through forms whose connections are not accessible to the conscious mind but are recognized intuitively as meaningful, then we are engaged in art. Common to both is the loving devotion to that which transcends personal concerns and volition."

ALBERT EINSTEIN
January 27, 1921

Albert Einstein, the Human Side: New Glimpses from His Archives.
Selected and edited by Helen Dukas and Banesh Hoffman. Princeton, Princeton University Press, 1979.
Printed with permission of the Hebrew University of Jerusalem, Israel

Preface

The sculpture of Kaare Nygaard is a three-dimensional statement of a personal philosophy. It reveals a world of thought and feeling that has taken shape during the course of a lifetime of active practice as a brilliant surgeon. Now, with this book, we have his words to elaborate on what the forms have meant to him and how the different subjects of his sculptor's tools have helped to shape his outlook on life.

To know Dr. Nygaard personally is a rare experience. He is proud of his Scandinavian heritage and is capable of drawing himself up to full height and proudly referring to himself as a Viking. He means, by this, that it is in his blood to face with courage whatever life has in store for him. But he is also heir to the world's culture and intellectual tradition, as evidenced by his broad reading in many fields of interest. He has been the much admired friend of famous men and women in his time, yet he considers as his own highly valued friends a large number of modest and humble folk who probably consider their closeness to him one of the proudest achievements of their lives.

Visitors to Dr. Nygaard's home are often taken on a tour of his works, which in many respects resembles the text of his book. And while explanations are given with flourish and relish, one never has the feeling that the sculptor, who is the tour guide, has a shred of boastfulness in his remarks. He never tries to say what is good about a particular work of sculpture, but rather what he had in mind when creating it.

It is rare for a person who is so accomplished in one field as Dr. Nygaard has been in medicine to have not only the ability but the commitment to pursue a serious creative career in the arts. The body of work described in this volume makes it clear that its author was one of those outstanding human beings whose life has been blessed by two strains of activity, which have both complemented and contributed to each other. And it is the creative part of his life, as revealed in his words as well as his forms, that may well prove to be his most enduring legacy.

K.K. Nygaard has always striven to achieve the highest qualities in living, working, and creating. He has seen the best and the worst of human existence but never, so far as I know, wavered in the affirmation of and the commitment to the values he holds most dear. His words and sculpture are testimony to the breadth of his vision and the depth of his faith in humanity.

David Finn

Introduction

In this book I intend to write about my own work. I know I am on thin ice. I have a vivid memory of a half hour TV interview by my friend Alexander Calder.

It did not come off readily. The interviewer was perspiring. Sandy was laughing and giggling, seemingly having a good time while being bent on syllables.

The interviewer finally brought out an intriguing mobile. "Please, Mr. Calder! There are millions of your admirers out there looking at this great sculpture of yours. Please, tell them. What inspired you? What does it mean?"

Sandy was still giggling. "I don't know. I just made it."

This scene is humorous. It did at the same time represent Sandy Calder in all his honesty and integrity, mixed with speech limitations because of his Parkinson's disease. He was telling it as it was. He did not know how it came to him. And he did not insist that it had any meaning.

Many artists feel exactly that way about their work. They do not consciously understand those crucial power packets of the creative act. It comes to them in mysterious and hazy ways, frequently agonizing, rarely ecstatic.

Must I, therefore, capitulate on this very first page?

I don't wish to do that. There must be more to it!

As for my own works, I am responsible for each of them. They did not escape from me with an alibi. They came gratefully into existence and by necessity, as if I had been pregnant with them, one after the other.

And as to that gestation period, I would like to add a few words.

What do we mean by creating?

Let us fall back upon an old saying: *To create is to do something out of nothing or out of a cumbersome material.*

Who is a creator? I believe we are all creative. I believe it is a basic common, biologic human characteristic. I believe creativity is a significant biologic power, which was and is an essential spark plug of the entire history of evolution of the human being and his mind—as well as all nature.

I strongly sense that there must be more to it. The ability to shape, to form, to express, to make things come into being, that ability might be great. Still, I sense that there has to be a second component in order to learn *what to express, what to shape*, and *why* and *how.*

That second system is to be found in the human brain's sensitivity to monitor and record the motion and the emotions of the world surrounding us and residing within us.

That biologic mystery is the radar system, common to all of us, traveling throughout our lives in stormy weather or through calm seas. We have learned that some of us have more of it—or too much. And some not enough. We judge it from the reaction and the behavior of humans in our daily encounters.

Do all artists have too much of that monitoring sensitivity? What about Carravagio? Vincent van Gogh? Edvard Munch?

I don't believe they were great artists only because they were harboring hypersensitive souls.

In the making of a great artist go multitudes of life factors to be added to the gift of creativity and recording sensitivity.

I feel those artists succeeded *in spite of*—not because of—their turmoil to execute an overwhelming richness of great art. I believe they succeeded in accomplishing it because in all of them occurred that rare constellation of ample supply of creative necessity coupled with a painful sensitivity to the occult avalanches outside and inside their vibrating minds.

Creativity and sensitivity in the right measures ensure what most of us strive for in our days.

If combined in haphazard measures, the results might be socially unfortunate products like so-called geniuses or mentally defectives. And the differential might be quantitative only—not qualitative!

Therefore, I have conjured geniuses out of my vocabulary.

I believe in human beings. I am part of and constructively engaged in humanity. Thus I have lived a life of a surgeon and a sculptor with no conflict between them. The two activities have been two forms of work in one man's plain brain, both supplementing and enhancing the other.

I can see a straight road in my life from my operating room to my studio. Whatever can enhance life—freedom of pain and distress, or the joy of beauty and art—is what rounds out my ambition.

Rodin, quoting Leonardo da Vinci, defined sculpture this way: *"The science of sculpture is the science of the bumps and hollows."*

My problem has not been to unite the two disciplines. The surgeon remains the surgeon. In his work, however, in order to bring it successfully to fruition, there is a formative necessity and ability that come into daily play.

If this formative, at times imaginative, urgency is intentionally nurtured, it might spill over from operating into the studio, from the bleeding flesh into the blessed material of clay.

And what is made to fill the bumps and hollows represents the challenge every artist is confronted with from that crucial moment on.

What he brings into his bumps and hollows will be a reflection of his entire personality, his associations, his experiences, modified by his emotions and his ability.

I have been forced to bring with me experiences and associations of a painful, at times drastic, character. This is common to all surgeons: the challenge, dramatized by the closeness of the final issue, to be or not to be—and if possible to stay alive and to remain without too excruciating pain and distress.

For me it has been a unique mountain to try to climb together with the rest of mankind. Some of these trials are probably filling hollows. There is misery in some of them. I have willingly let it come through.

If my figures are filled with associations, I expect they are not foreign to my fellow man.

If they are expressing representational forms of a conventional flavor, I do not ask to make excuses on their behalf.

Pictorial art does not have the primary responsibility to carry within its boundaries all the miseries of the age. Nevertheless, it may not afford to exclude it all. This leaves the door ajar for my entry into the studio with soiled garments and an urgency to communicate.

I am aware that thereafter all depends upon *who* is trying to communicate, *with what means*, and, crucially, *with what message*.

If my work somehow can do that, through pure forms—or lack of forms—through subject matters, disguises, or simple statements, these figures should not mind having been incarcerated in the frozen form of bronze.

And neither should my words.

In the Sweat of Thy Face Shalt Thou Eat Bread

The first and cardinal sin was committed in the Garden of Eden. They disobeyed. Broke the word of God. They partook of the forbidden tree and its knowledge.

They learned the wrath of God who spoke thus: "In the sweat of thy face shalt thou eat bread, till thou return unto the ground; for out of it wast thou taken: for dust thou art, and unto dust shalt thou return" (Genesis 3:19).

God knew Adam. God meted out his punishment: throughout the globe over the ages, for Adam and all his myriads of descendents—hard labor. Throughout their waking hours, throughout their dark and anxious nights—hard labor.

The *tree of knowledge* is felled. Eden erased. By some, even God is assumed dead. His punishment upon a disobedient humanity still prevails in the sweat of its face.

In my not short span of life I can testify to the sweat, to the hunger for longer minutes of sleep through anxious nights. In wonder, also, that work has been gratifying to me and maybe meaningful to others.

Nonetheless, I shall be fully aware: God's decree of punishment is ravaging through human minds begging for mercy and redemption.

21″ × 11½″ × 17″

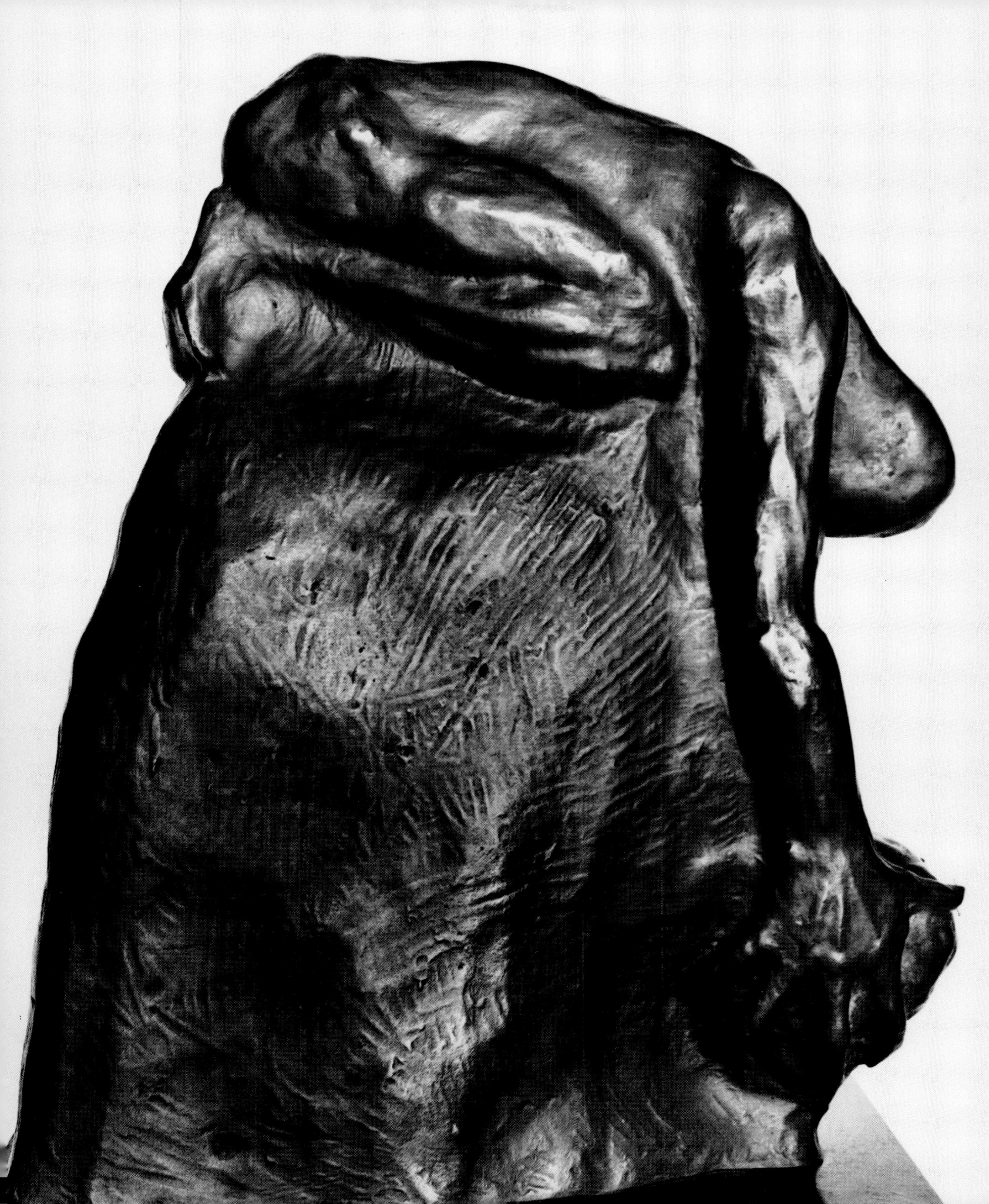

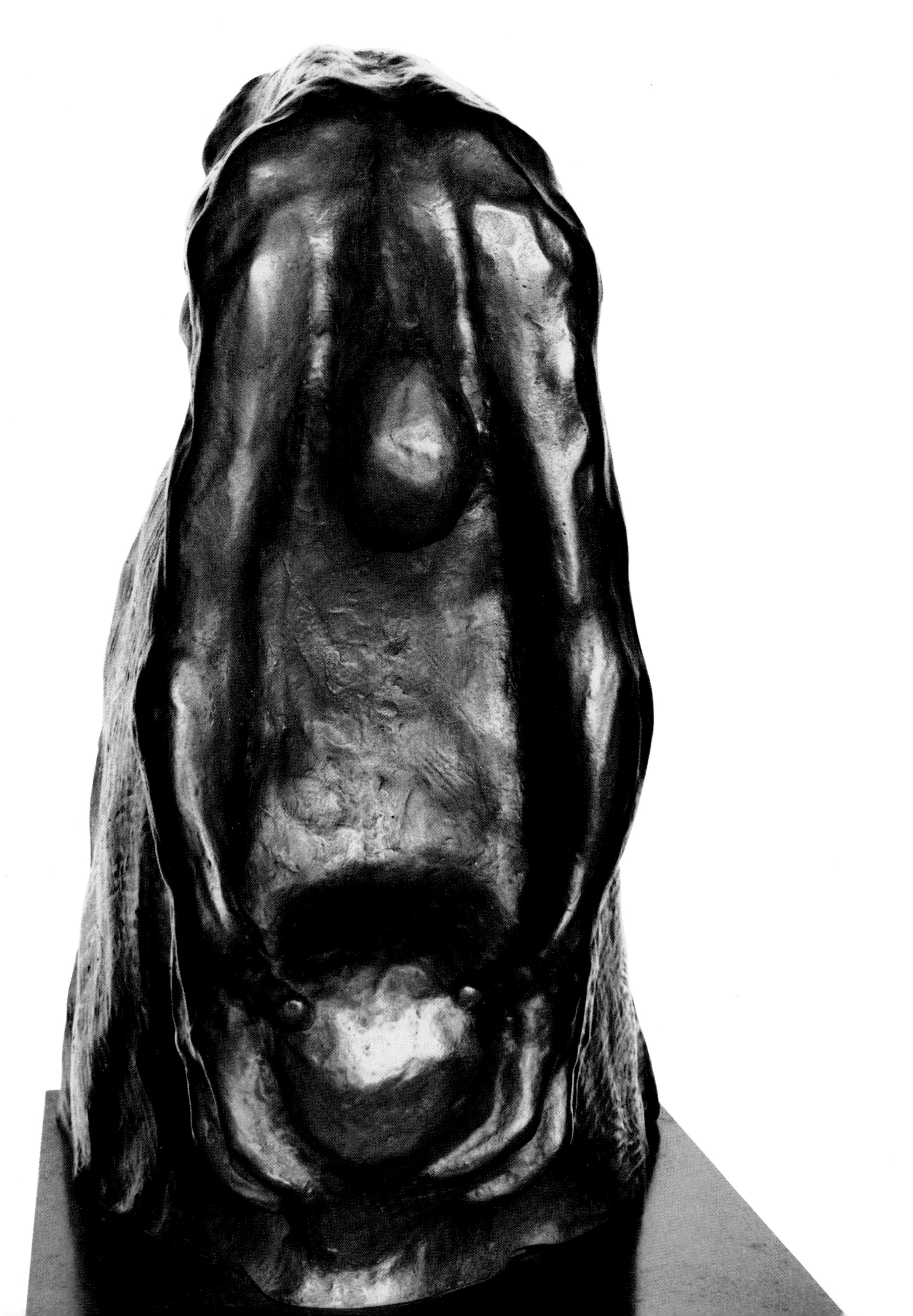

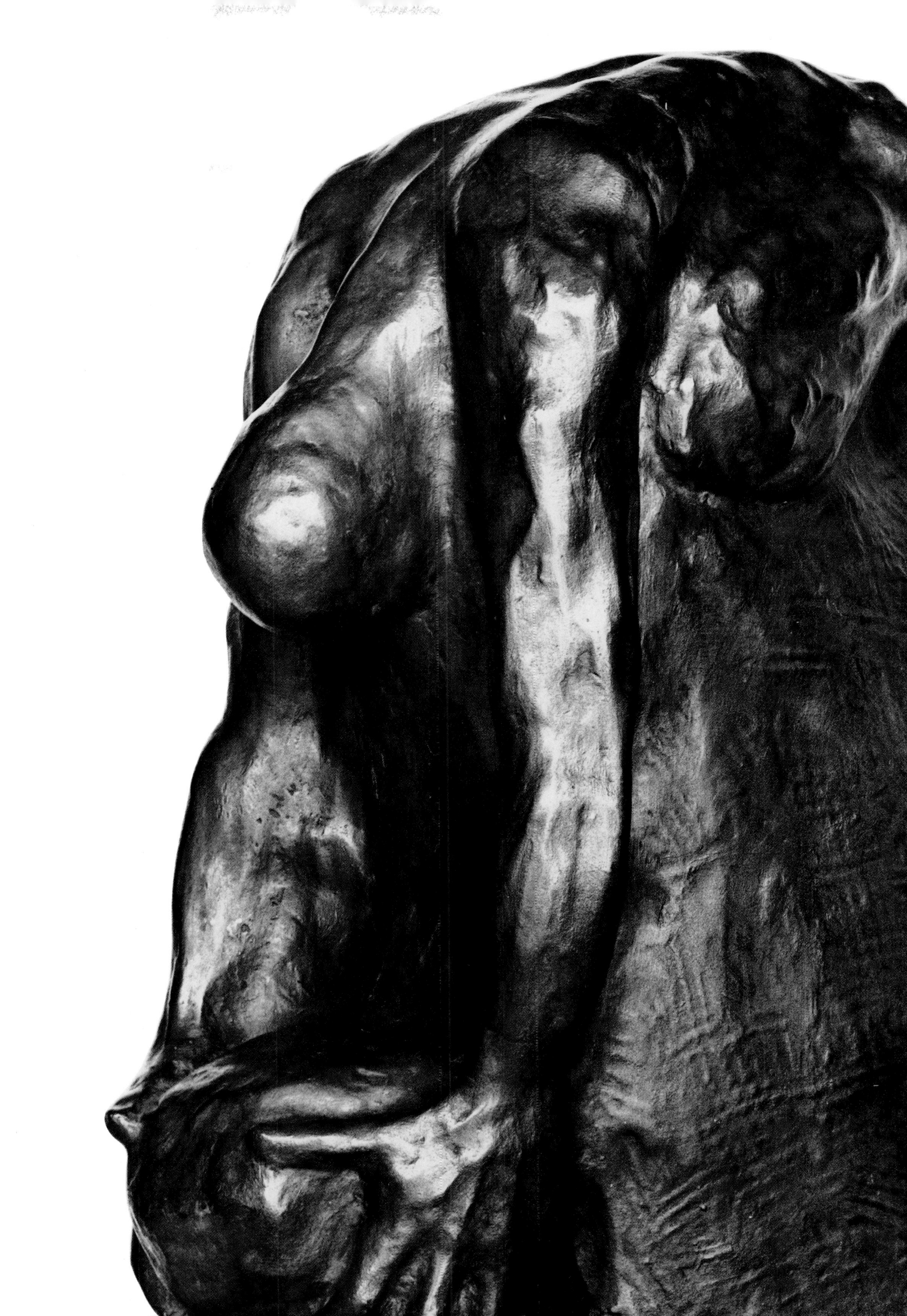

Walt Whitman

There can be monumentality
in a leaf of grass.
There can be grandeur
in misery.

15″ × 6″ × 6″

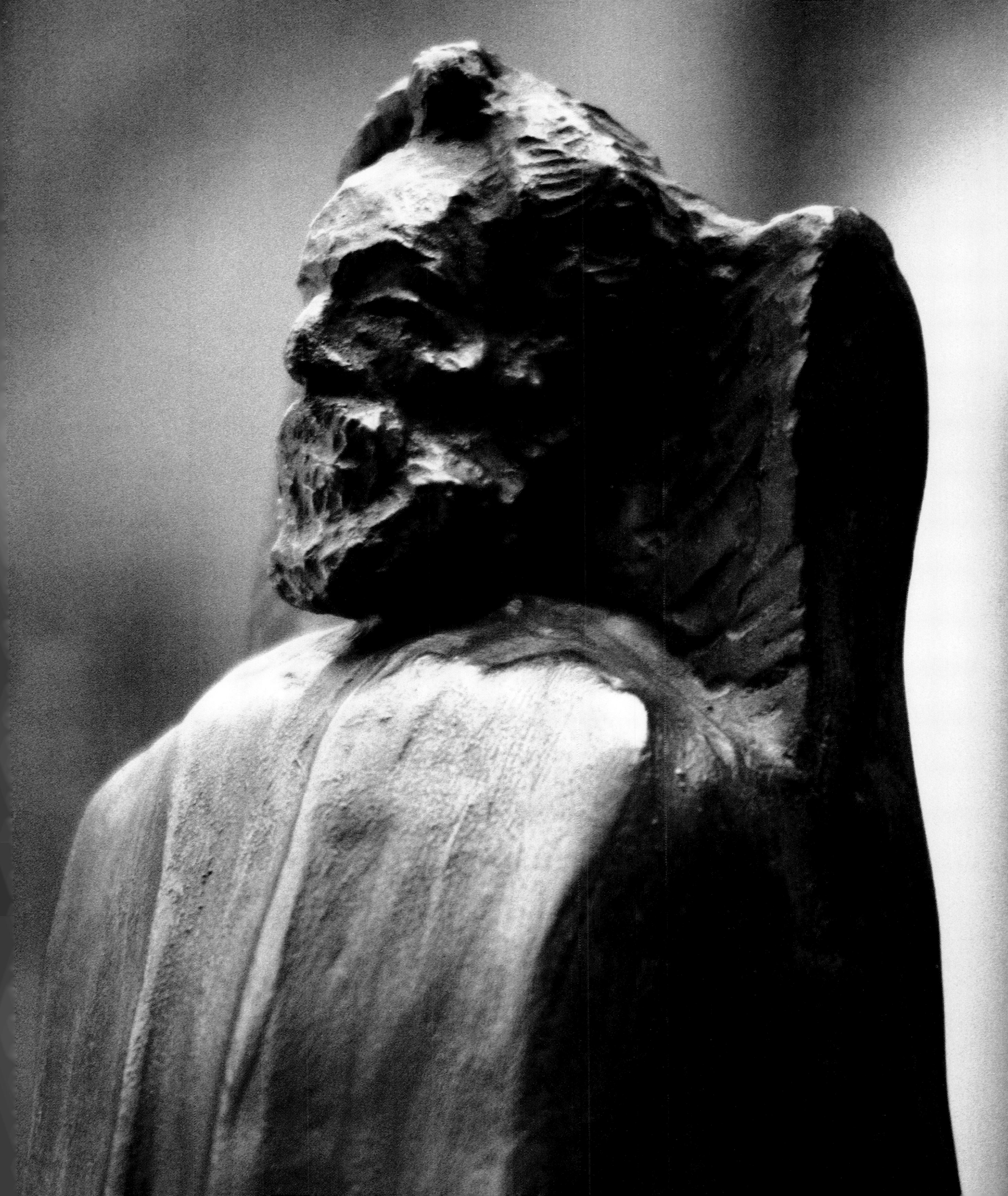

Moses

LET MY PEOPLE GO

35″ × 33″ × 24″

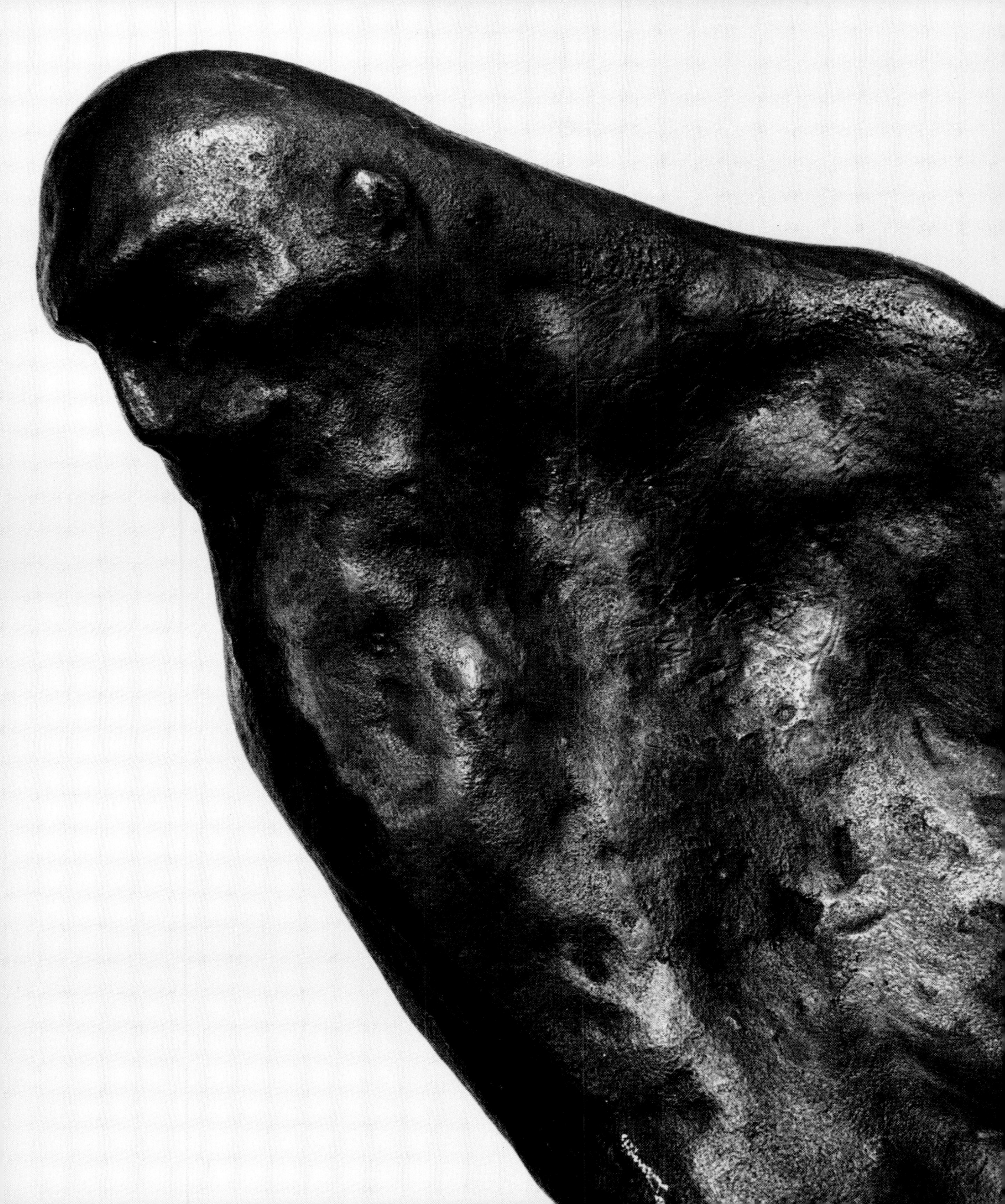

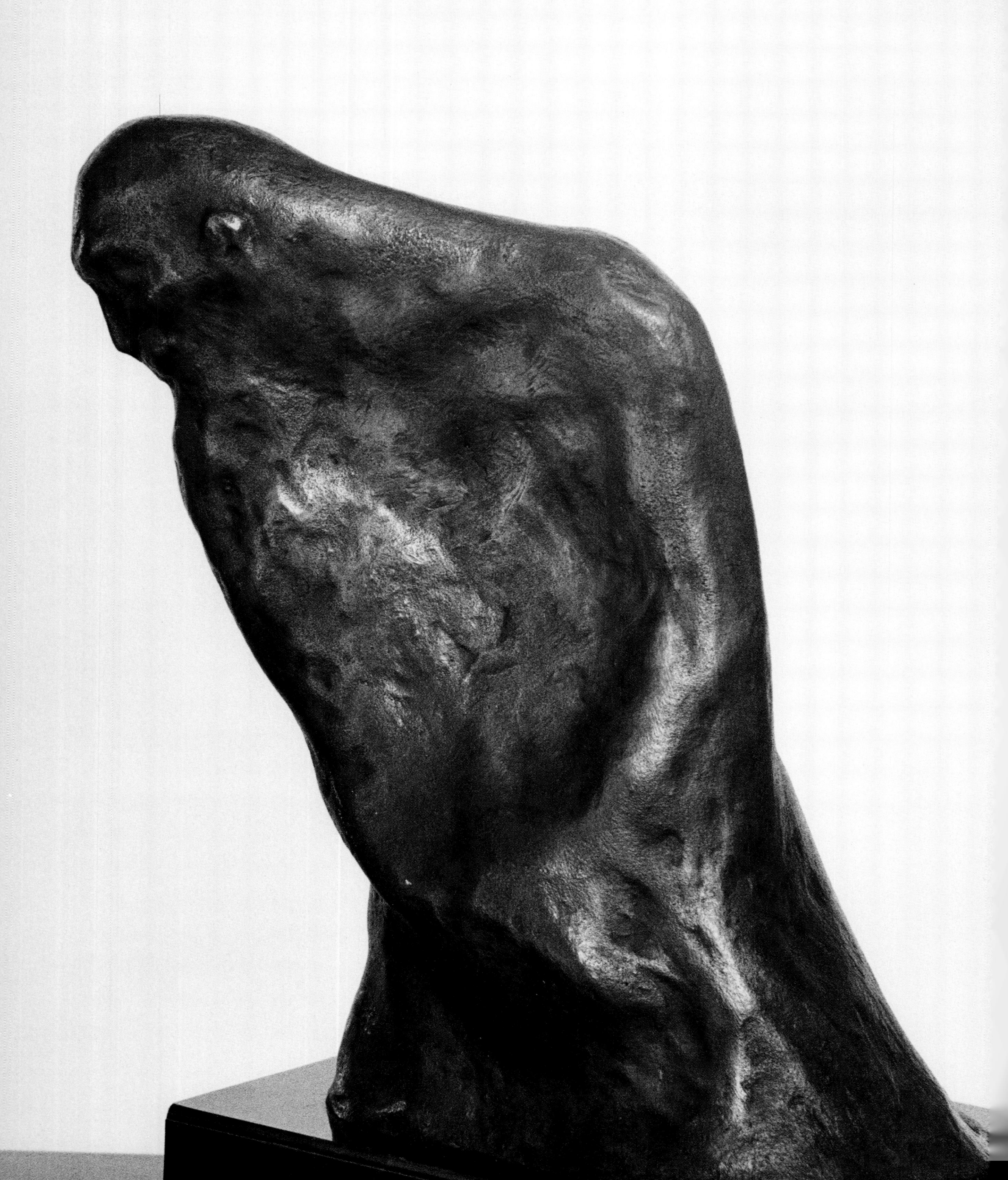

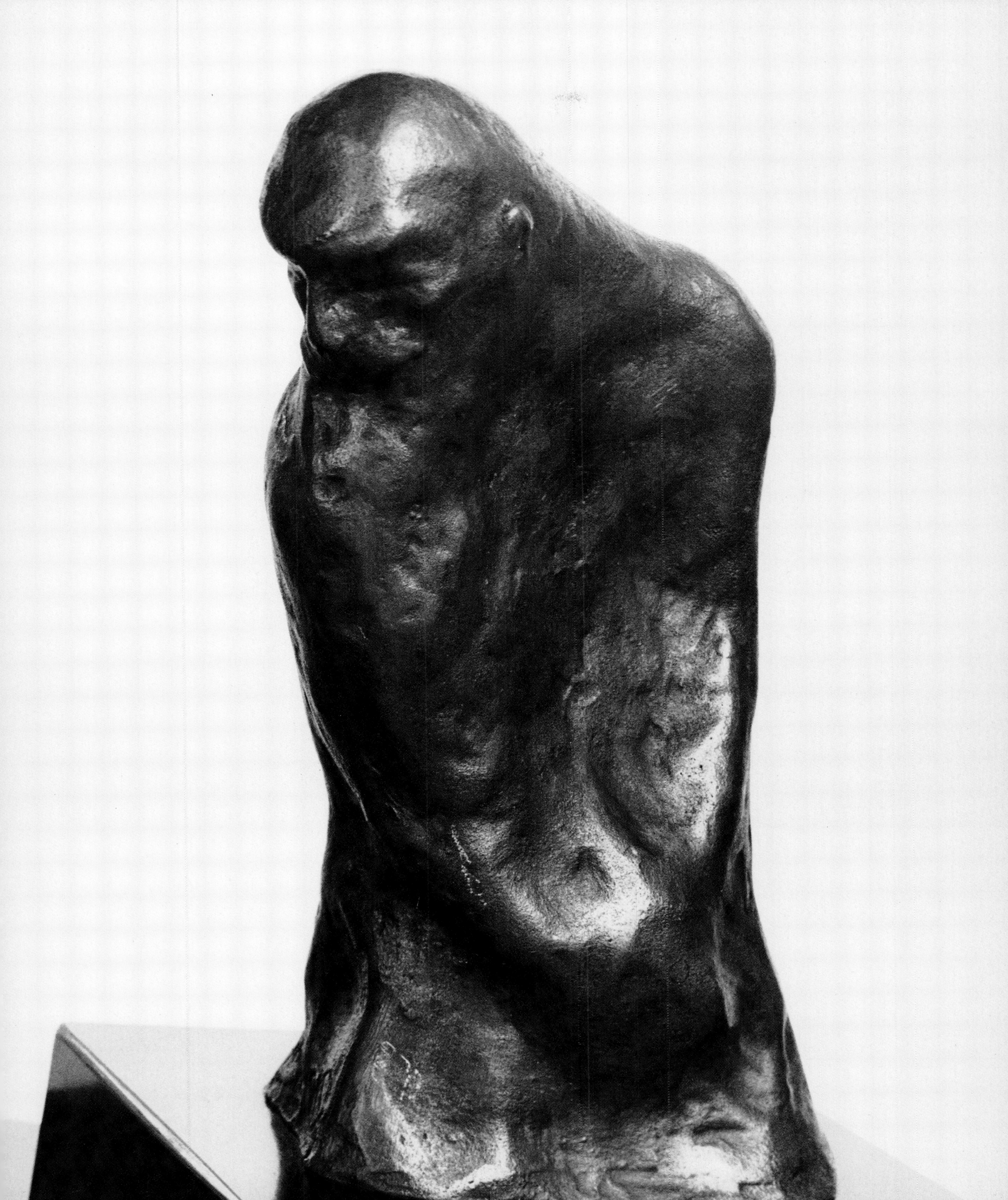

Rodin

The main thing
is to be moved;
to love;
to hope;
to tremble;
to live.
Be a man
before being an artist!

24″ × 16″ × 21″

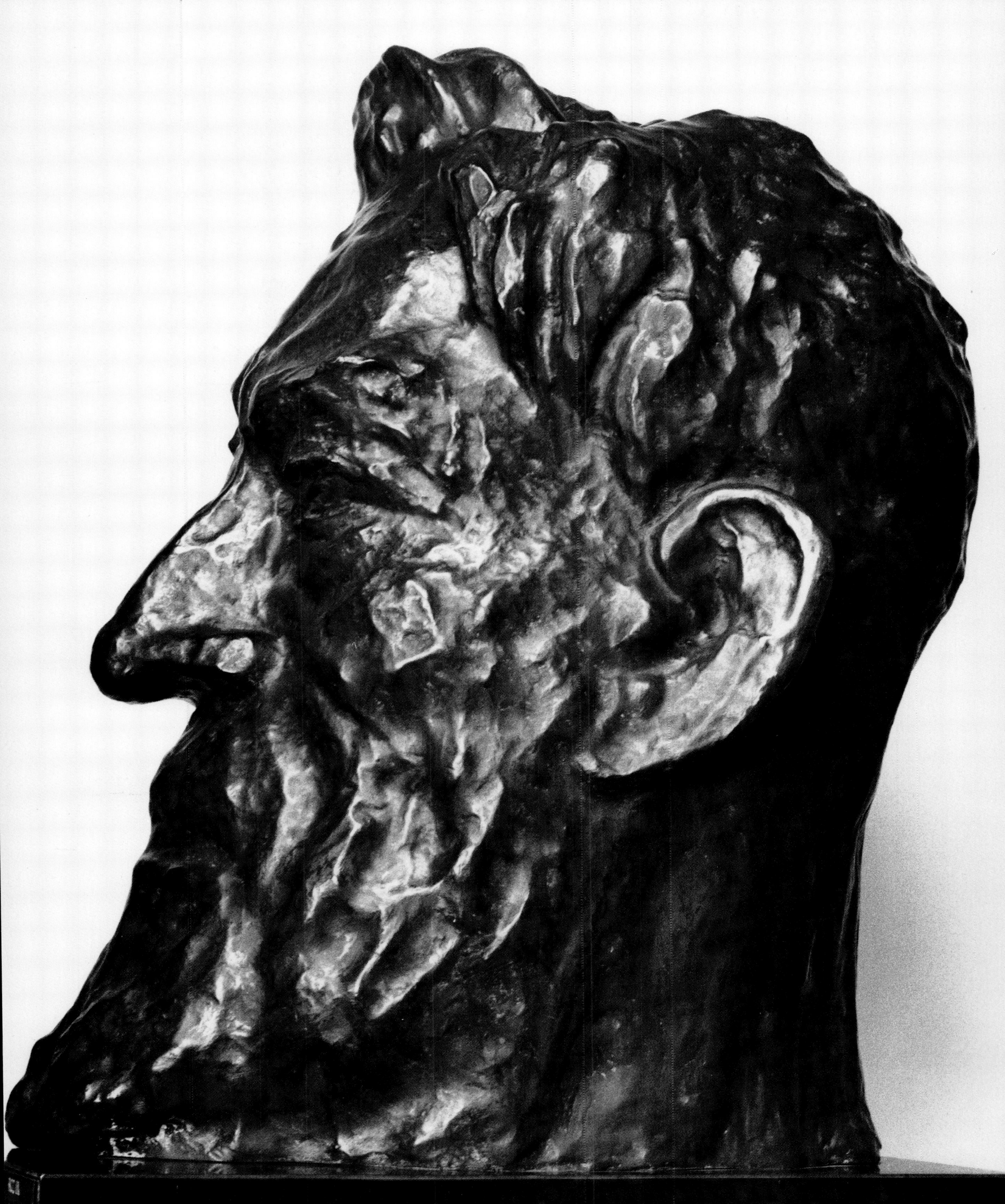

The Bifocal Marcel Duchamp

I learned to know Marcel Duchamp when he was in need of medical advice. Subsequently I learned to know him as an artist and as a human being. I should add he was not an easy man to learn to read. His highly organized, sensitive, analytical intellect seemed tuned to the beauty of logic.

Society as we are confronted with it today seems irrelevant to logic.

Art likewise.

Chess is.

I sensed that the beauty of chess was Marcel Duchamp's true love.

Why the bifocals? The bifocals represent a sculptural compromise.

Marcel Duchamp saw the world and all its incongruities through a multitude of focals, and not all benevolent ones.

He gave me one of his books: "To K.K.N. Artist-Carver of the Invisible. Affectueusement, Marcel Duchamp, White Plains, 1963."

He gave me a meaningful encouragement one day, and added: "You have, as you have told me, been working under the blessing and the luxury of anonymity. Please, don't give it up too soon. Hang on to it. It can be a remarkable blessing."

Marcel might have been meditating on his own career.

For forty years following his exhibit of *Nude Descending a Stairs* at the Armory Show in New York in 1913, there had been no exhibit of his work until the 1952 exhibit at the Musée d'Art Moderne in Paris.

During those forty years, however, he was not anonymous. During those years he grew to be the prophet of the "ready-mades" and modern art—and I suspected he never considered it a worthwhile accomplishment.

In his years of revolt in about the second decade of this century he declared art superfluous.

Life itself remained the only significant value.

In his later years, deep in the inners of this prophet of modern art, I believe he had not changed.

Life was the only meaningful value of existence—until death do us part.

22½″ × 10″ × 11½

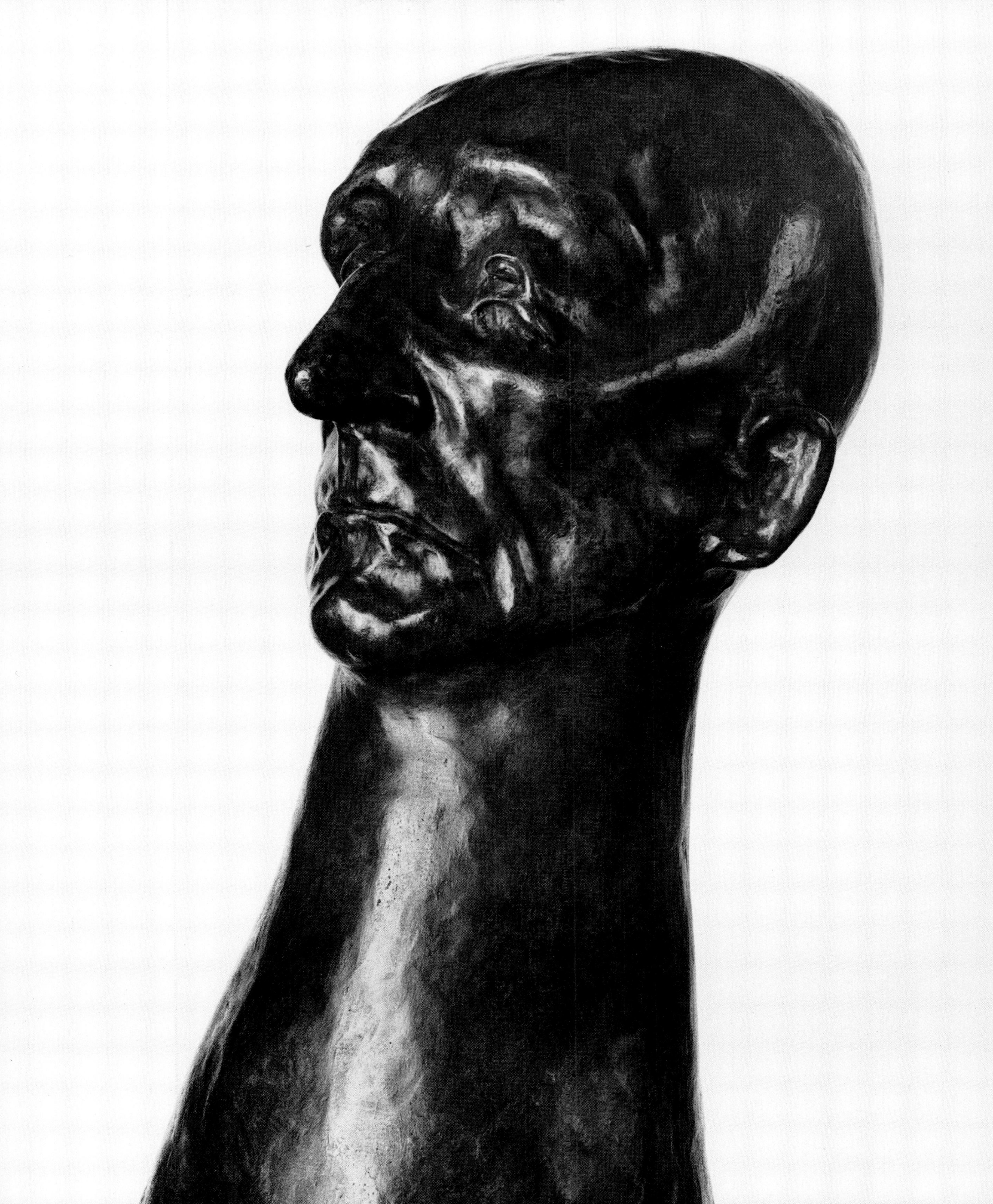

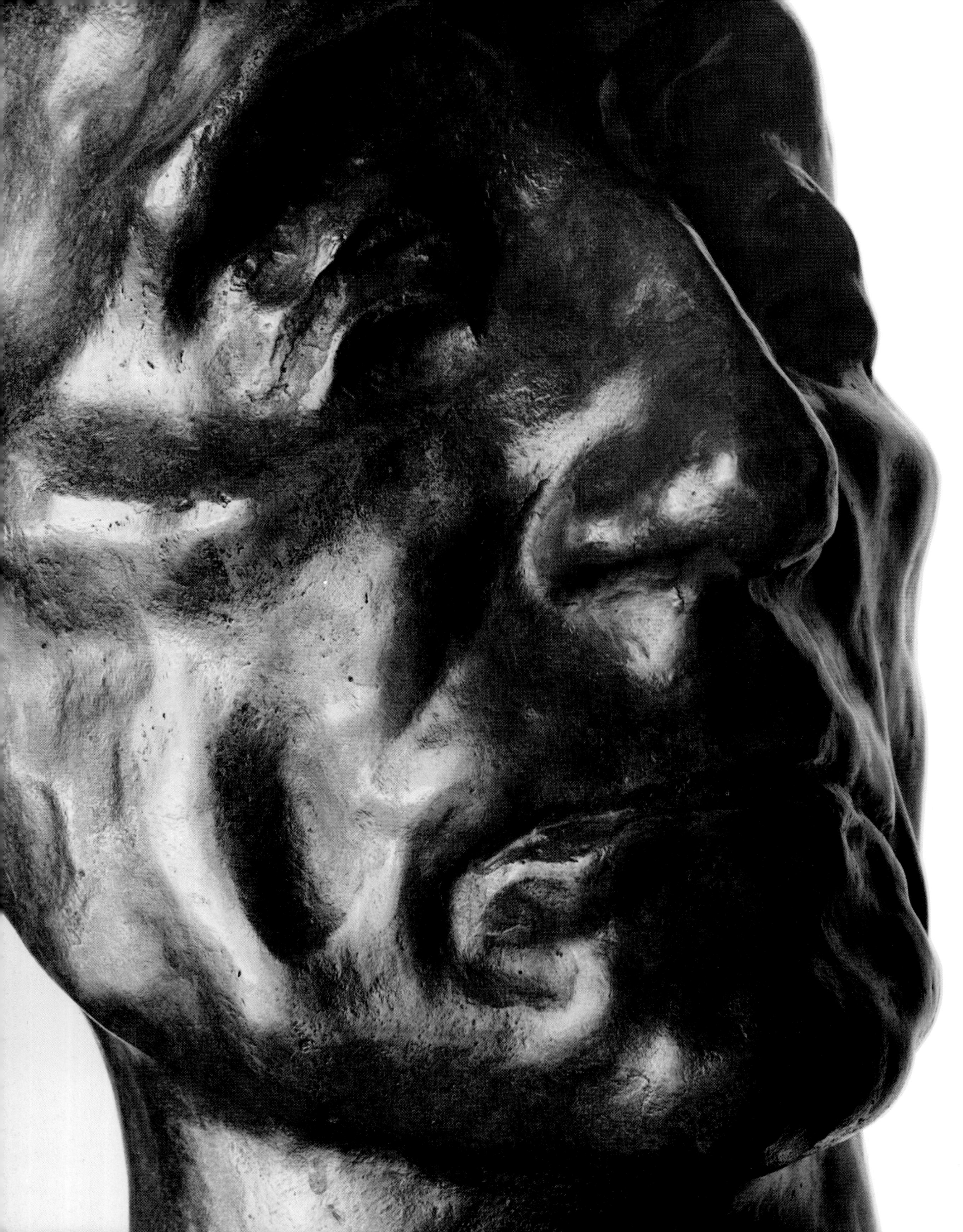

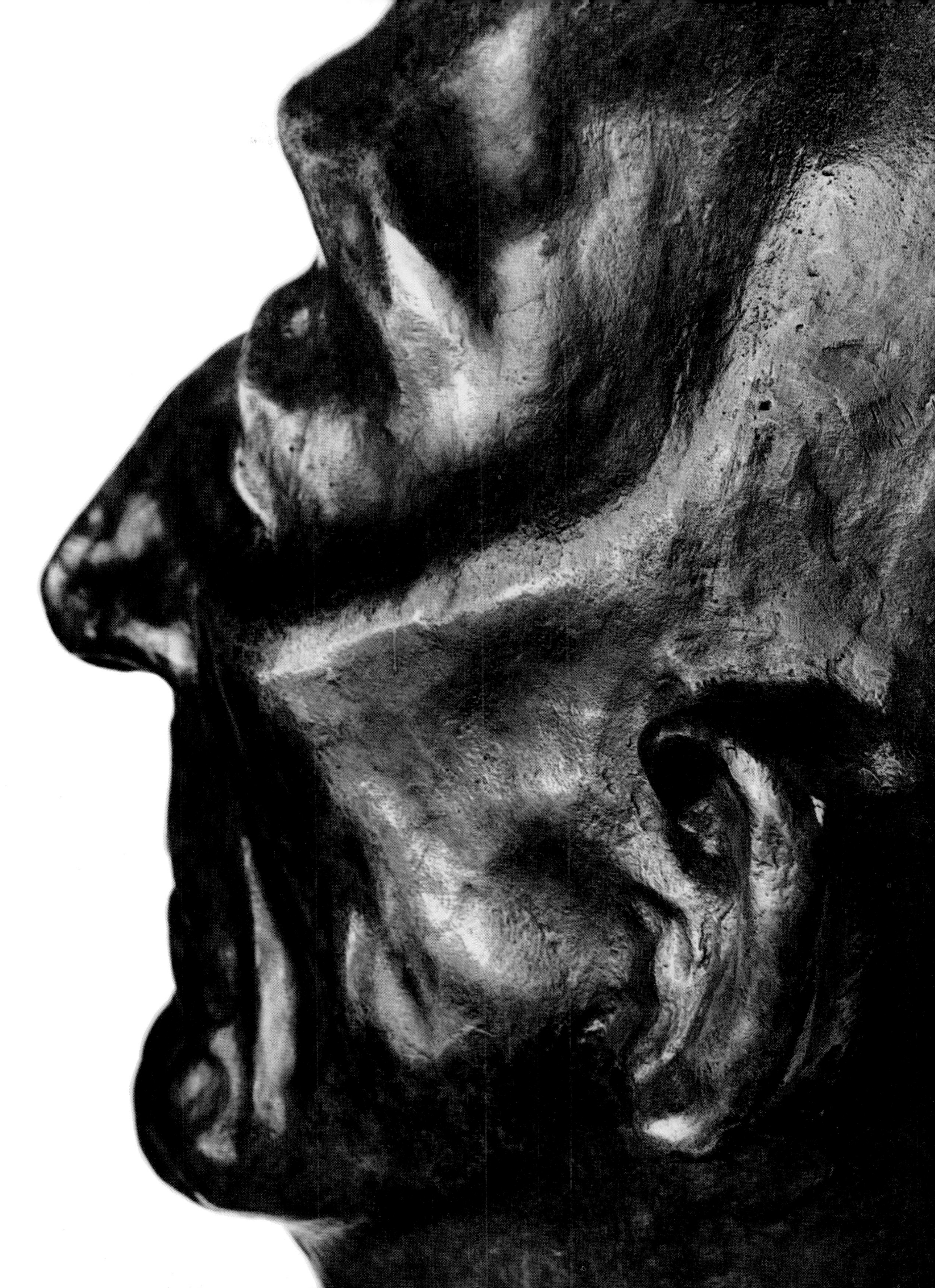

Nietzsche

Practically all of my bronzes are works "in the round." In order to obtain an all-comprising visual impression, one has to walk around them, so to say. The bronze is not meant to be placed up against the wall. It is to be viewed in an open space.

Nietzsche is one of the exceptions. *He* is to be up against the wall. I want him *en face*. I do not trust him. Even after my cutting off the back of his head and his neck, the mask conveys a proclamation of superstrength while permitting no human nuances and inviting no negotiations.

His forte was the ultimatum as presented to the Almighty God—and to humanity itself—by a Superman escaping from Nietzsche's brain with fancied images of greater Superworlds.

The escapee was relatively nonmalevolent until decades later, when some of his visions were picked up by the Nazis and he was proclaimed by Hitler's decree to be the philosophical creator of the new Superrace—the *Herren Volk*.

Since those years I have had him on my desk, straight in front of me, as a reminder.

There will be other prophets coming and yearning to be above everybody and not part of anything. History repeats itself. When it does, it seemingly and invariably tends to grapple for ideals and ideas crawling within the illusions of a superman. We'd better be there. We'd better be ready for him again!

11½″ × 4½″ × 5½″

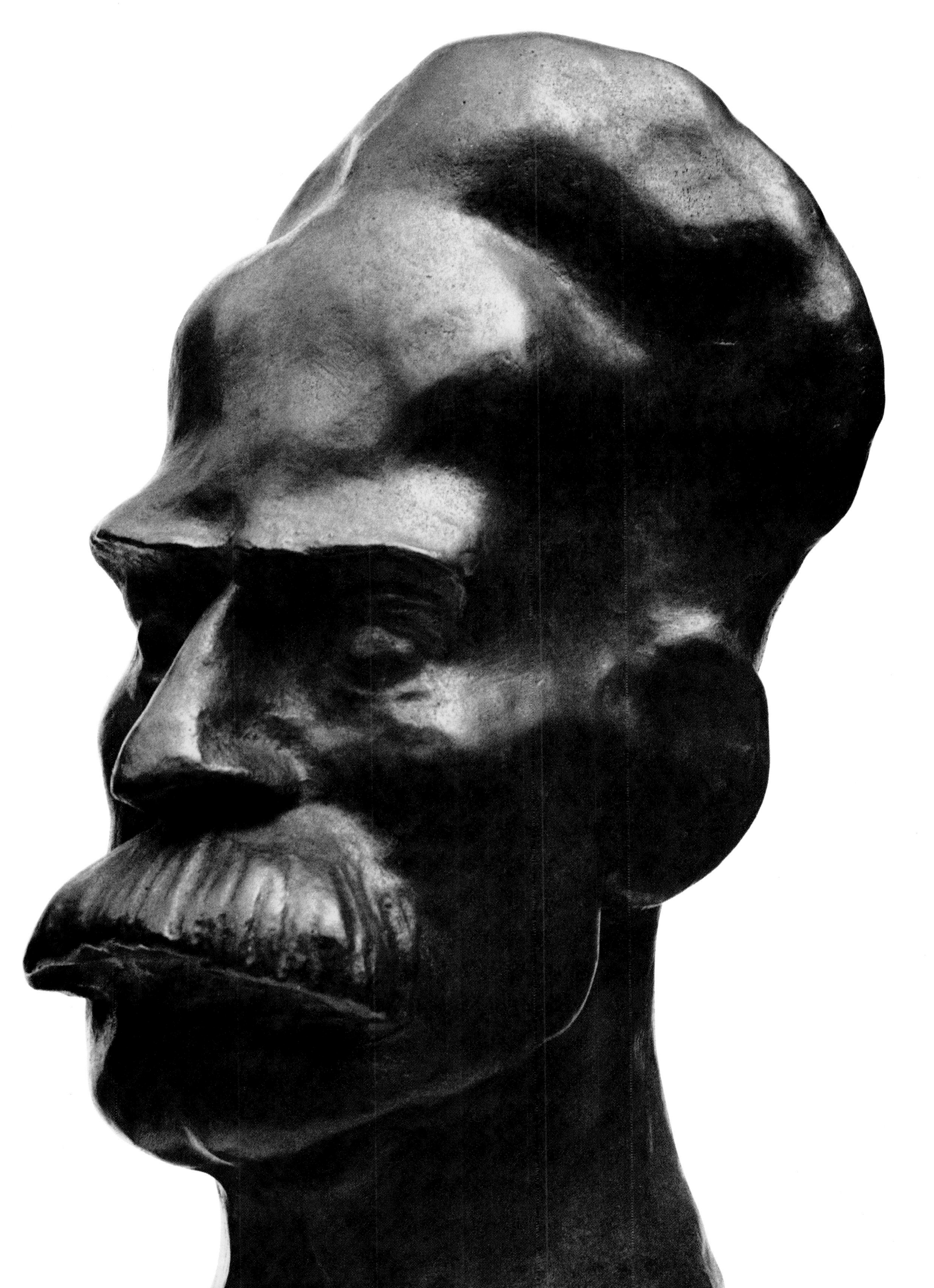

The Museum Director

Our society harbors great men—and some small men.

Sometimes there is a fascinating and confusing mixture of both in one person.

He may have a similar difficulty himself.

I touch upon this dichotomy in the present work.

In one aspect the subject may seem somewhat bombastic and pompous.

In another direction, however, his prestigious critical power shines forth gloriously.

It may be a bit dislocated by a strong ego manifestation, yet soon regains absolute dependable control.

Until a small firecracker interrupts it all.

I intend no malice.

There are situations where my sense of humor cannot be repressed.

I have happily discovered that even bronze is willingly curving into a smile.

26″ × 22″ × 16″

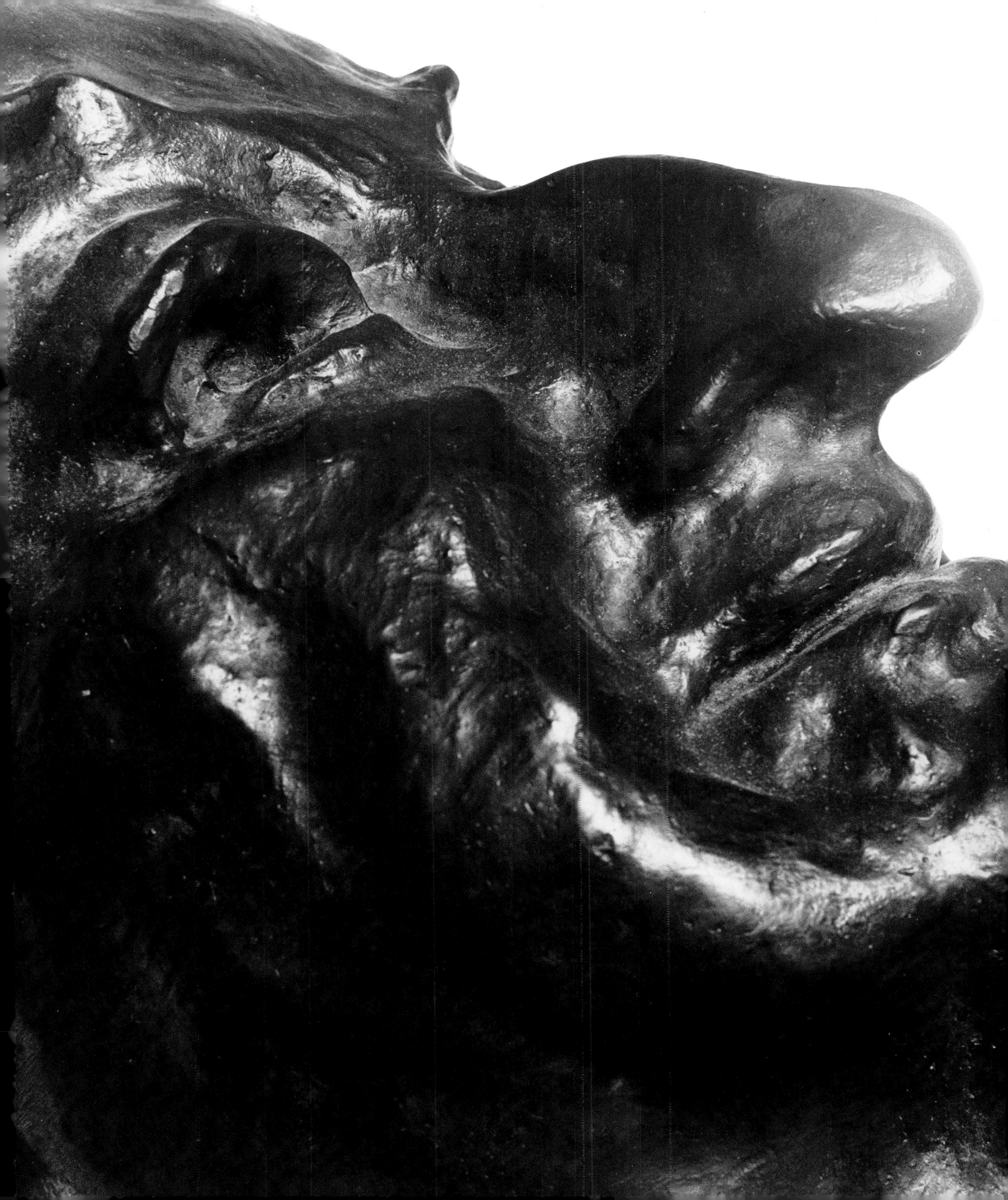

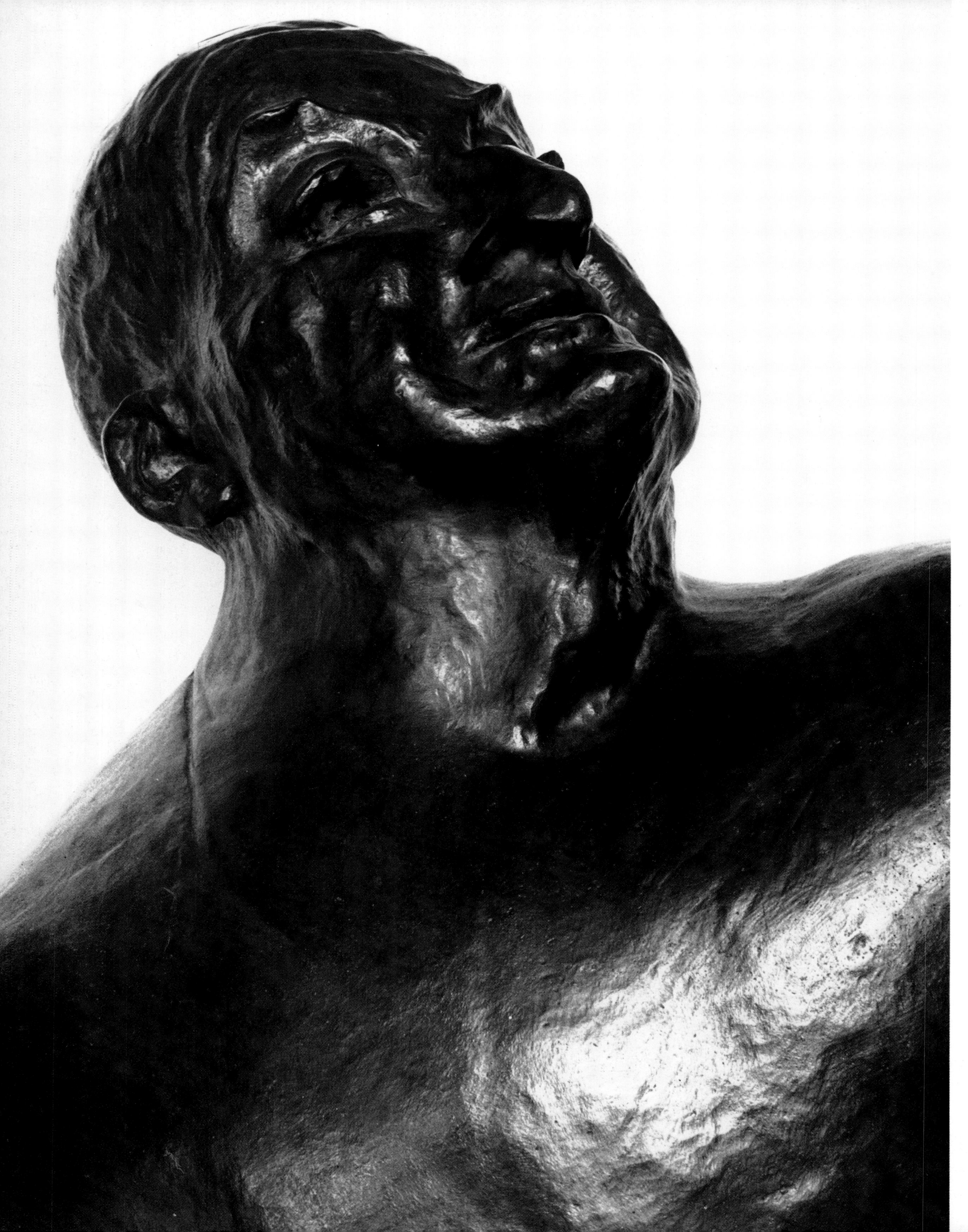

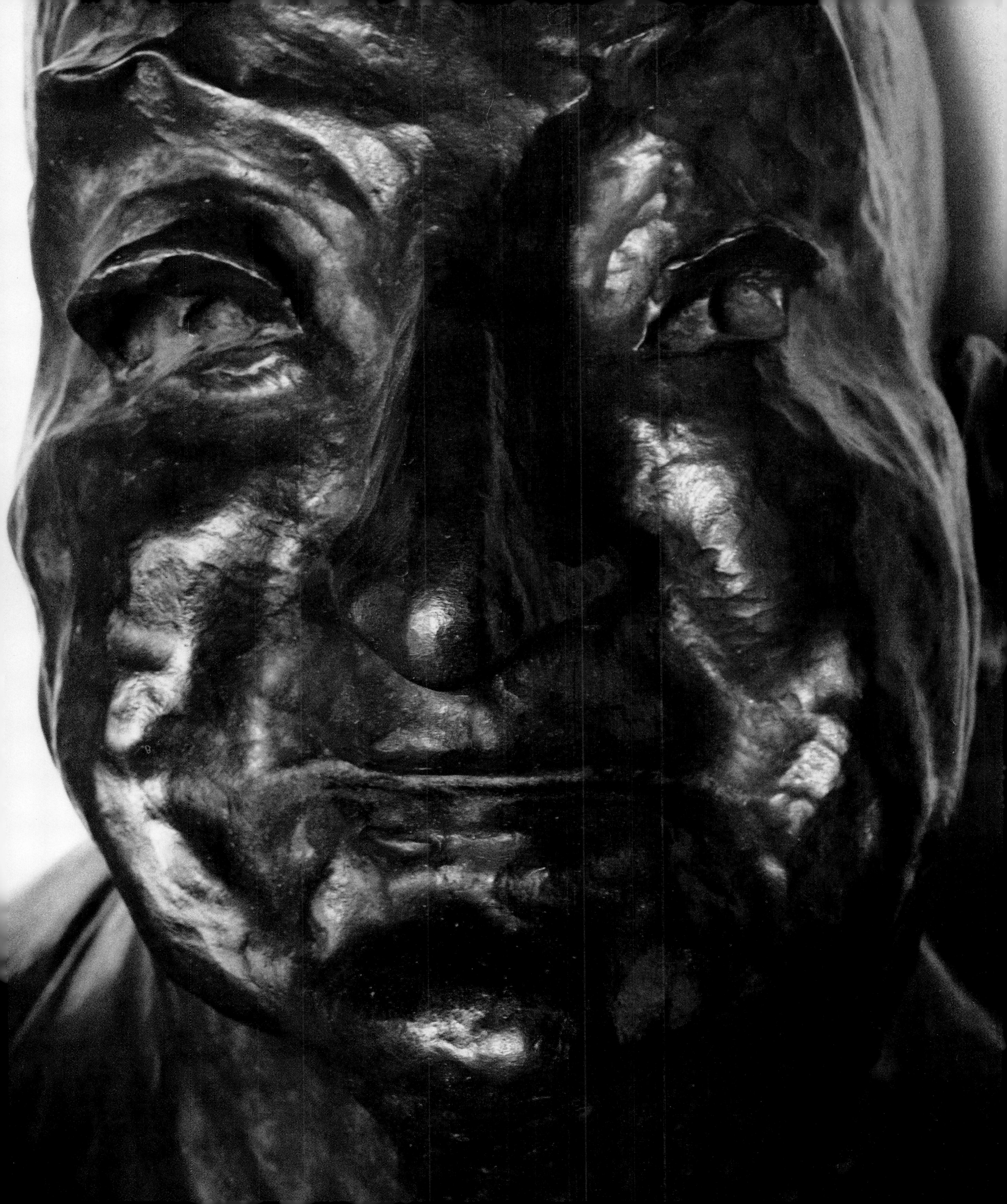

The Art Critic

In a light moment someone defined surgery as the intricate art of tearing things apart and fitting them constructively together again.

If this is so, I think there must be a certain resemblance between the art critic and the surgeon. The critic is apt to tear things apart. There is a difference: at times the critic can permit himself the luxury of not putting things together benevolently.

I should say that I have no small respect for his profession. Some critics I admire. A few I love.

Through the sensitivity of their eyes and their accumulated knowledge, by the subtlety of their mind, they are up on the firing line every day on behalf of the written and spoken word, to record the heat of their cultural environment—or lack of such.

To observe, takes a clear retina. To learn to possess the enigma of art, takes a pursuit of art, in love.

To convey it to others takes a sophisticated pen. The rub is: while we observe through a biologically well-established organ common to us all, we interpret what we observe through an organ that varies so much from the average that we might call it uncommon.

If that brain of his is additionally gifted with a sense of humor, the mixture of serenity and smile might come to us as a therapeutic relief even though he might have failed to reconstruct those pieces so miserably spread about by his keen analysis. And thus, in this bronze, we find the art critic and the surgeon roaring together in laughter.

14″ × 8″ × 13″

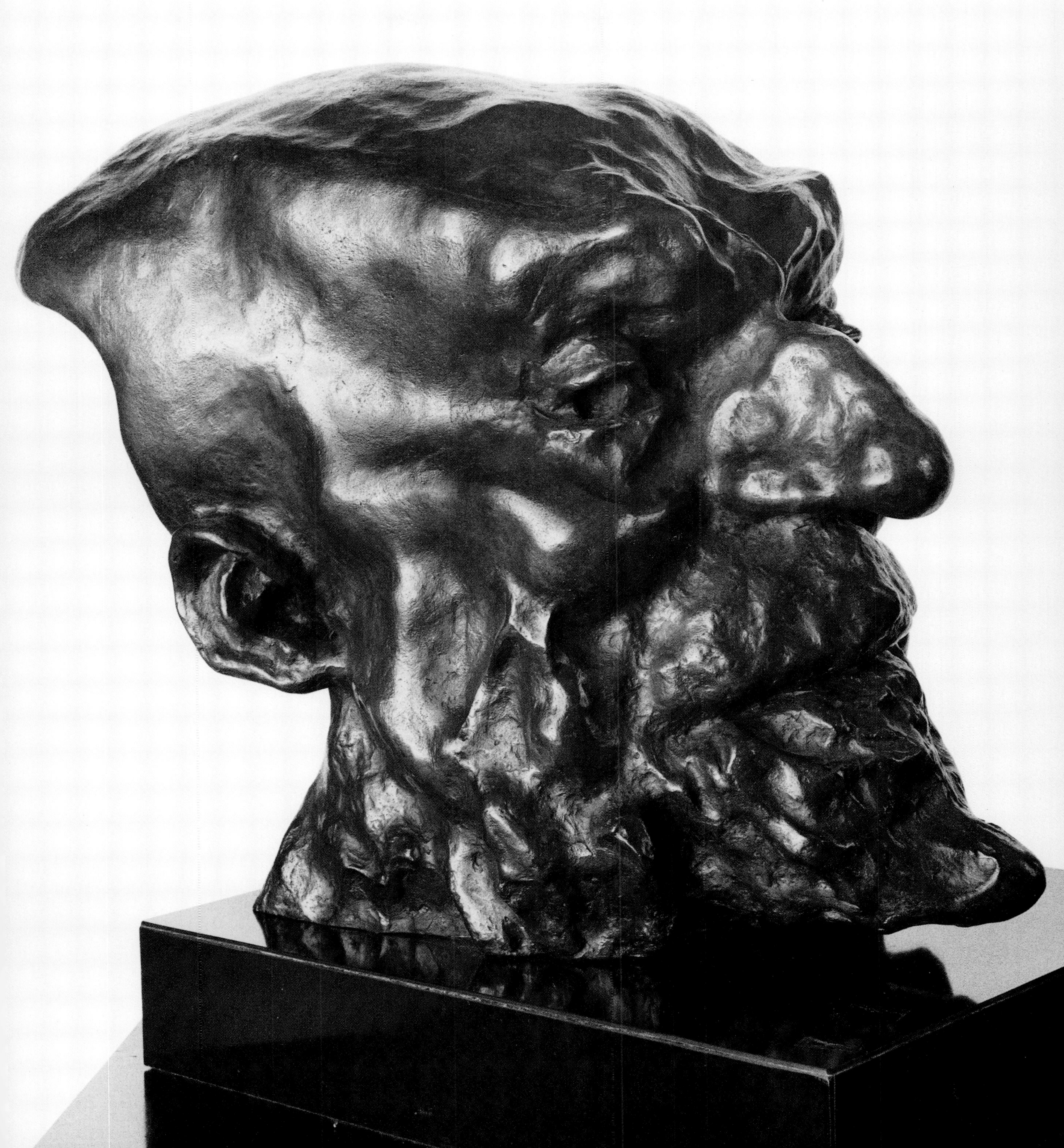

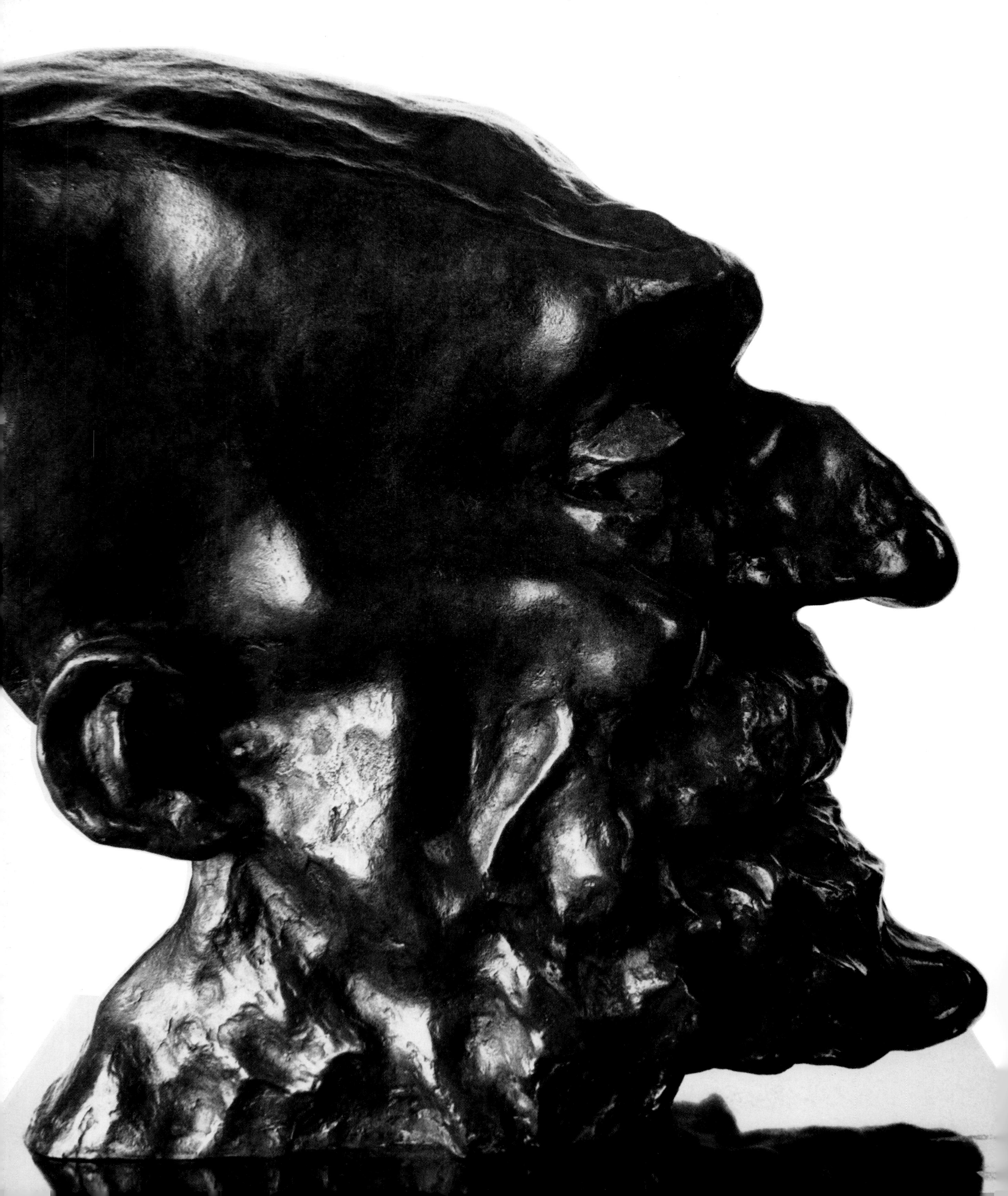

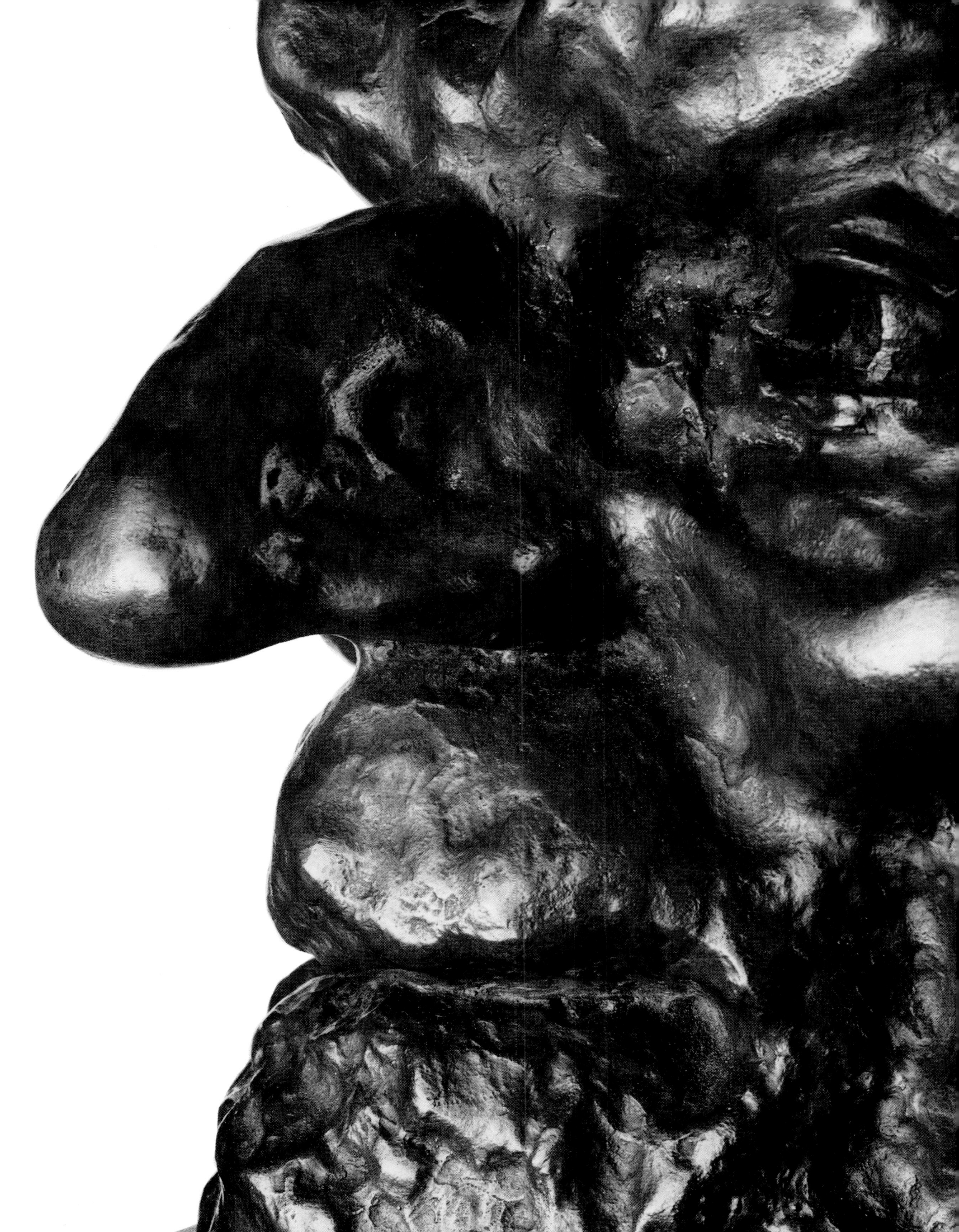

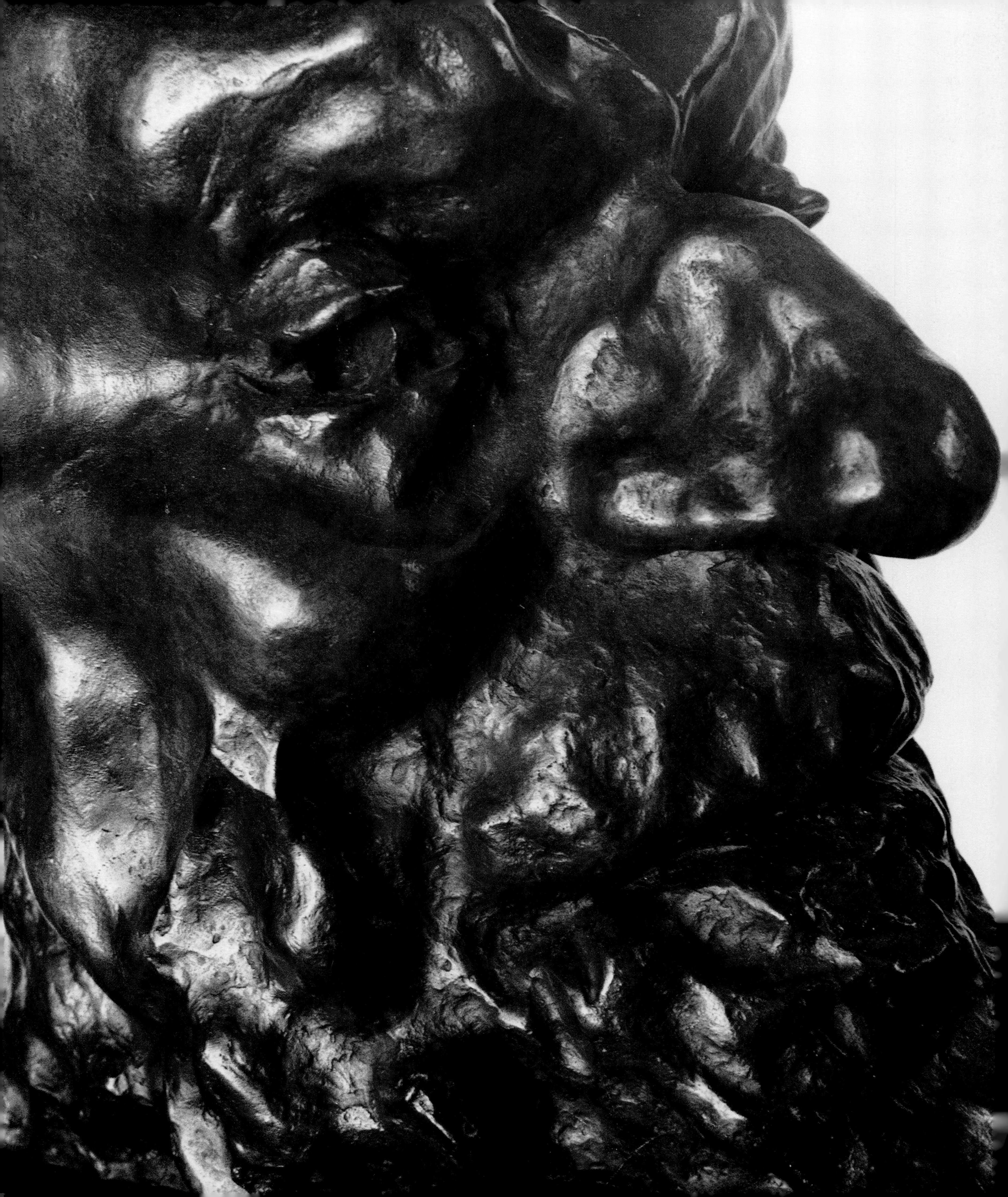

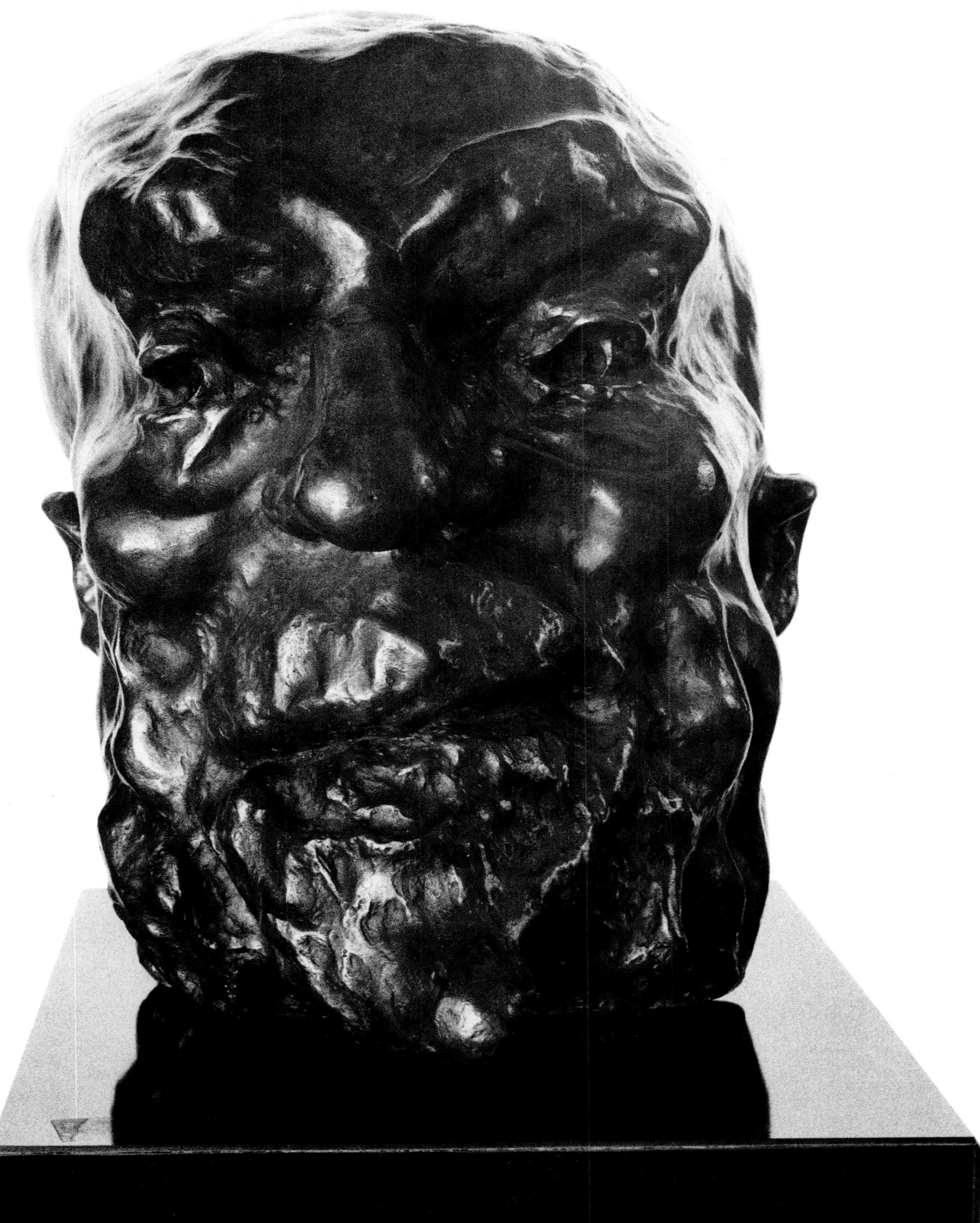

Homage to Vincent van Gogh

In admiration, in veneration, in love,
I have executed two bronzes of Vincent.
In the present one he is compressed.
He has no volume.
No power or strength.
No ambition.
He is confined within a strait jacket.
Tainted with psychiatric overtones.
He holds no palette.
He handles no pigment.
He has no friends, except brother Theo.
He has no life.
Exodus impends.
And it is not retroactively preventable, even
by the subsequent glory of a museum bearing his name.

19″ × 6″ × 4½″

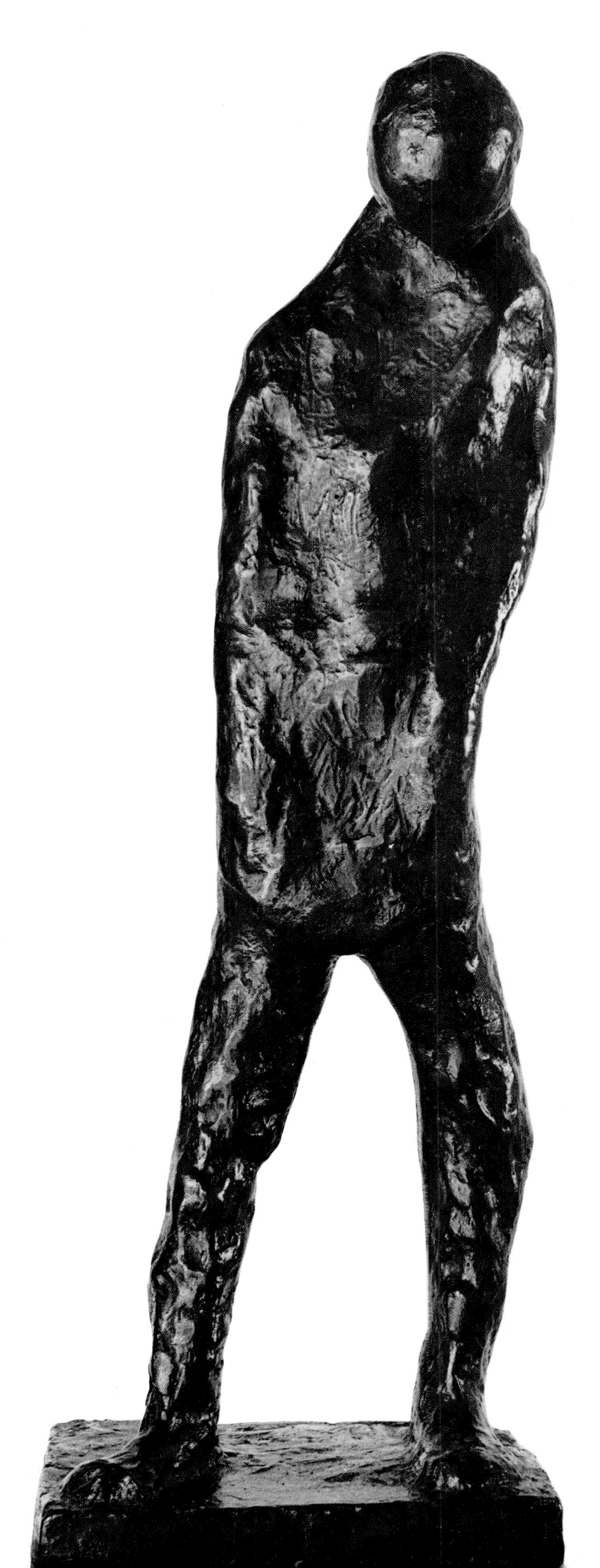

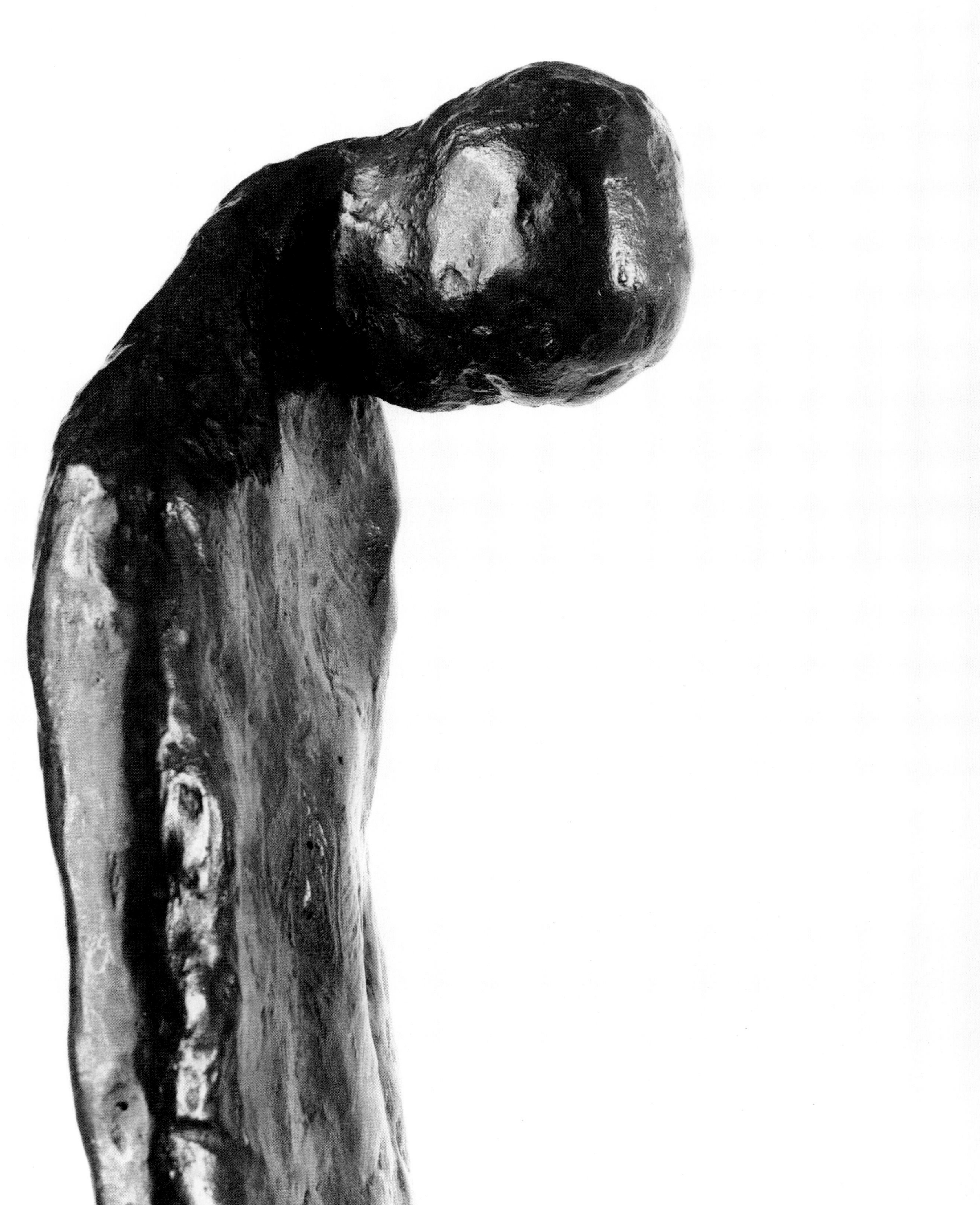

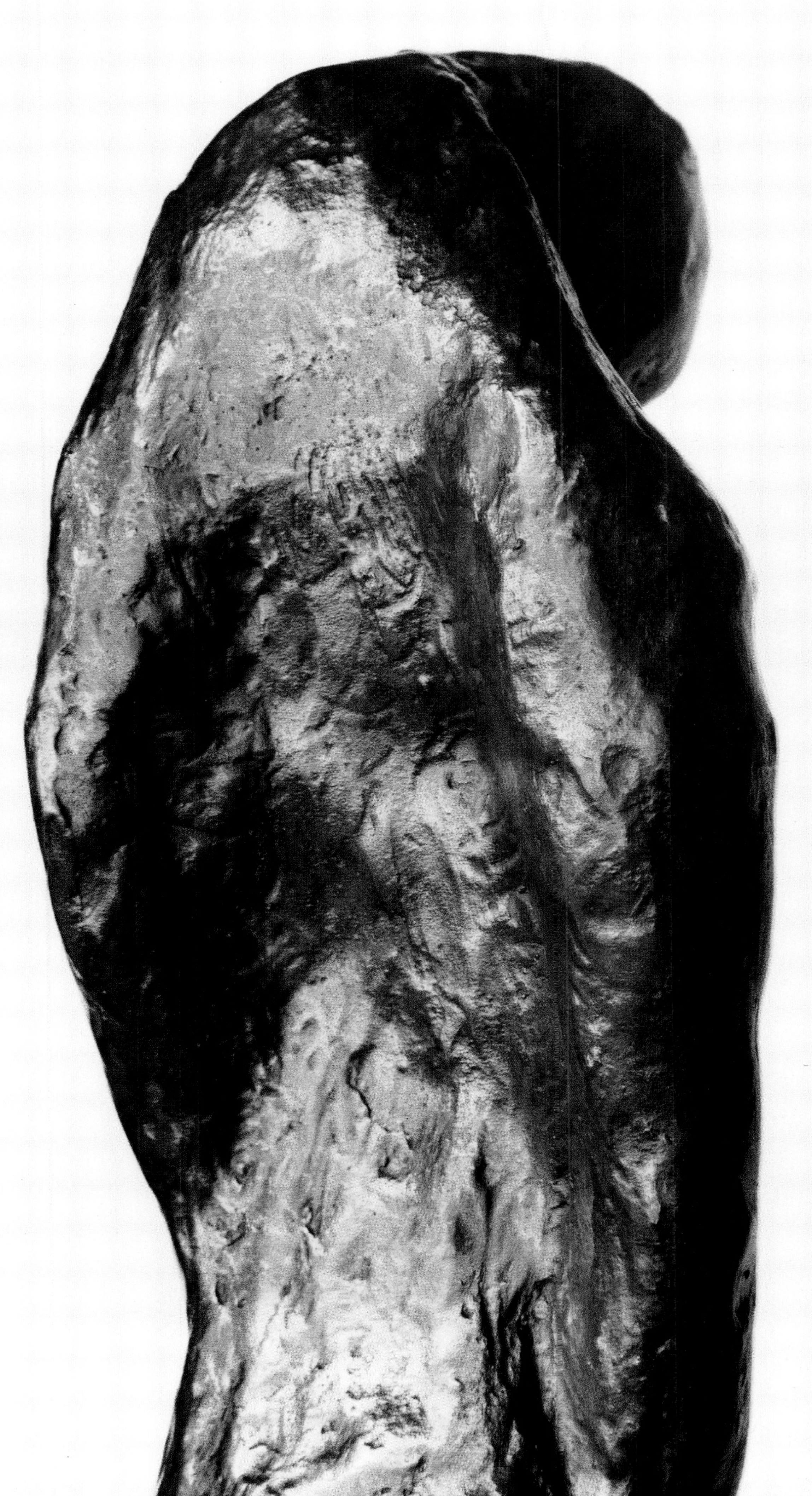

Homage to Paul Gauguin

Throughout his life Paul Gauguin protested against the degenerative influences of our civilization.

Trying forcibly to escape them, in Tahiti, he also met the degenerative influences of syphilis in Paris.

He failed miserably at nurturing his talent for learning to live.

By pure obstinacy, however, he succeeded eminently in governing his talent for pigments on canvas.

My little sculpture is not kind to Paul Gauguin.

Nor are these photos. They trace unmercifully the lines of disruption and despair in his distorted face.

I have an obligation to remember this face.

In some ways it is part of us all.

9″ × 6″ × 5½″

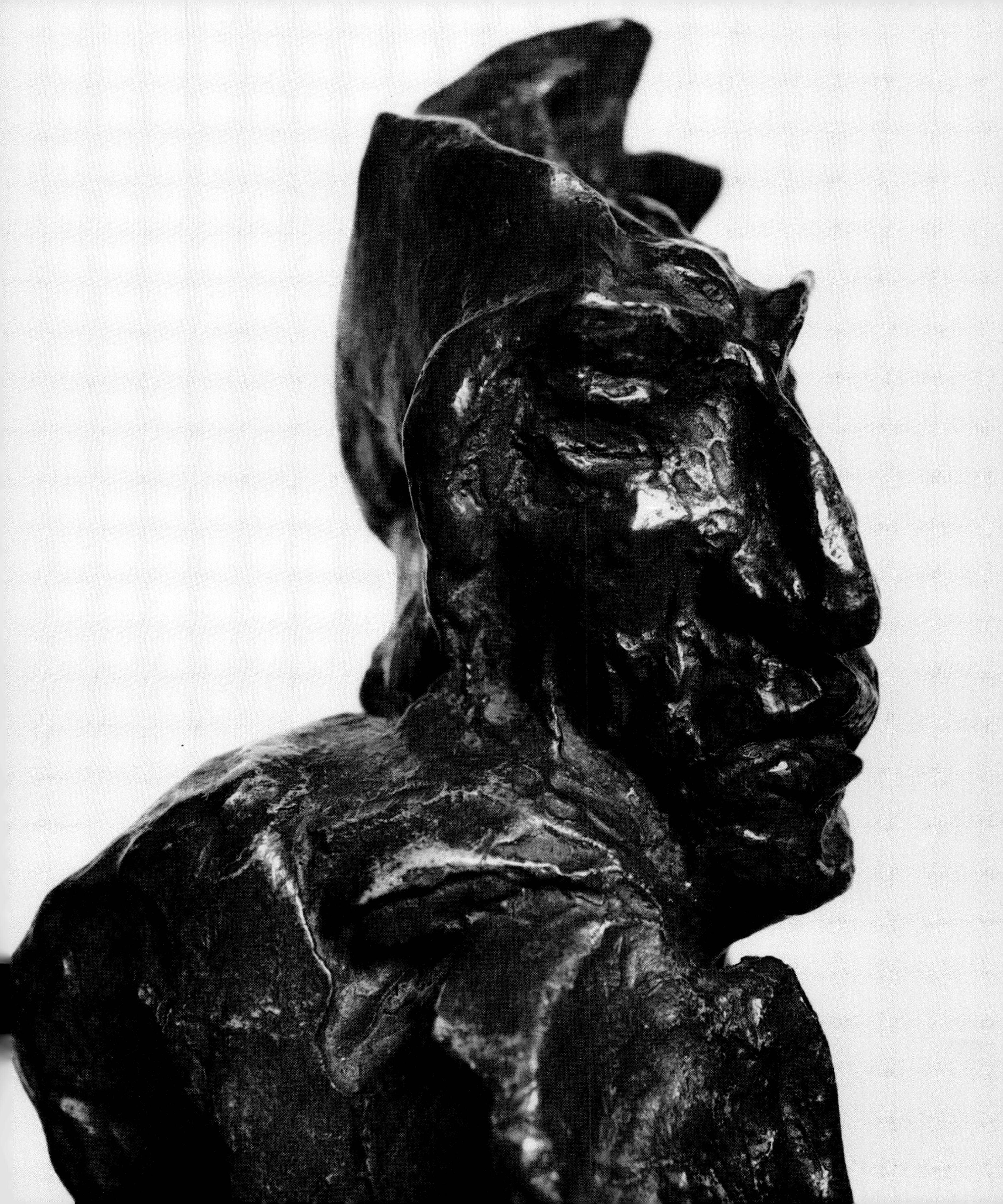

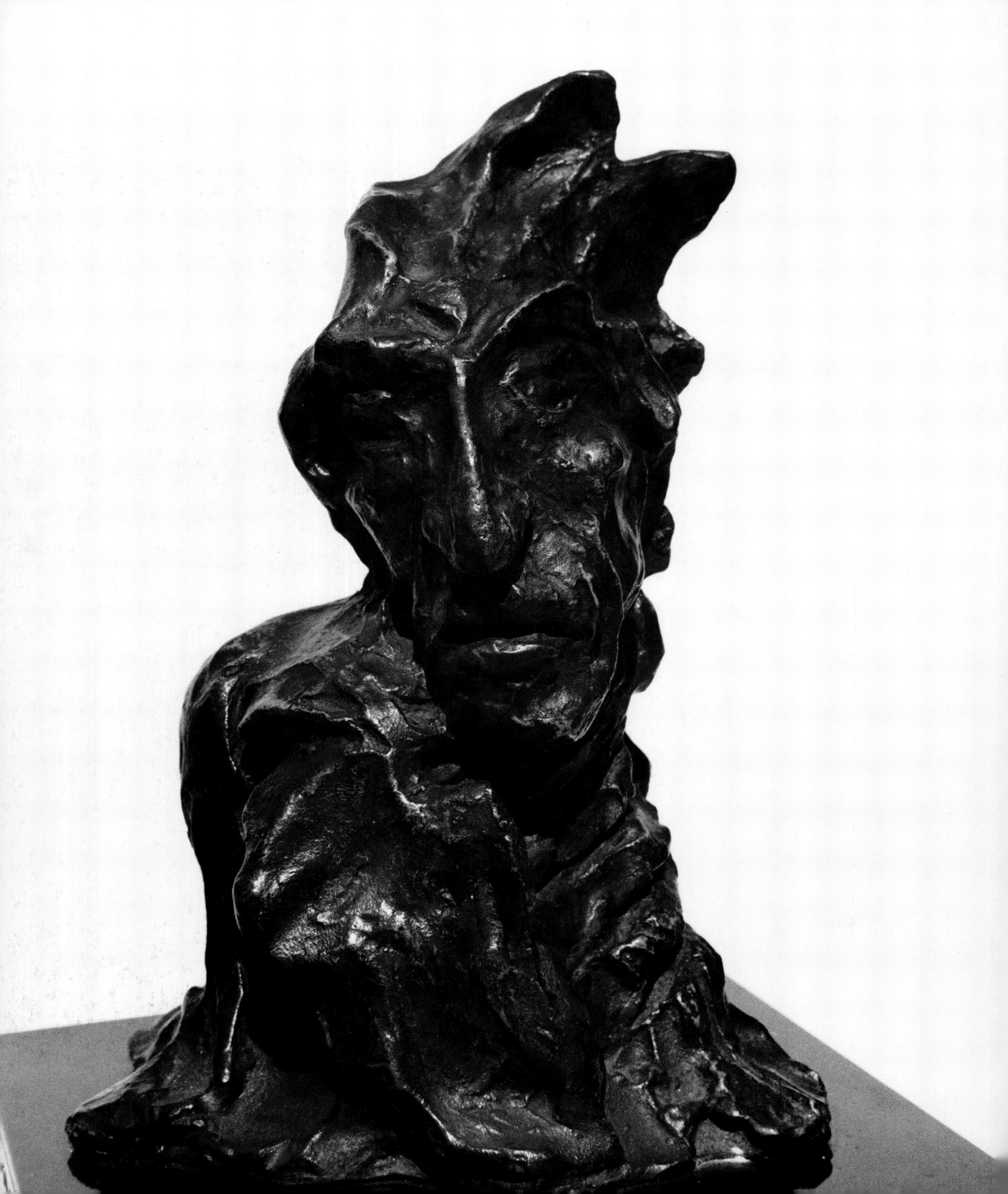

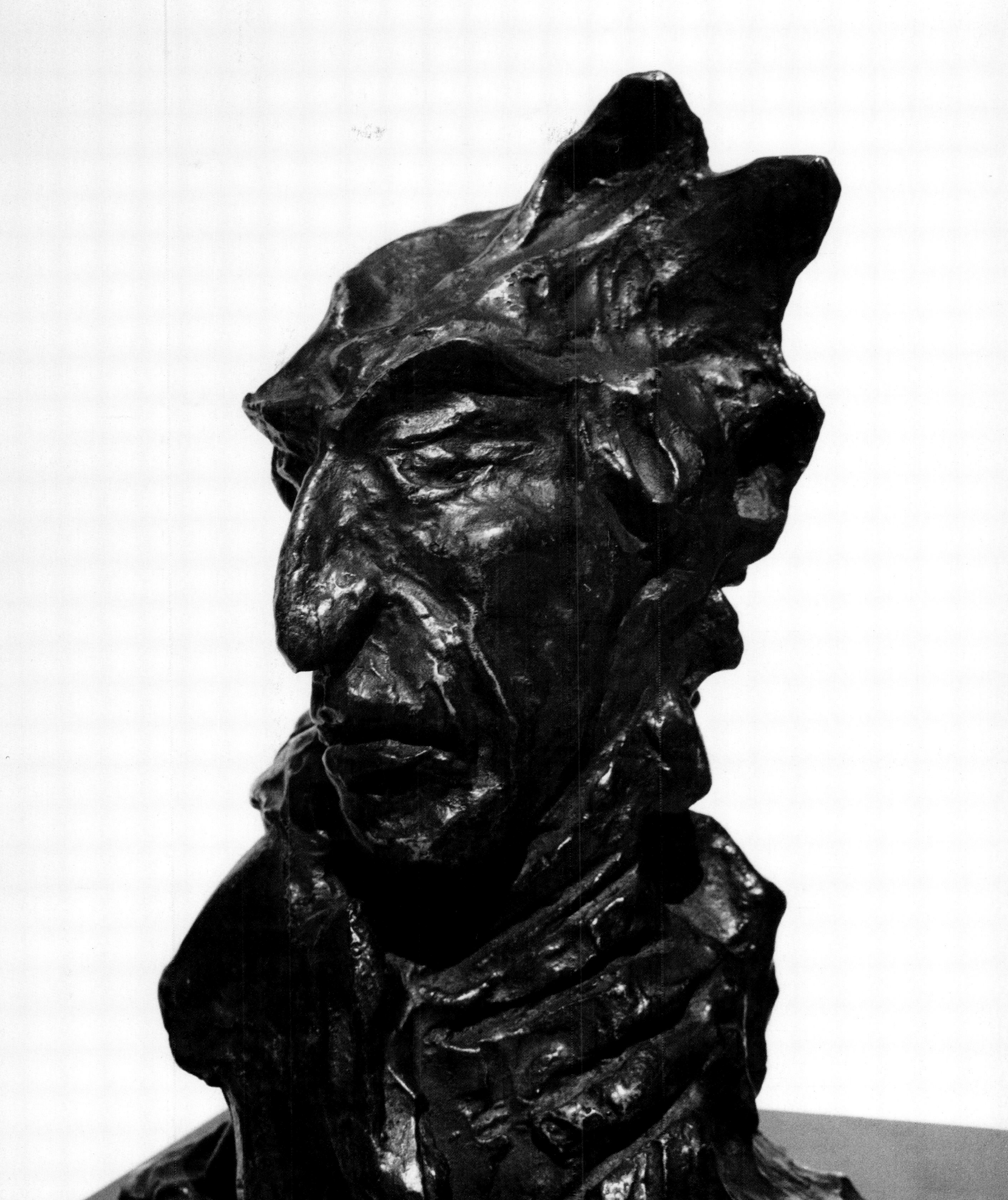

The English Barrister

When you look at the back of this sculpture, it seems only a round lump covered with monotonous, horizontal, parallel lines. The lines flow toward the front of the sculpture but do not meet; they are kept apart by the serene, plain, and plainly-shaped face of a man. It seems tucked in from all sides.

I can describe him in detail: he is middle-aged or a little beyond that; quite intelligent, if you trust yourself to make a diagnosis by the face only; a bit emaciated; stern but not completely forbidding. But he is no fanatic.

Since the title says he is a lawyer, you may believe you know what to expect of him.

You may think him cruel in his interpretation of the law, if he is against you.

If he is for you, you may think him wise.

If you are the sculptor, you may think of him—and try to depict him—as the human interpreter of the horizontal lines and paragraphs of abstact law.

Here is my simple reading of the barrister: an abstraction in one aspect, a human being in another.

Or, said differently, laws and legality on one side, interpretation and humanity on the other.

18″ × 16″ × 9″

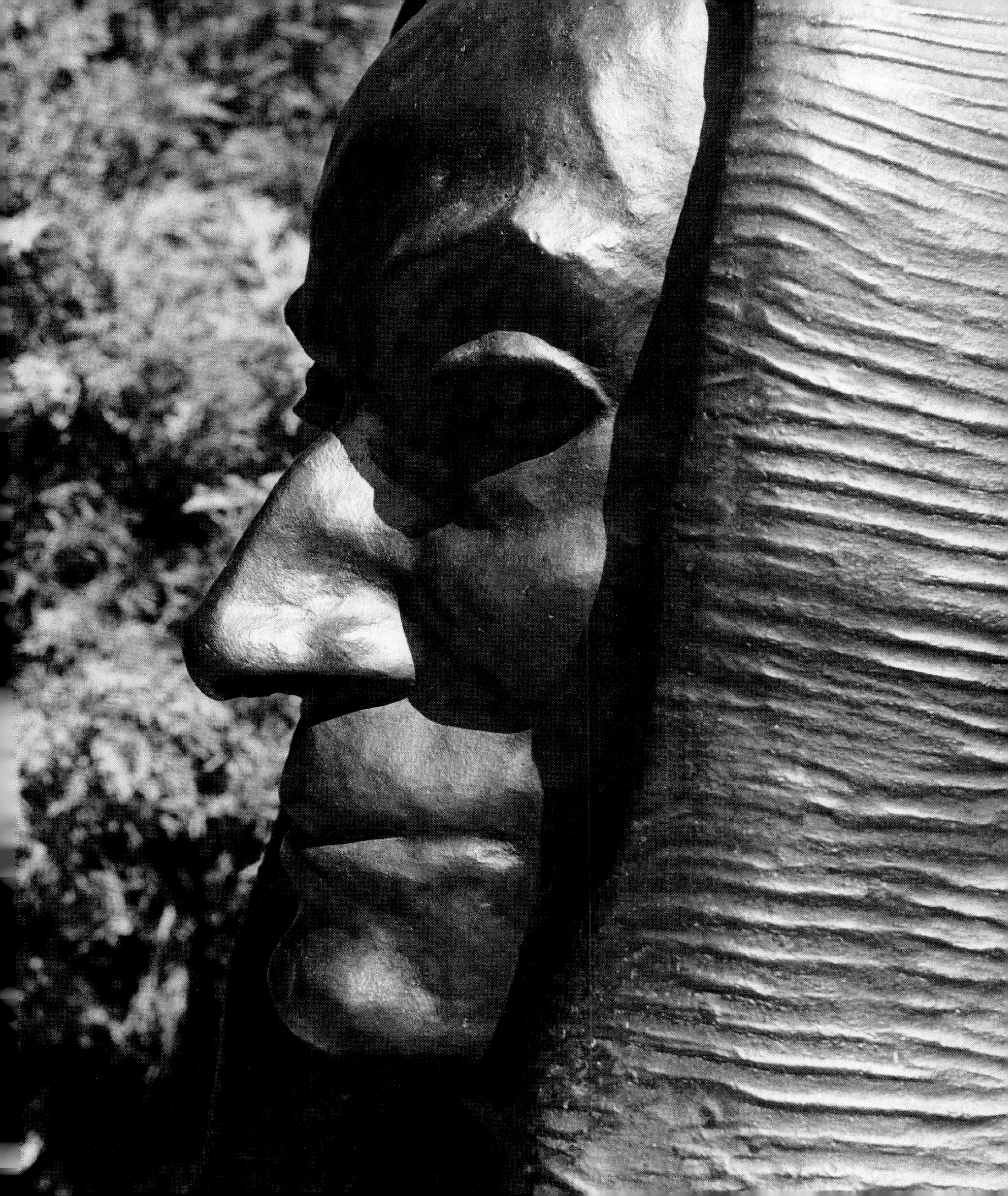

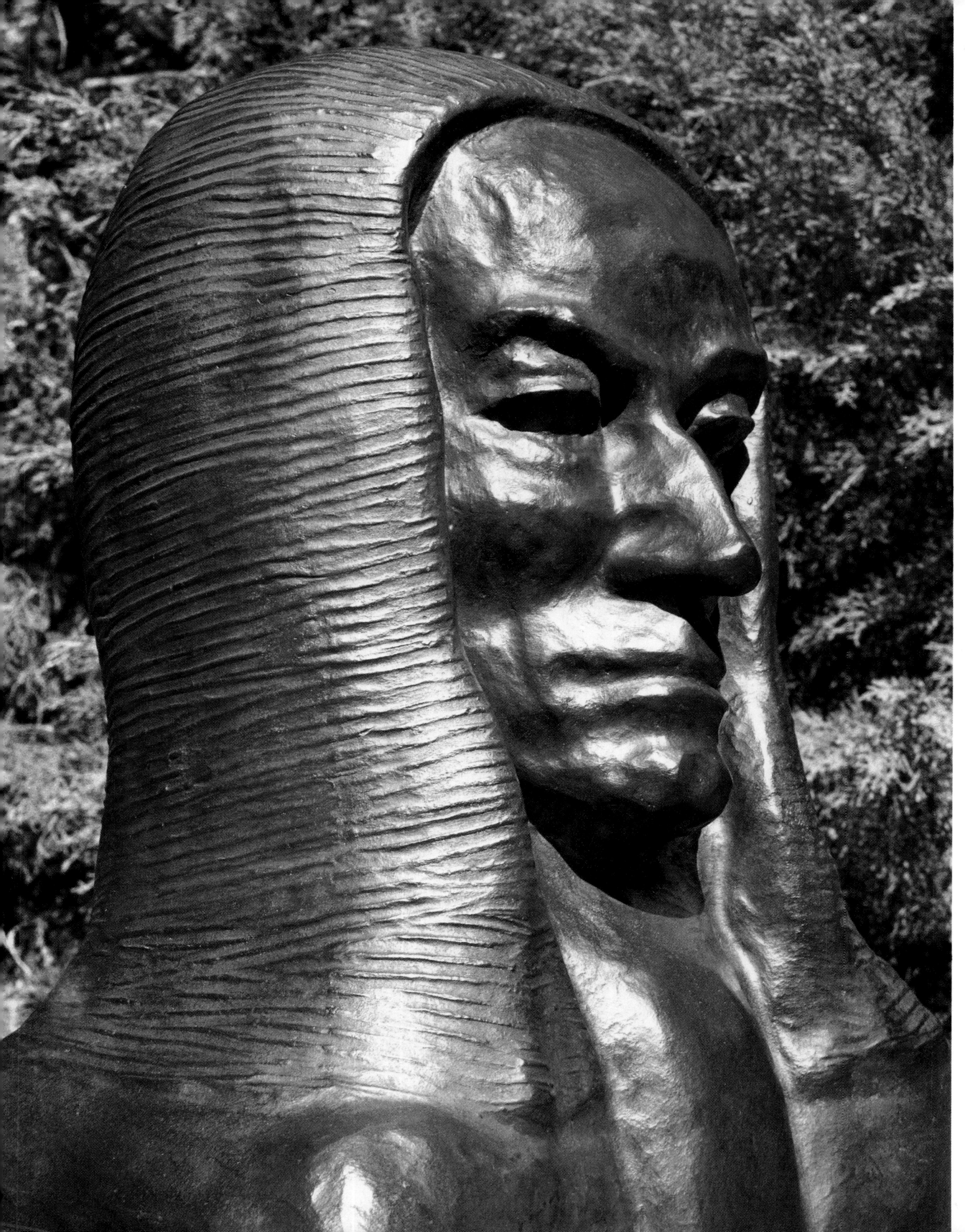

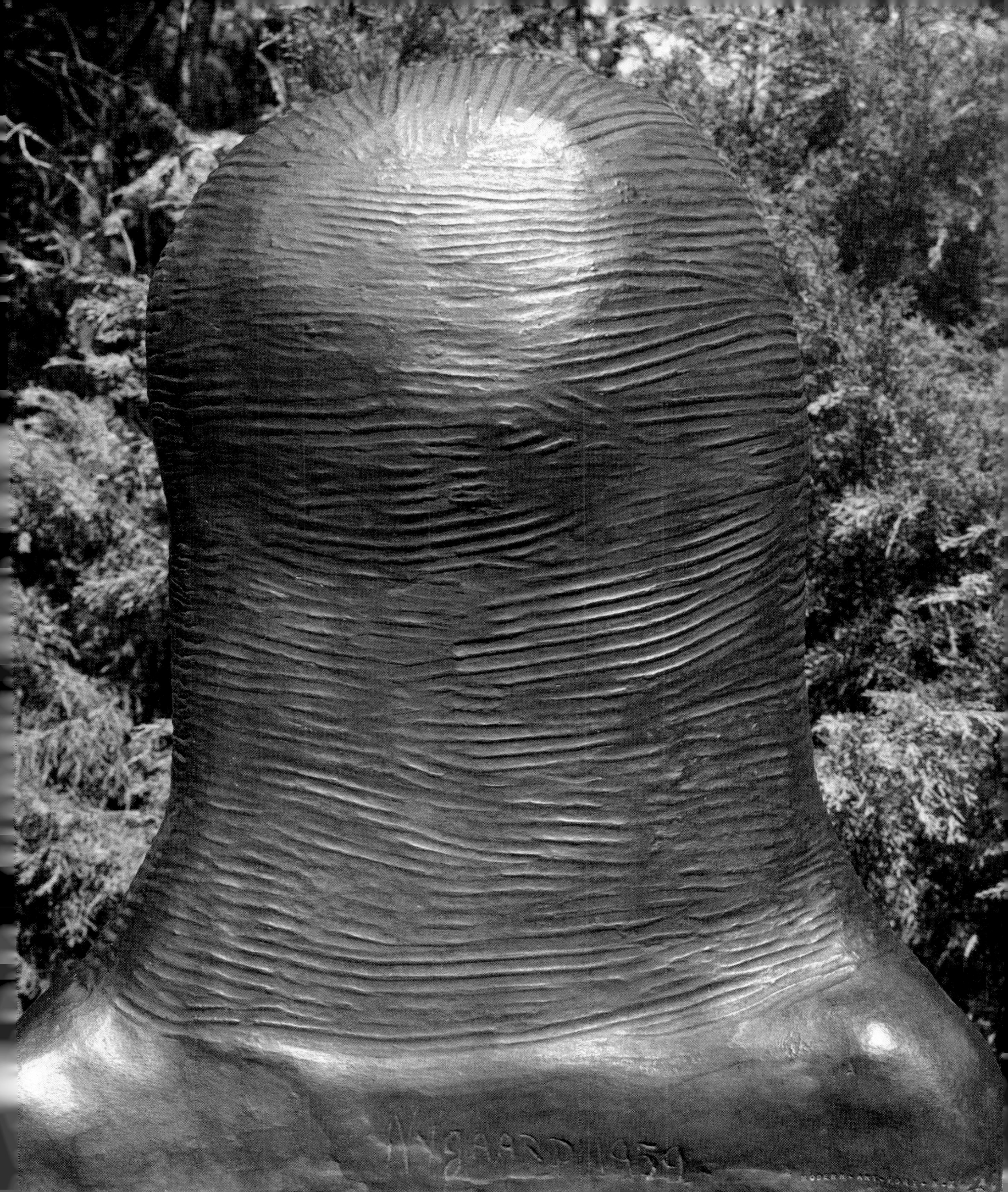

The Poet and Pegasus

I had in mind a tribute to Herman Wildenvey, Poet Laureate of Norway.

His poetry gripped me in my younger days. It still does.

In its fabulously musical, rhythmical lines—and between them—I find precious human notions and essences of wisdom and visions.

A benevolent muse had ever so lightly touched his lips.

He sublimely blessed the summer, sun, and life under a frosty blue sky.

I knew Herman.

I operated on Gisken, his wife.

In return he wrote me a poem.

We both sensed we dealt with human values.

His lighter-than-air vehicle was the word.

Mine was the knife.

I did not ask the poet and the horse to carry any burning message.

I wished to transform poetry into bronze.

Of course, it cannot be done.

Still, there does exist in any beholder that vague, fine network of human nerve fibrils willing to embrace, in a unity of transcendent sensations, the metaphors, rhythms, and spirit playfully reflected in the lines and planes of *The Poet and Pegasus*.

34″ × 10″ × 14″

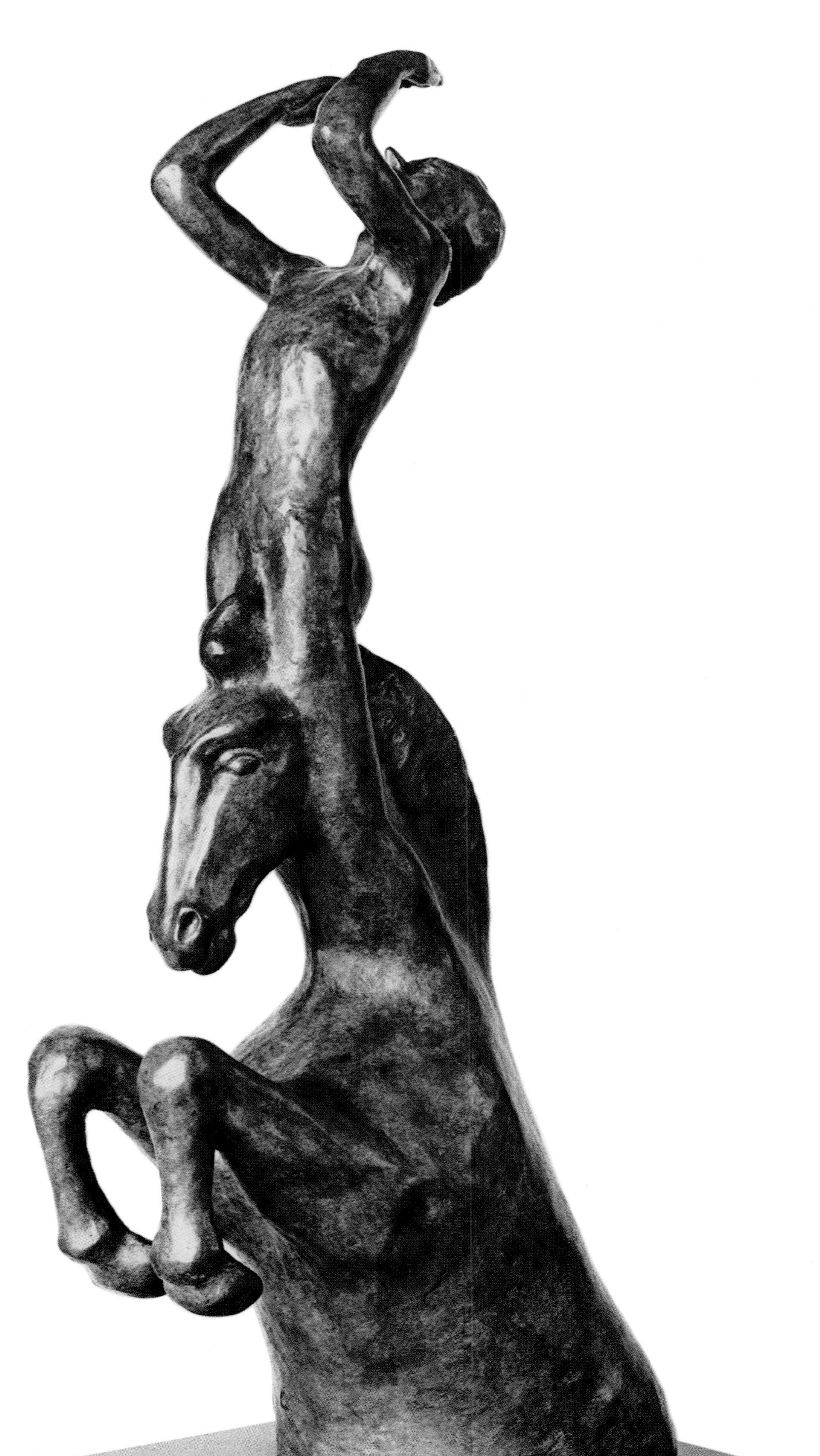

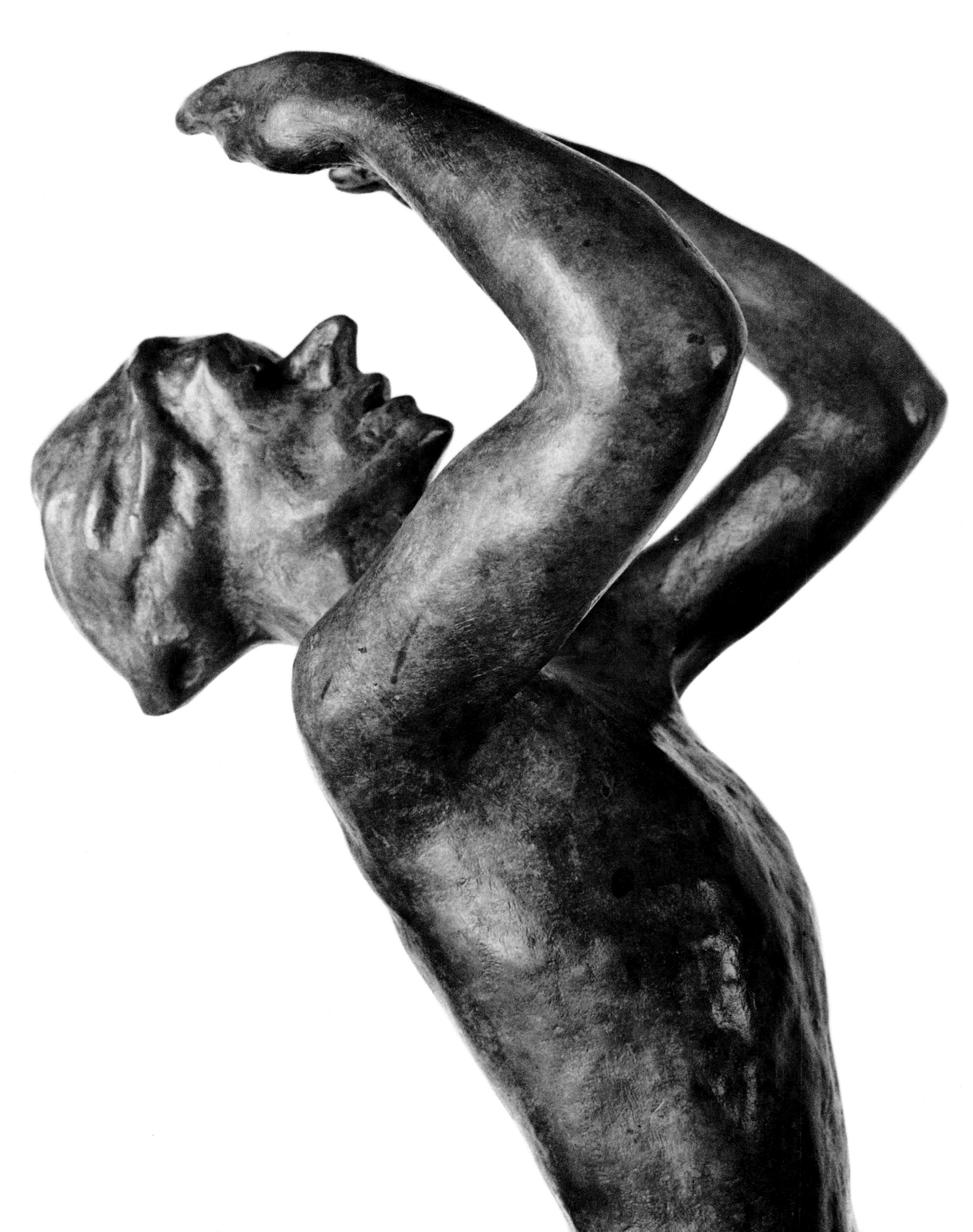

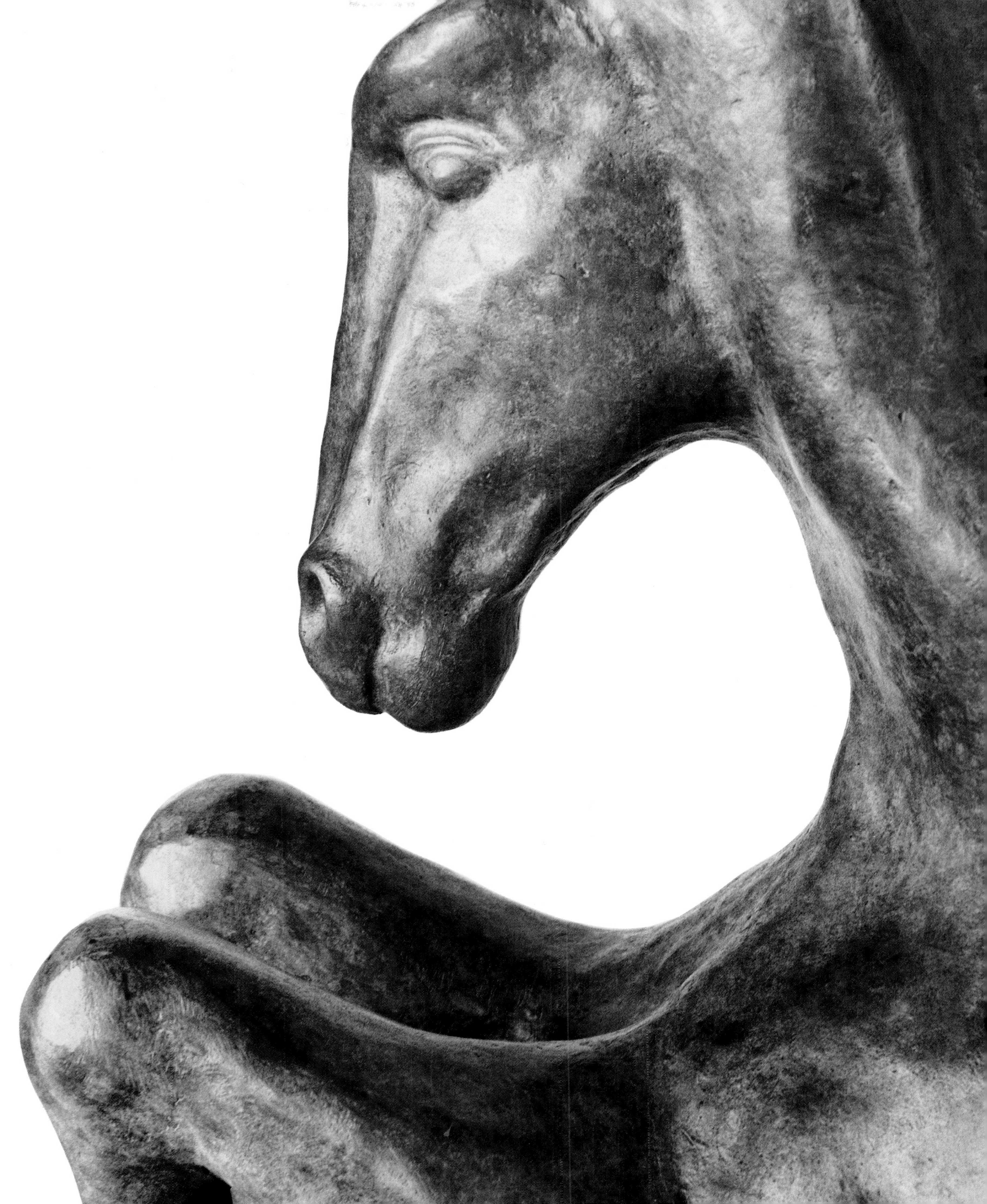

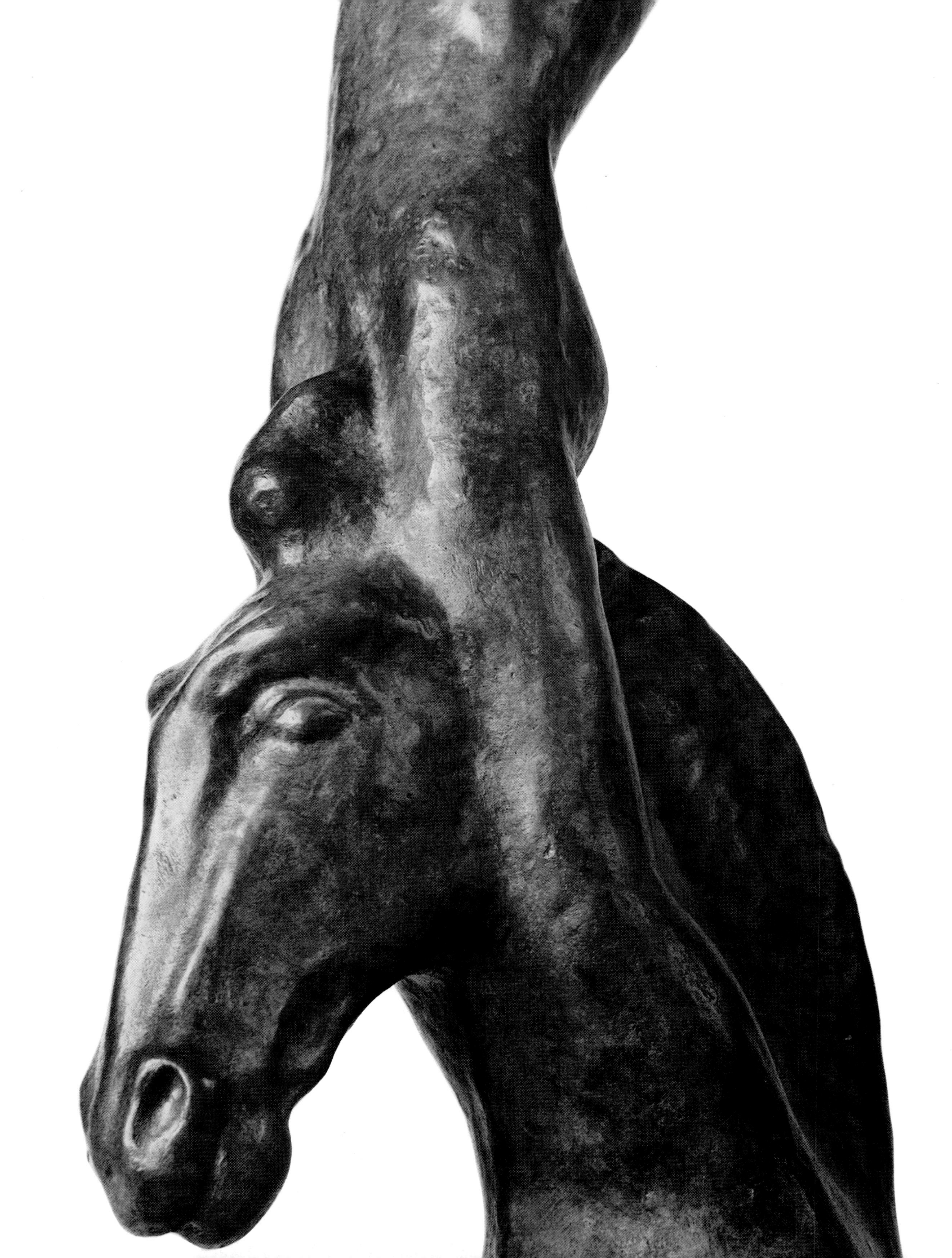

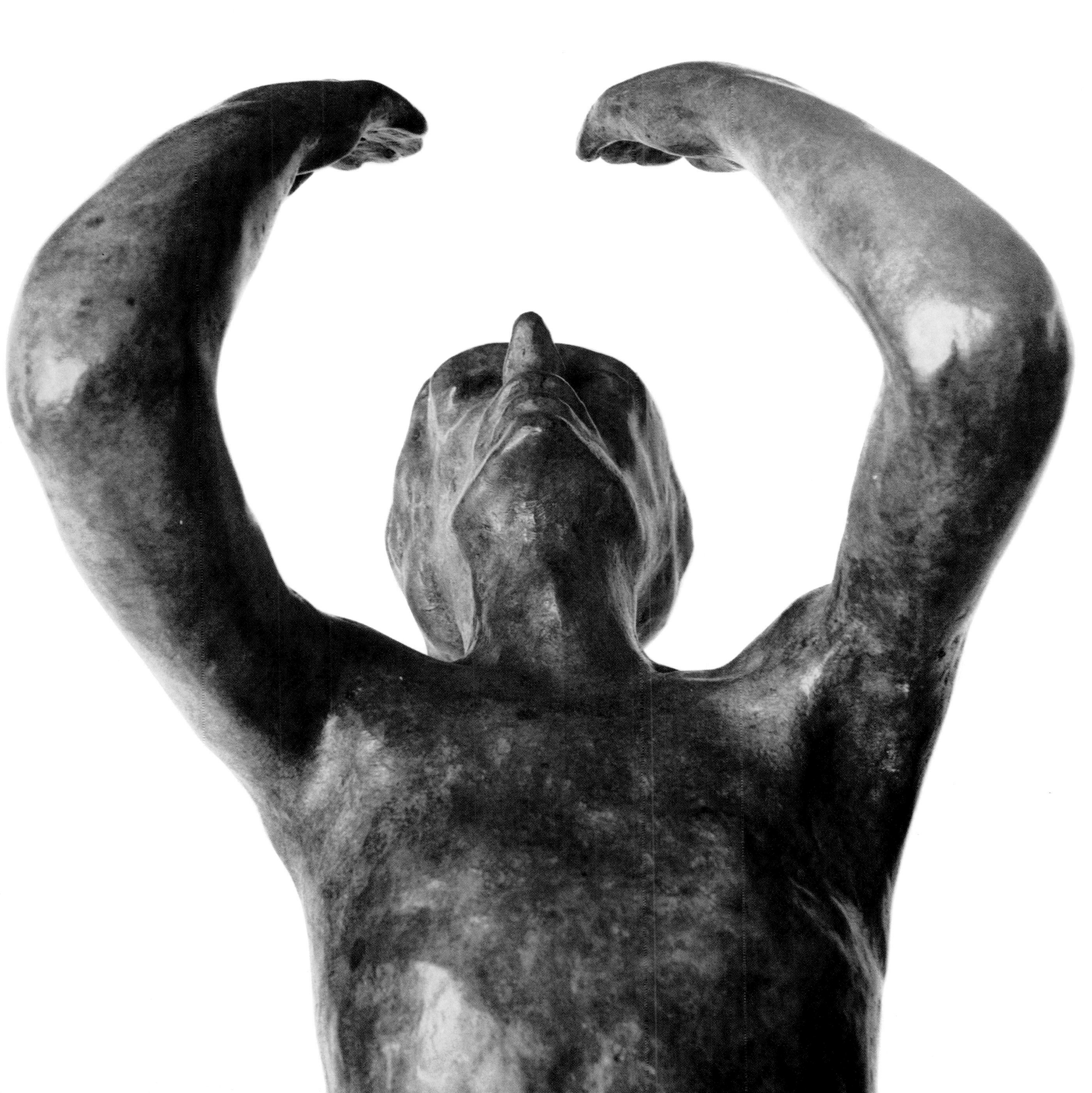

Hamlet

"O God, I could be bounded in a nutshell and count myself a king of infinite space, were it not that I have bad dreams."

William Shakespeare;
The Tragedy of Hamlet, Prince of Denmark
Act II, scene 2

18½″ × 14″ × 9″

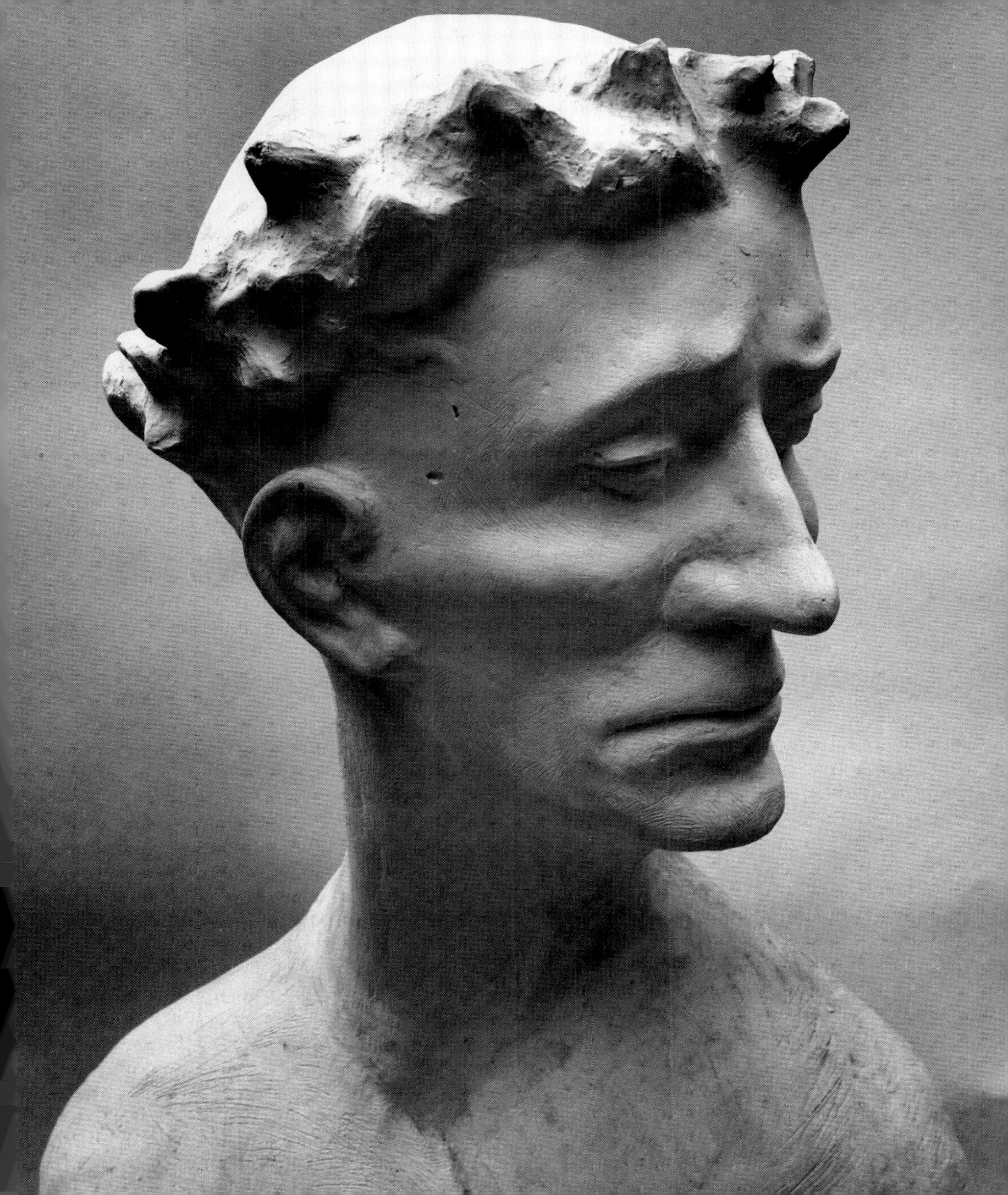

Lamenting Hamlet

"To die, to sleep—no more—and by a sleep to say we end
The heartache, and the thousand natural shocks
That flesh is heir to. 'Tis a consummation
devoutly to be wished. To die, to sleep—"

William Shakespeare
The Tragedy of Hamlet, Prince of Denmark
Act III, scene 1

16½″ × 8½″ × 12″

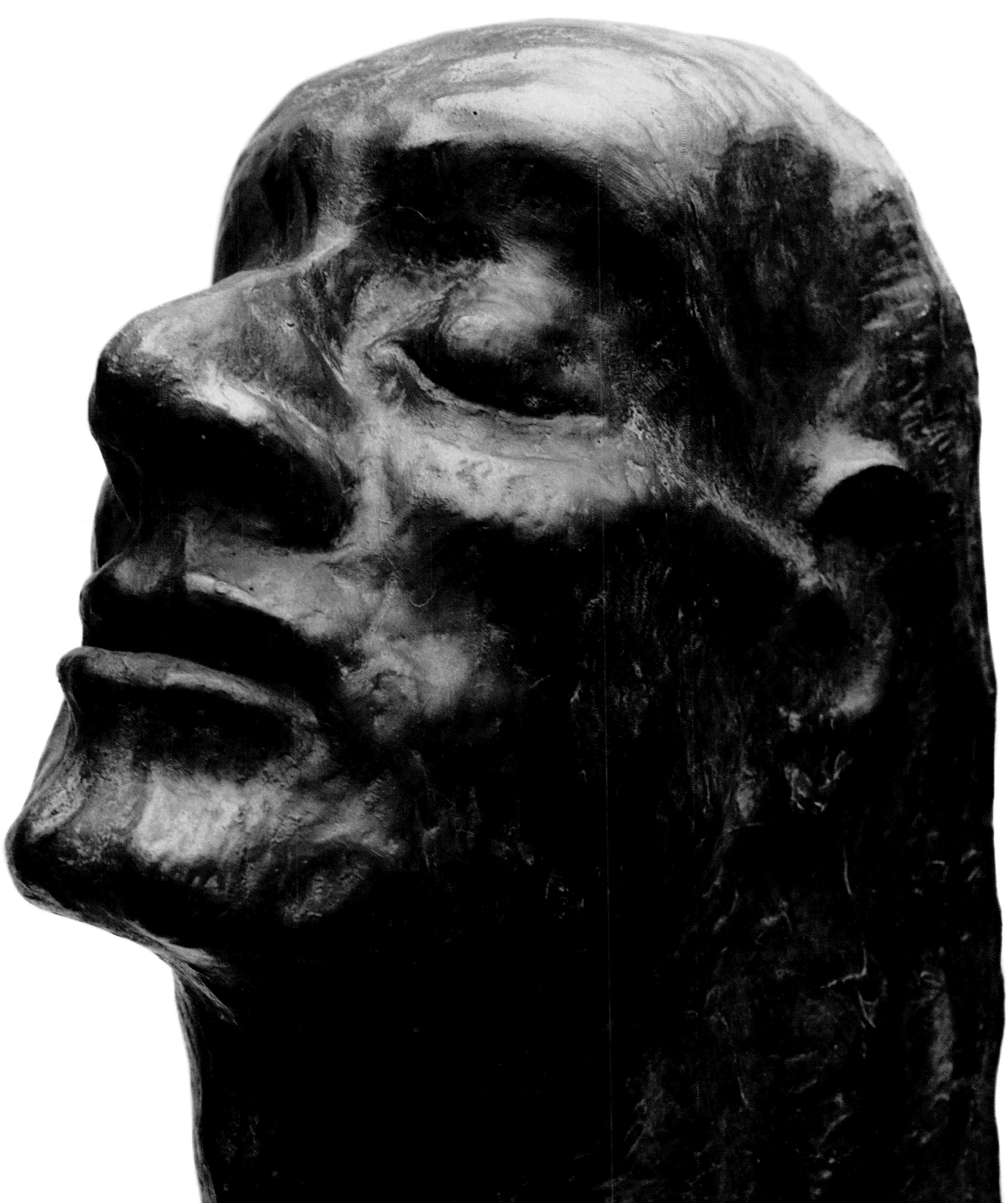

Pietà

The theme of Pietà, Holy Virgin and dead Christ, has figured in European art since about 1300. It originated within clerical circles as no such story is to be found in the Bible.

In medieval times great variations on this motif were not permitted. Thus, in Michelangelo's first *Pietà*, finished in 1500, the Holy Mother is holding the body of Christ across her lap, her right arm supporting his head and shoulders; limp arms and legs hang helplessly; the head is turned back, to the right.

We witness a silent and serene scene: tenderness and sorrow of a mother confronted with the ultimate tragedy of a dead son.

For the Christian Church this scene has had one meaning:

"Holy Mother. This is your son.

They crucified Him.

Now He is yours—and ours."

Some years ago I must have been meditating about this theme of Compassion Mariae.

I wanted to see what I could do to express it in present-day metaphor.

To try to dress this theme in modern clothing would probably offend the Renaissance spirit. Yet, I felt some transformation might be permissible since our heart probably feels a different and less intense relation to this Renaissance subject matter.

It is not that we are strangers to mother love or to the sorrows of death, but that our multifaceted and multicolored culture perhaps neutralizes for us the overwhelming impact on the Renaissance audience inherent in a Compassion Mariae.

If so, a variation on the theme might today be permissible.

I might have been reminded by similar phenomena in music: variations on old themes, providing surprising and charming insight into music of past ages, hauled out of its hiding places to be given new life by a creative mind.

Brahms did this in his variations on St. Anthony's Chorale and Respighi in his Gregorian themes and his ecclestiastical modalities. There are many more such examples.

Such transformations are successful because the composer is a master in his own right.

I noted this as a warning. Still, I could not help trying. And here is my *Pietà*, in its structural simplicity.

One horizontal: the dead son, in anatomical outline.

Behind him rises a triangle: the Mother, the Holy Virgin, motherhood itself, an abstract figure as abstract as sorrow itself.

The group breaks one significant rule.

Art requires unity.

The group should have been all abstract, or all objective.

But death itself breaks rules.

It interrupts the continuity of life.

It prevents unity.

It leaves an emptiness, with form and reason and hopes well obscured.

It leaves more!

Compassion Mariae speaks in her own tongue: "Death does not annihilate. It creates."

23″ × 48″ × 22″

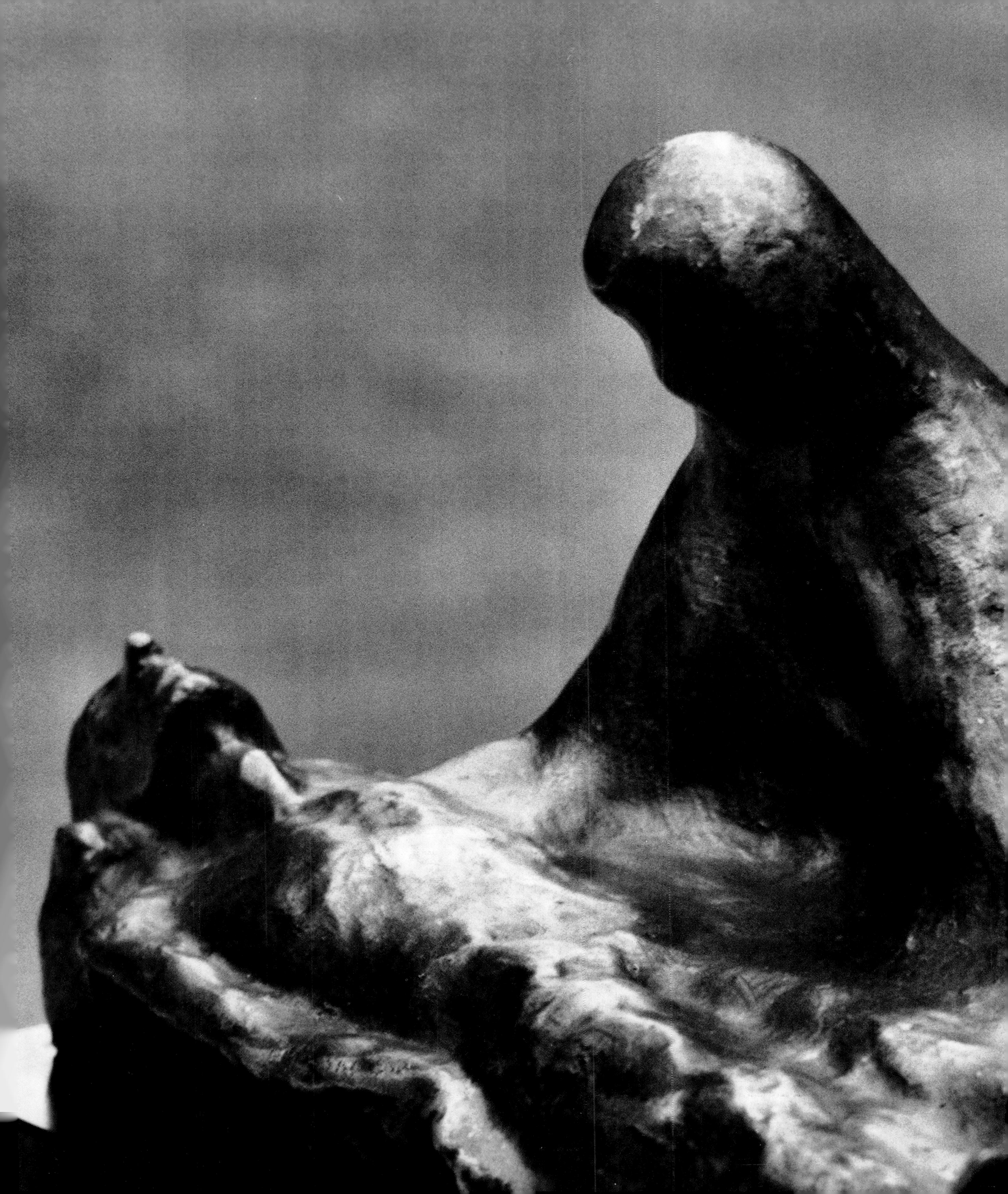

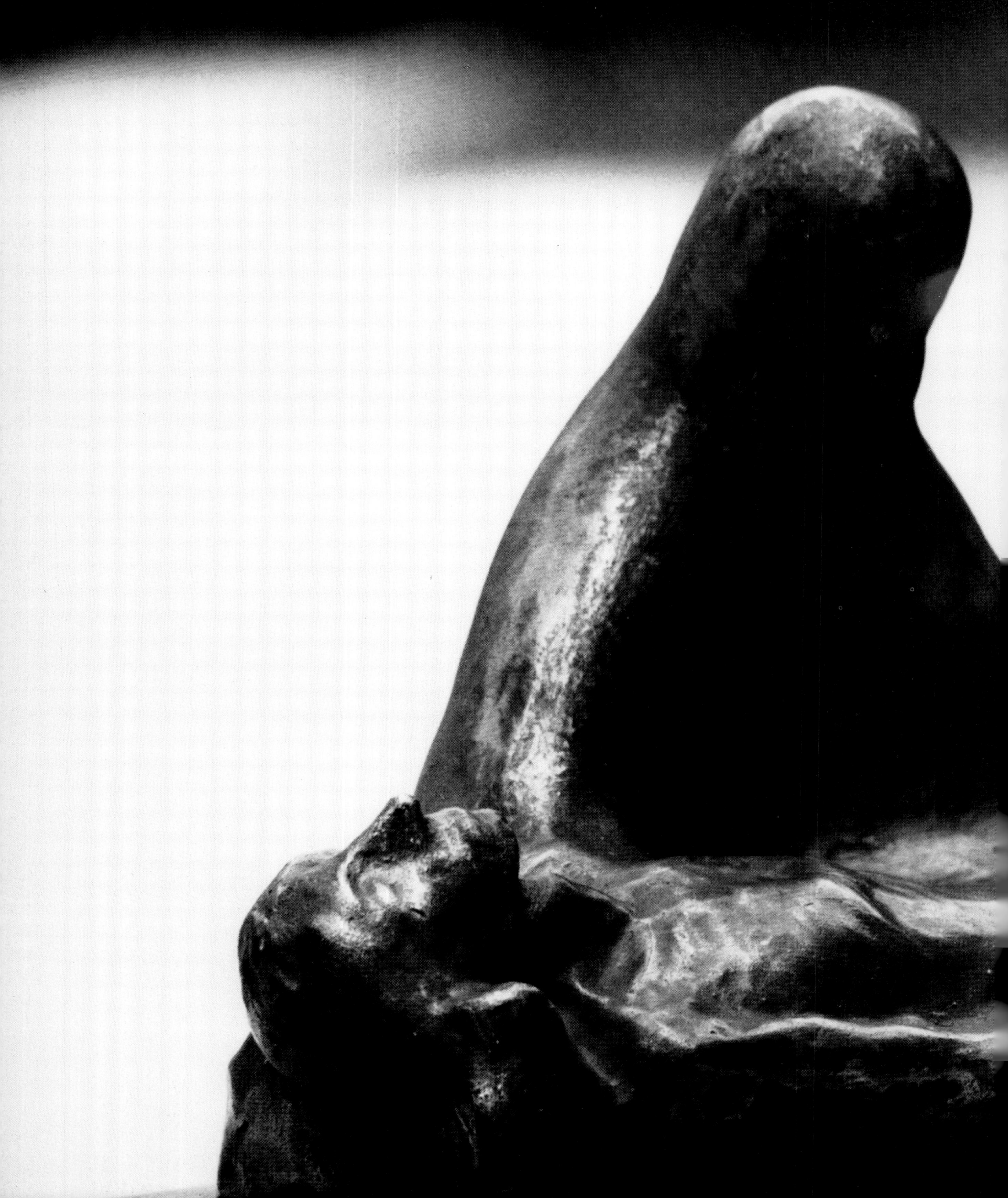

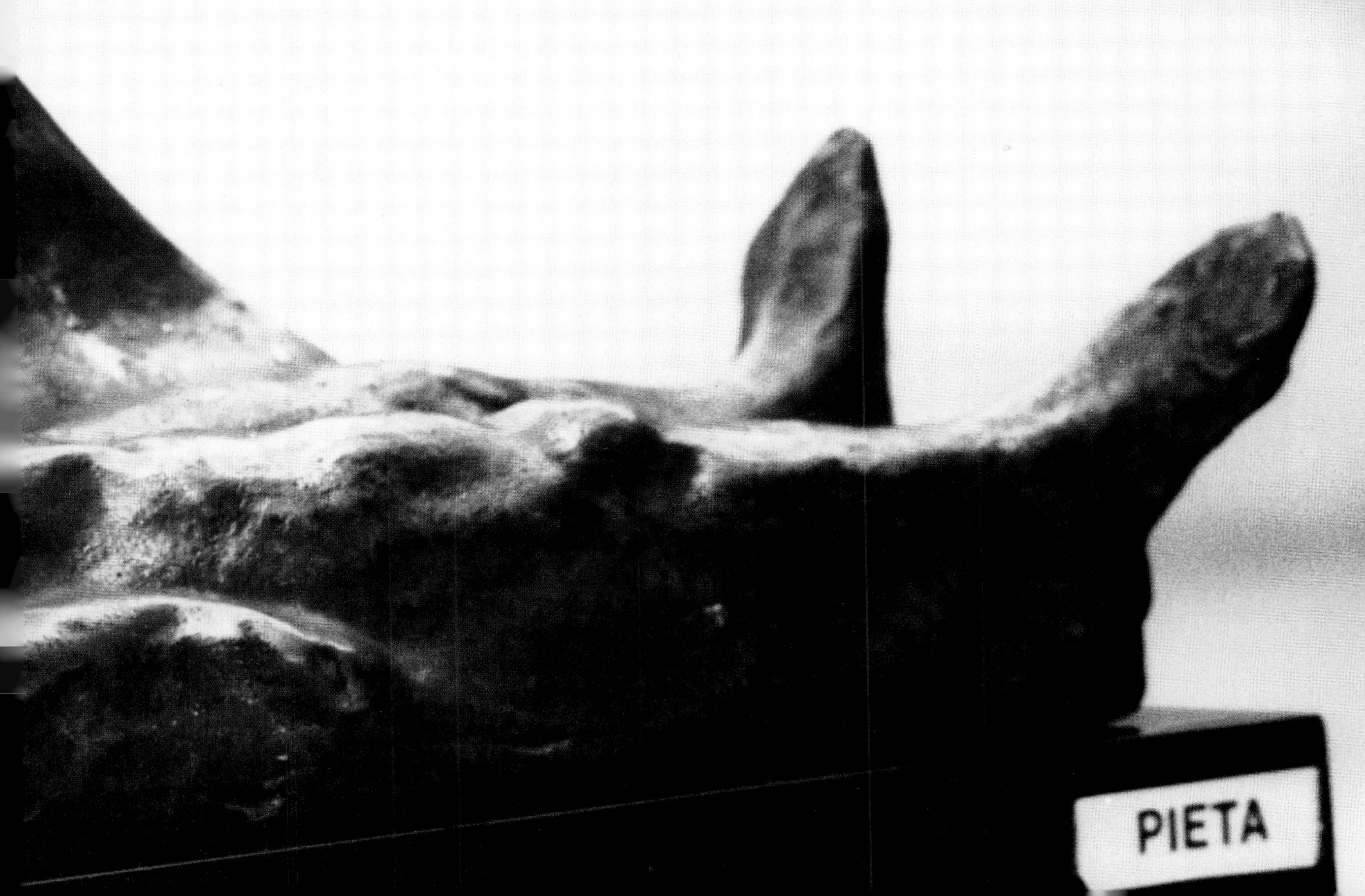
PIETA

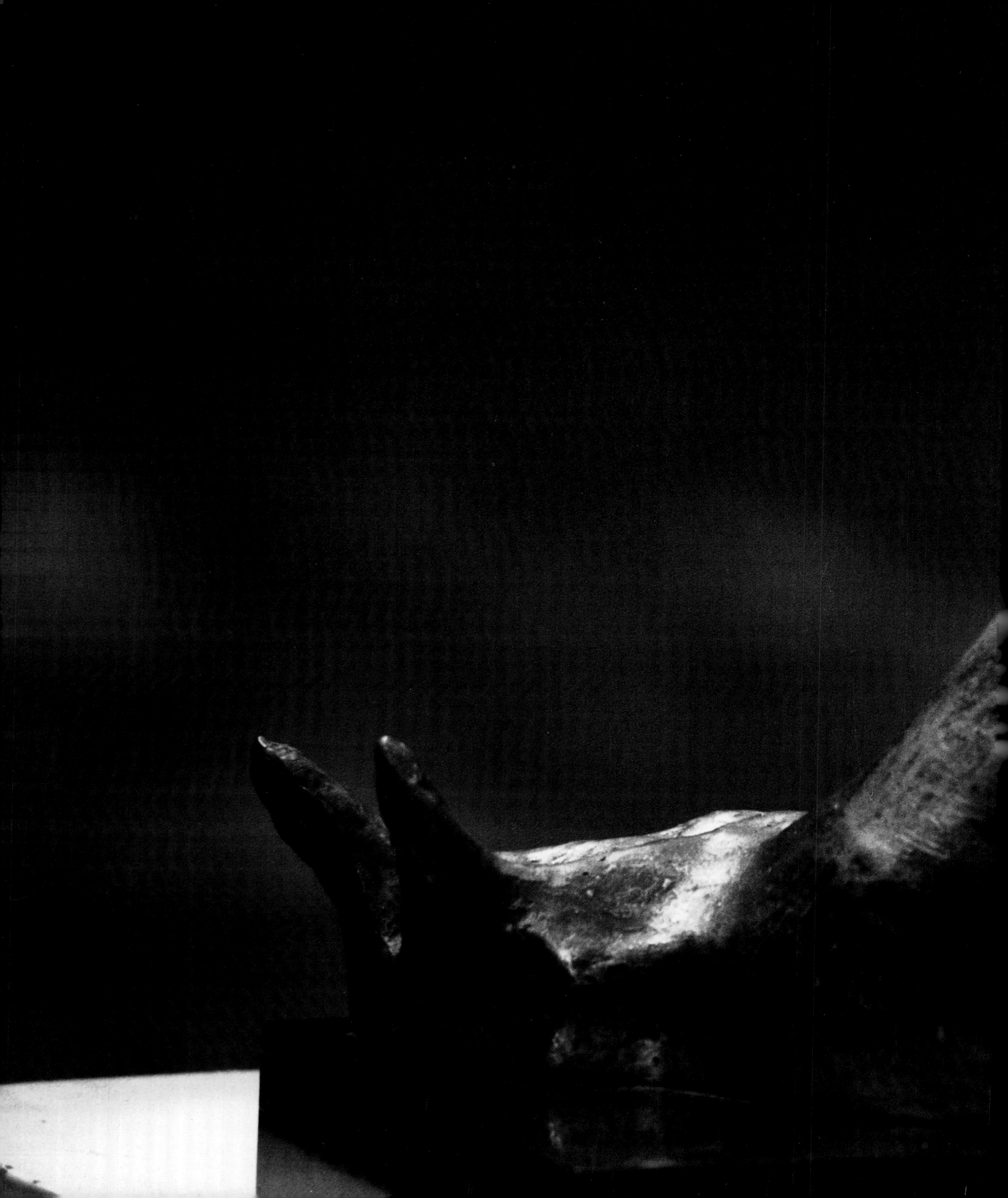

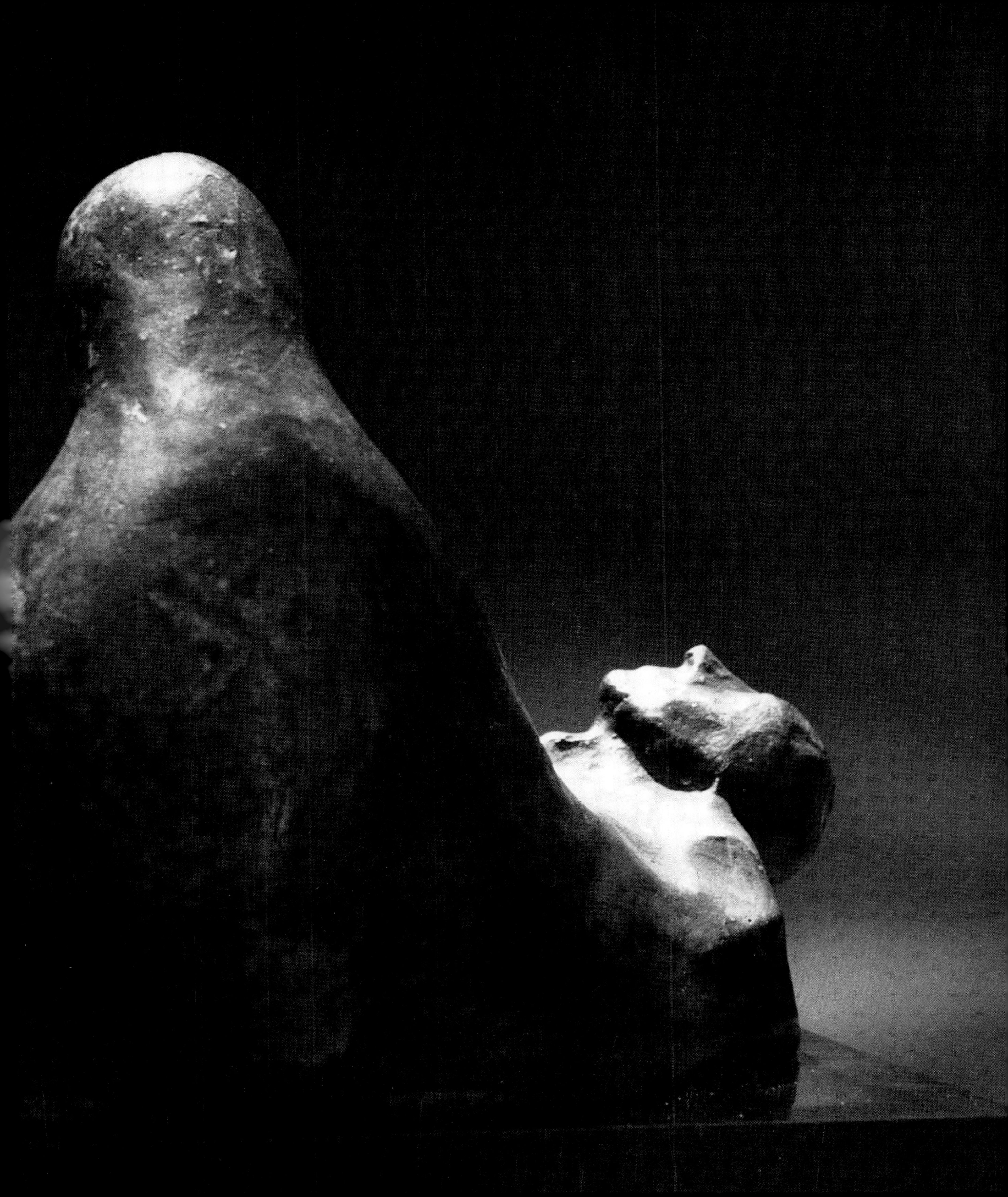

Knut Hamsun

Knut Hamsun, Norwegian poet and author, Nobel Prize winner for literature in 1920, is the subject for this bronze.

The work got a bit complicated by necessity as well as because of Hamsun. There are in all ten figures in the group. Hamsun's life and his literary production, many-faceted and voluminous, were highly complex.

He was born of plain farmer stock and was herding sheep as a youngster. In his teens, he tried and failed as a writer. Came from Norway to the Middle West. Continued his literary efforts while husking corn in the Dakotas, and continued to fail as a writer as well as a starving streetcar conductor in Chicago.

He worked his way back to Norway; to more striving, more starving. He finally broke ice with a memorable work that one cannot readily get out of one's system. You will remember his *Hunger.*

Subsequently he committed what he termed "fist novels." They are an angry young man's protests against the Establishment, against world-famous men on the literary horizon, excepting Walt Whitman, in a way.

During many fertile years, blessed by love for the soil, the genuine, the unadulterated, and in haughty revolt against humbugs of many kinds, he poured out his heart and his brain in an impressive literary work.

He went to his grave an old, proud, disappointed man, not greatly honored by his countrymen, who were sincerely disappointed at his somewhat ambiguous attitude: during the Second World War and the Nazi invasion of Norway, the soul of the nation was at stake—and he was not at the center of it.

It is an enigma that this literary giant and intellect—during times that were testing men's souls in all their extensions and limitations—should be found lacking in essential character valuables when the fire was burning through the house. It is in times like these when the world is searching for, and finding, its genuine giants. At that time Hamsun was not counted among them.

In literary men, as it must be true in all men, it is not necessary to realize the very weakest points in men, except in special conditions. The world is filled with them. It seems that in our system, in our history, it is inherent to emphasize and extract strength and force as the constructive means by which the world moves forward. However, something is moved by all. Sometimes also by the weak, but moved it is. And blessed be those that move.

I have no small interest in this man of word and poetry. He came out of some place that some call nowhere. He created something which is found in people's souls, in their daily life, in their dreams, in their work, and in their hopes and prayers.

There is the young boy slinging his arm around the curved horn of a proud ram projecting its head directly out of the block. There is the angry fist. Here are two lovers from Victoria. Here is the dreamy poet's diffusely outlined face, his head gently bending to his shoulder as his mind is strangely perfused by tender and archaic memories of ages past.

The main and center group is made up of three figures. In the center I have placed the mature, dominating artist. To the right, he is closely tied in with the emaciated young man whom he is upholding with his right arm, lifting him, steadying and

68″ × 72″ × 76″

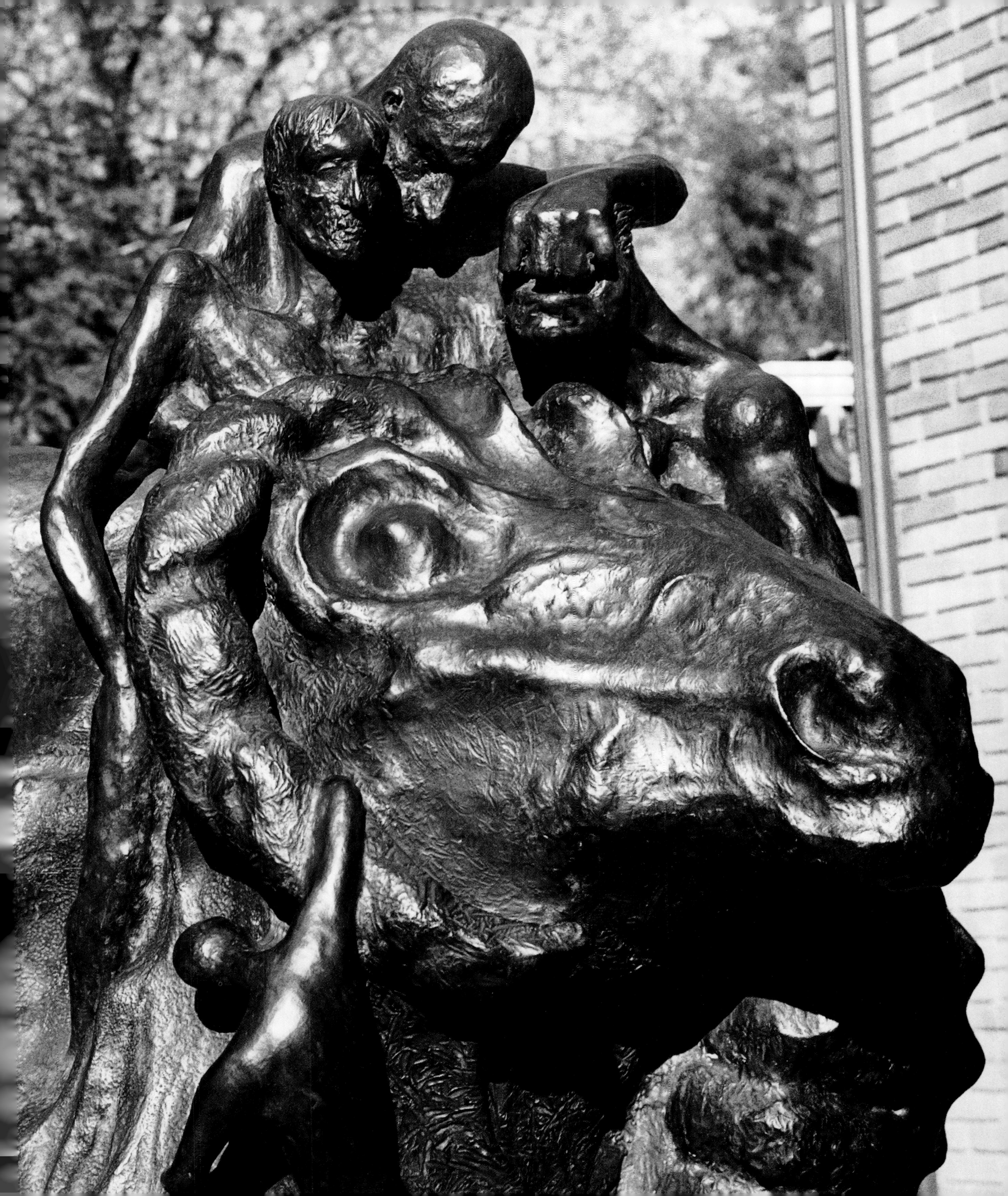

protecting him. The master's left arm is strongly bent forward, and his left hand is forcefully dug into the mouth of a storming-on genius, who, with bent neck, lunges into the universe yelling to be heard, while being restrained by the dominant master who is urging clear utterances and songs, not only screaming. The lesson: geniuses are not born, they are made.

Admittedly, a sculptural group like this one is in direct competition with a complex story that might require words instead of bronze.

Hamsun did not ever have to try to turn himself into sculpture. He expressed himself otherwise, and in masterly fashion.

Expressing him and his work as pictorial art, I admit, is inconceivable.

Still I have ventured to try to extract in bronze a small part of him as a challenge to the mysterious act of sculpting. That is where I might have committed a cardinal sin. But I was anxious to risk it. And it was fun.

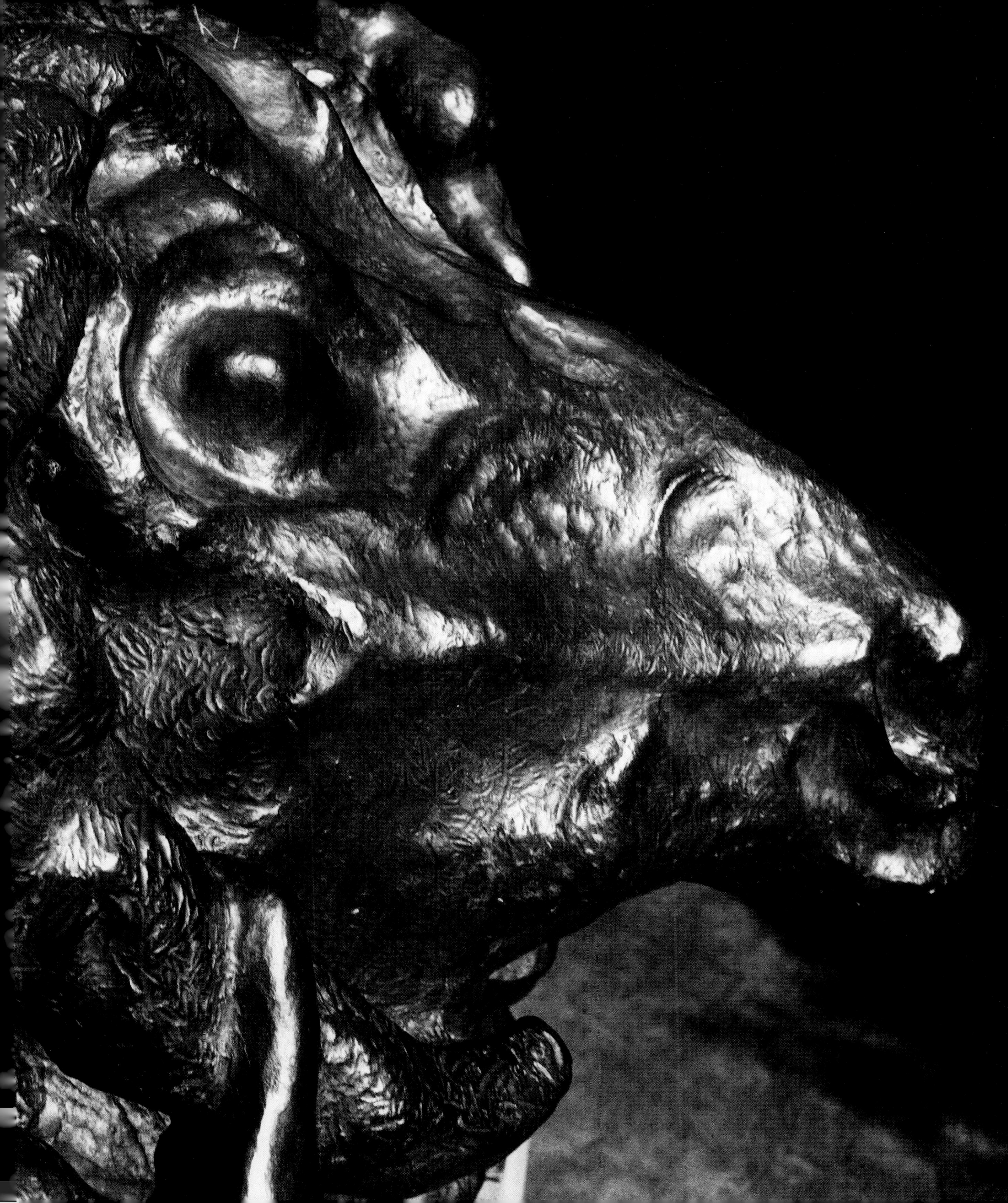

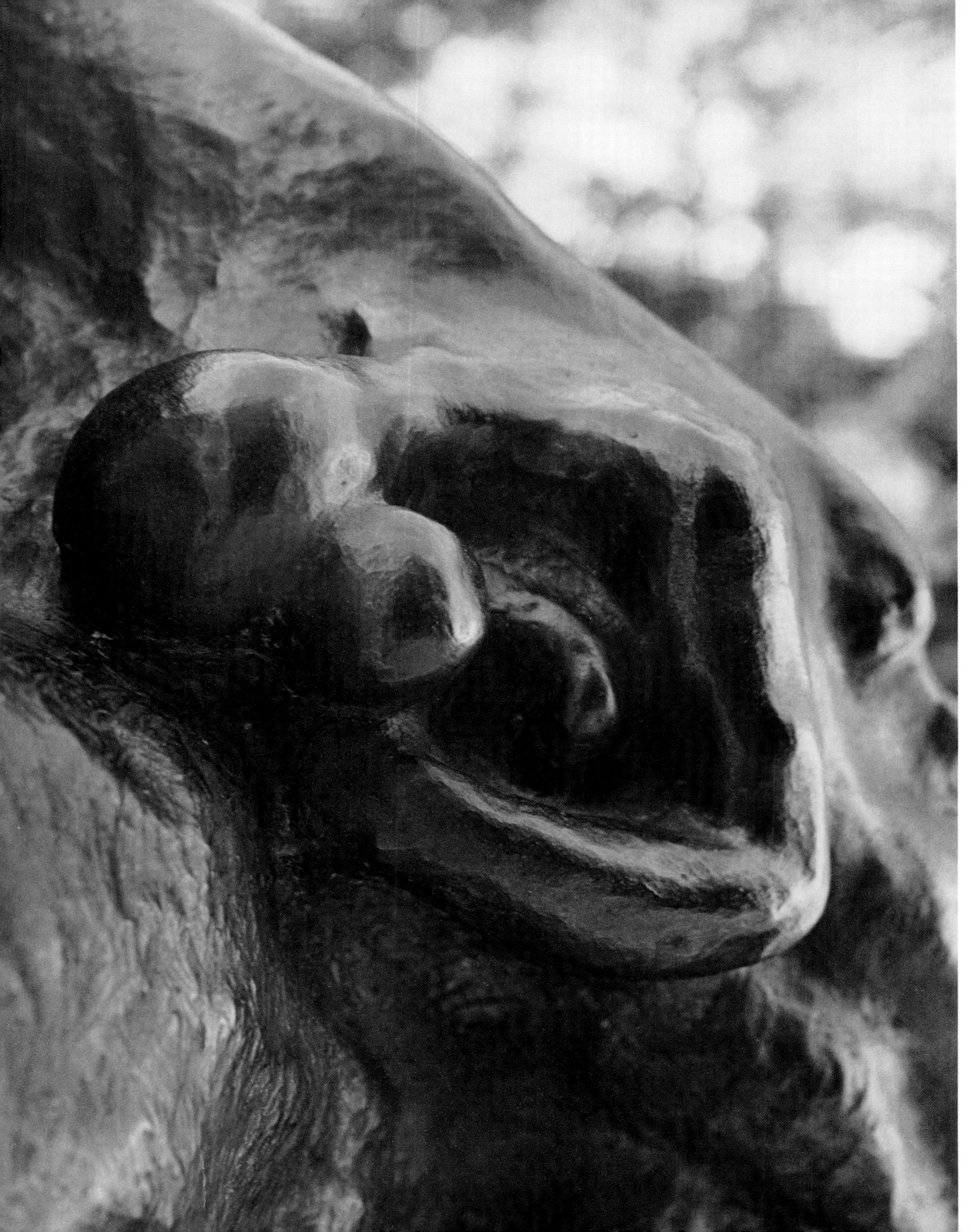

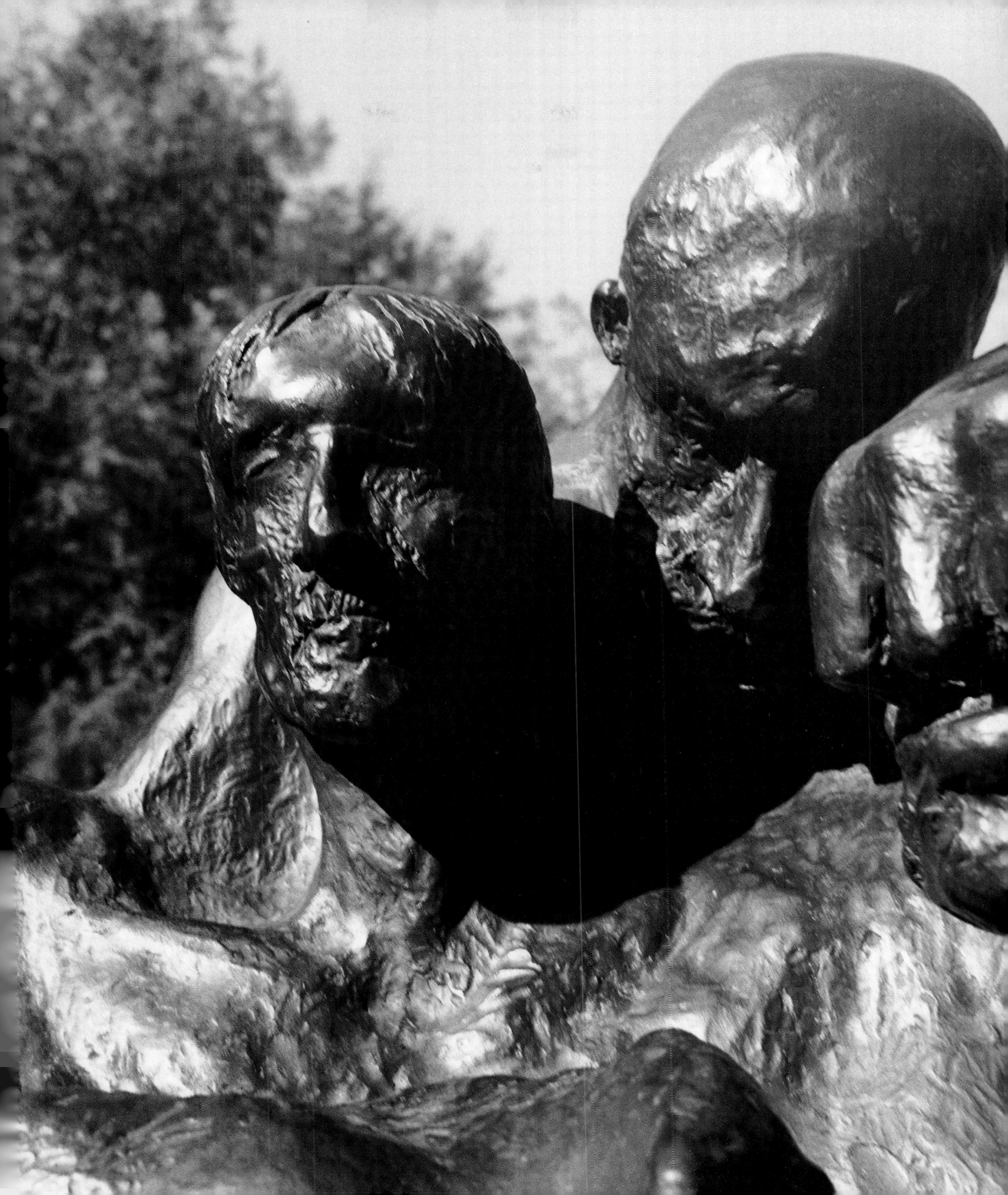

The Death of Savonarola

On May 23, 1498, Savonarola was hanged and burned in the Piazza facing the Palazzo Vecchio in Florence. The present-day Florentines pass the very place every day. The city has marked the place of execution with a commemorating bronze plate among the cobble stones of the wide Piazza.

The date may be thought of as a watershed in the history of the Catholic Church. The past and the future were in conflict. The issue of the Church, and the state of Florence and other states, seemed gravely in doubt. The politics of the state and the affairs of the Church were played on the same stage and often in the same play, be it comedy or tragedy, indistinguishable in tactics, in aims, and in intensity. Only differentiated by semantics.

Savonarola was a Dominican friar. Within the Church he reached his eminent position as prior of San Marco in Florence. During the last five years of his life he was not only a prior to the Florentines of his time. He was their prophet and their political leader as well. And that was at the crest of the Renaissance.

Worst of all, he was the scourge that intended to chastise and to renovate what he considered a guilty Church.

He was condemned to death by the Medicis and the Borgia Pope, Alexander VI.

The Renaissance was the flowering base of our Western cultural world. The Catholic Church, the Medicis, Botticelli, Leonardo da Vinci, and Michelangelo were active, but few had to go to their death with papal and Medici decrees, as did friar Savonarola.

His sin might have been his urge to cleanse from within; the sin of the Church might have been not to allow him.

In the thirty years after the last whiff of smoke had evaporated from the Arno following his burning, another Catholic monk was preaching, writing, meditating, and overcoming. Martin Luther was not for burning.

This is in a nucleus what the sculptural group *The Death of Savonarola* may be able to touch, admittedly in a peripheral way.

This segment of history, and similar ones, must be told by words. A thousand words are infinitely more expressive than any picture. But pictorial art may be permitted to touch upon it ever so lightly, as I have tried to do in my own way in this work.

I have tried in sculptural form to tell a story about Savonarola, hanged and burned, and without jury trial. I have included the responsible parties—the Medicis and the Borgia Pope. Lorenzo de' Medici was dead by four years at the time of the burning. It was his family, his party and their secular interests that combined with those of the Pope to make the deed possible, in a so-called legalized manner.

I have used the image of Lorenzo de' Medici, Il Magnifico, as expressed in a well-known bust by Verrocchio as part of the present group. A Florentine might readily understand this constellation of eminent Renaissance figures.

In present-day art, over a few decades, it has been considered good manners not to burden art with the telling of a story.

However, it seems that it is not possible to make an image without at the same time touching upon a story. I am seeing a simple thread made to hang from a ceiling, maybe with an attached bead at its end, swinging lightly in an exhibition hall. That item

34″ × 16″ × 17″

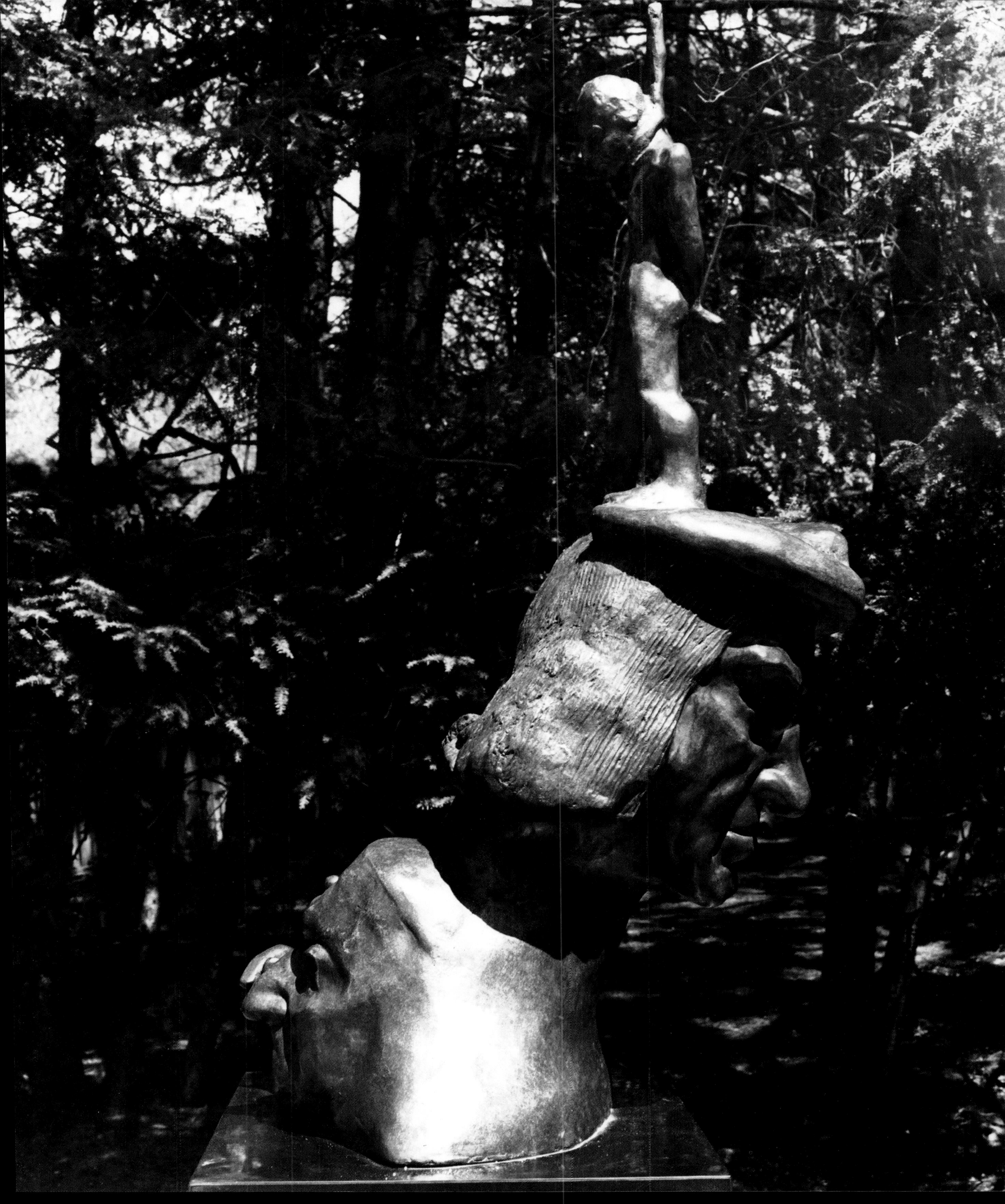

expresses something. It may be inclined to say: "I am nothing." It may also insist it represents Newton's Law, or "I am art now." Whatever it is claiming to say, or doesn't say, it still tells a story, threadbaredly so perhaps, but still telling.

In this sculptural group of mine, I have fallen back upon the idea of the Indians and their totem pole. The political Renaissance conglomeration seems to fit my plan to execute a vertical sculpture.

The Borgia Pope is at the base, lifting his hand in conventional blessing. The Medici is almost unnoticeably growing out of the Pope's anatomy while turning his determined face in exactly the opposite direction of the Pope.

A small, naked Savonarola, in size completely out of proportion to that of Lorenzo and the Pope, is standing on top of the Medici's flat-bottomed hat. Savonarola is facing in the identical direction as that of his superior, the prelate of the Church.

He is emaciated. This probably is of little ultimate consequence as Savonarola already has the noose around his neck; in addition, as was decreed, there is around his neck an iron chain: the flame after his hanging shall burn through the ropes, but he will still hang.

This is the way I see him, just before he is lifted aloft. His well-developed legs defiantly stand apart in full anatomic and mental equilibrium as the last seconds of his physiologic life are ticking away. Those seconds of the beginning of his next historical life are waiting just around the corner at the Ponte Vecchio: his ashes were thrown into the river flowing under the bridge. The Arno River and the sea, which they finally reach, could not have been greatly enriched by those meager remains.

We have.

The sculptural group, in all its surrealistic manifestations, may represent a realistic reminder.

History always repeats itself.

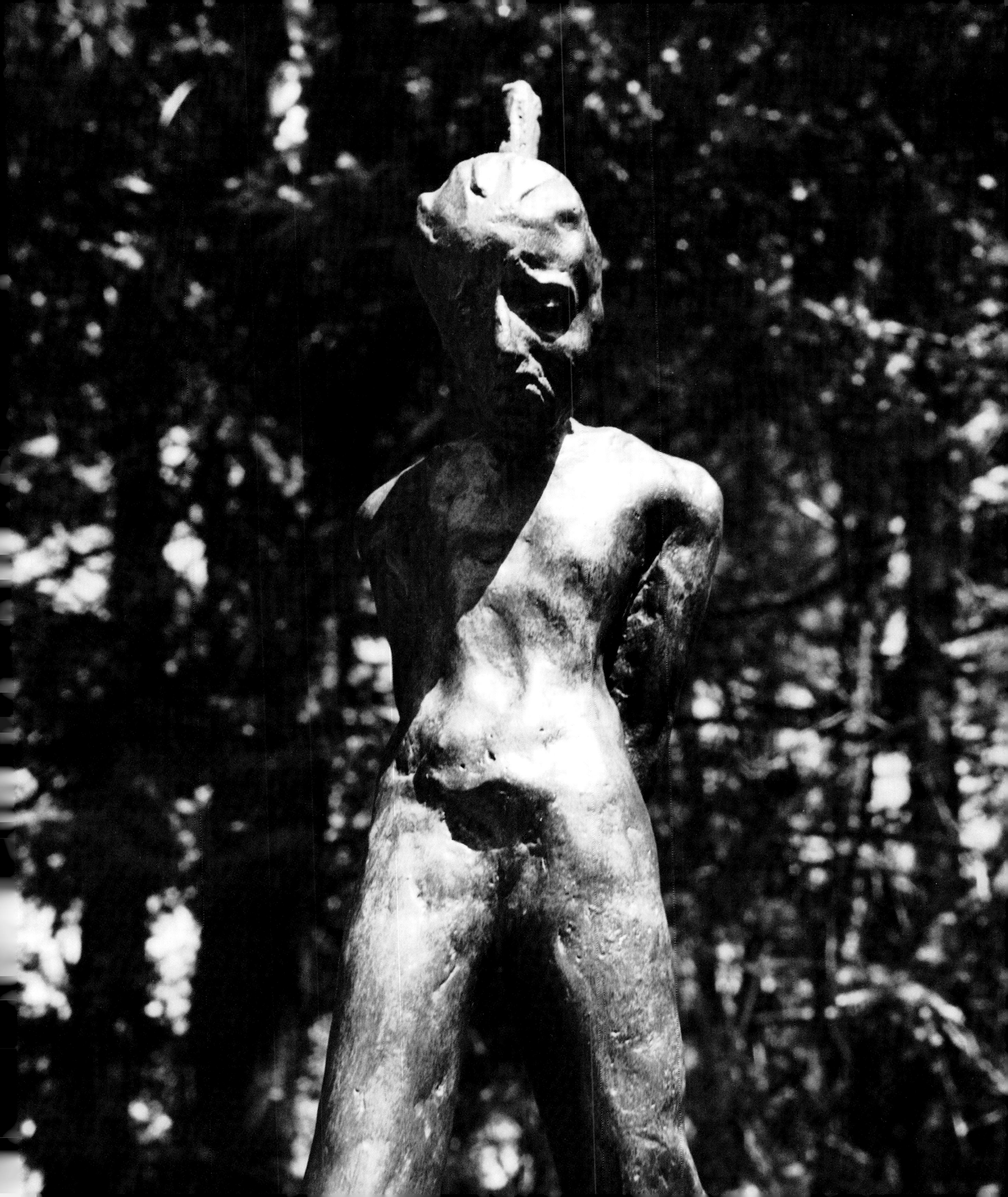

The Virgin Mary

Some of us will reckon it a blessing to have been exposed to the Renaissance art filling the galleries and the castles of Florence, Rome, Paris, Leningrad, Washington, and New York.

In these art collections the Virgin Mary is an ever recurring subject matter in ever-varying constellations and iconographies, while constantly and always remaining the biblical deity: the Mother of Christ, the Child of the Holy Ghost, and as such venerated by and loved by women, by men, by artists.

Our present age is different from the lushly flowering decades of the Renaissance.

I am not prepared to think we are better. In some respects we may not be worse. In one way we are not the same as the Florentines of the time of Savonarola and the Medicis.

During their life, a close, intimate relation between the population and its Church existed, which shaped the daily life of the urban and rural countryside.

It shaped the life of the artists.

Michelangelo stated that an artist without God would never create great art. And great art was produced in abundance during those times.

If we were to bring her up to the present day, how would the Virgin Mary appear to us today?

This occupied me for some time, admittedly more like a metaphysical challenge.

But seemingly, as if something was maturing, I started to glimpse in our society the presence of the Blessed Virgin in many places, and in many occupations. She was still alive. She was real. Real in all her grace and femininity. Vital in her strong dedication to be, to serve.

I saw her in the hospital one morning. A child had been brought into the emergency room. A wild dog had attacked him and his face, his trunk, his arms were macerated into a bloody pulp.

She gently leaned over him. She folded her arms about his disheveled existence and safely lifted him from the stretcher over to the bed from the intensive care unit.

Here was our present day heroine and deity.

Still the Blessed Mary.

I got to my clay in the late evening.

The delivery lasted less than half an hour.

I had been pregnant with her for some years.

And now the folds in her garment are gently flowing within the cloth of bronze.

POSTSCRIPT

It has obliquely been indicated to me that my essay, "The Virgin Mary," shows a befuddled thinking relative to central theologic concepts—and worse—the writing uncovers alledgedly a moral blindness and an absolute irreligiosity.

Therefore this P.S.

This is a late date in my not brief life.

I shall therefore not feel inclined to a strong personal defense.

I have lived this life with struggles common to us all.

I believe I have also lived it with good intentions molded in Christian morality and with an acute awareness and responsibility to the *existing seconds* and the gratitude for the *now* given me.

Still, I am anxious not to withhold valid thoughts and historical and fundamental theologic concepts against which my writing might dramatically have committed cardinal sins.

41″ × 24″ × 9½″

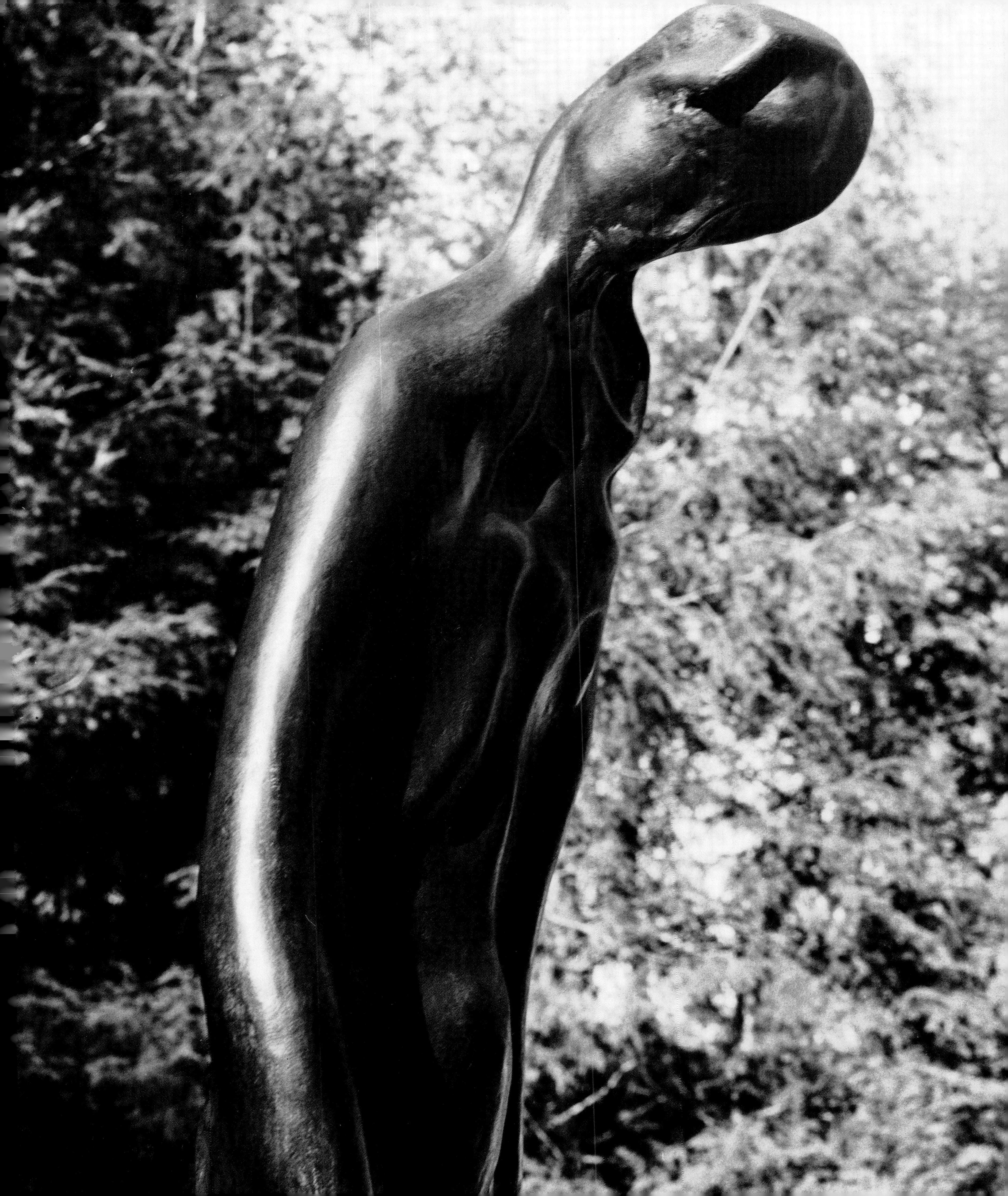

I am listening to Father John:

"A human being, versed in morality and in Christianity is living a life molded by our Deities.

The Almighty God, His Son Jesus Christ, the Holy Ghost, the Mother of Christ, the Blessed Virgin Mary.

These are the Deities of the Church.

They are not to be construed as replicas of men and women, to be searched for and found among people.

They are Deities.

They are transcendent figures in the Heavens.

They are not only symbolising—they are collectively exercising and executing God's blessing upon humanity.

Through the Christian Church and our Holy Deities, this blessing upon humans is to be extended into Eternal Life, when these offerings are accepted by the virtuous life of each one of us.

Thus our Christian Deities are to be found among us wherever we are—and whenever we are searching for them in true spirit.

However, it must be understood: the Blessed Virgin Mary is not expected to appear even during the worst catastrophies in the emergency room.

She is not to be transformed into the sinful soul of a human of her gender.

She is not to be catapulted from the Deity existence which is hers.

She is a pillar in the Basilica of Christ.

She is not to descend onto earth to succor and give a hand.

The Virgin Mary is God's own choice.

She is the Mother of Christ.

She lives in the Heavens—and in receptive hearts.

She is not to be enrolled as a paramedic."

Thus spoke Father John.

And the Bible speaks thus: "Thou shall not make unto thee any graven images, or any likeness *of anything* that *is* in heaven above" (Exodus 20:4).

I promised no defense.

But I must be privileged to present a confession: this confession deals with two personal and constructive weaknesses.

1) Throughout my days I have slowly learned to sense the potential value of the time—and the seconds—granted me.

I don't any longer say that I have only one life as if I were complaining that there should be many more.

I have had more than one life. I have had myriads of seconds—and packed within them potentials that I have learned to understand must be fulfilled to the best of my ability and, if feasible, to the best of the value inherent in the seconds.

I am grateful for slowly learning to understand those great potentials.

They are to be cared for *now*. For that reason a longing for eternity has been greatly weakened in me.

I like to think that I must be responsible for my life *now*.

2) I have accumulated a great admiration for humanity, in all its weaknesses and miseries, in all its inhumanities, as if, like a constructive silk worm spinning a protective, glorious layer of texture about us all, we were cocoons with myriads of potentials.

Thus I have learned to live in Christ and to believe in life—and somehow to believe in me and beyond. Thus ends my Postscript.

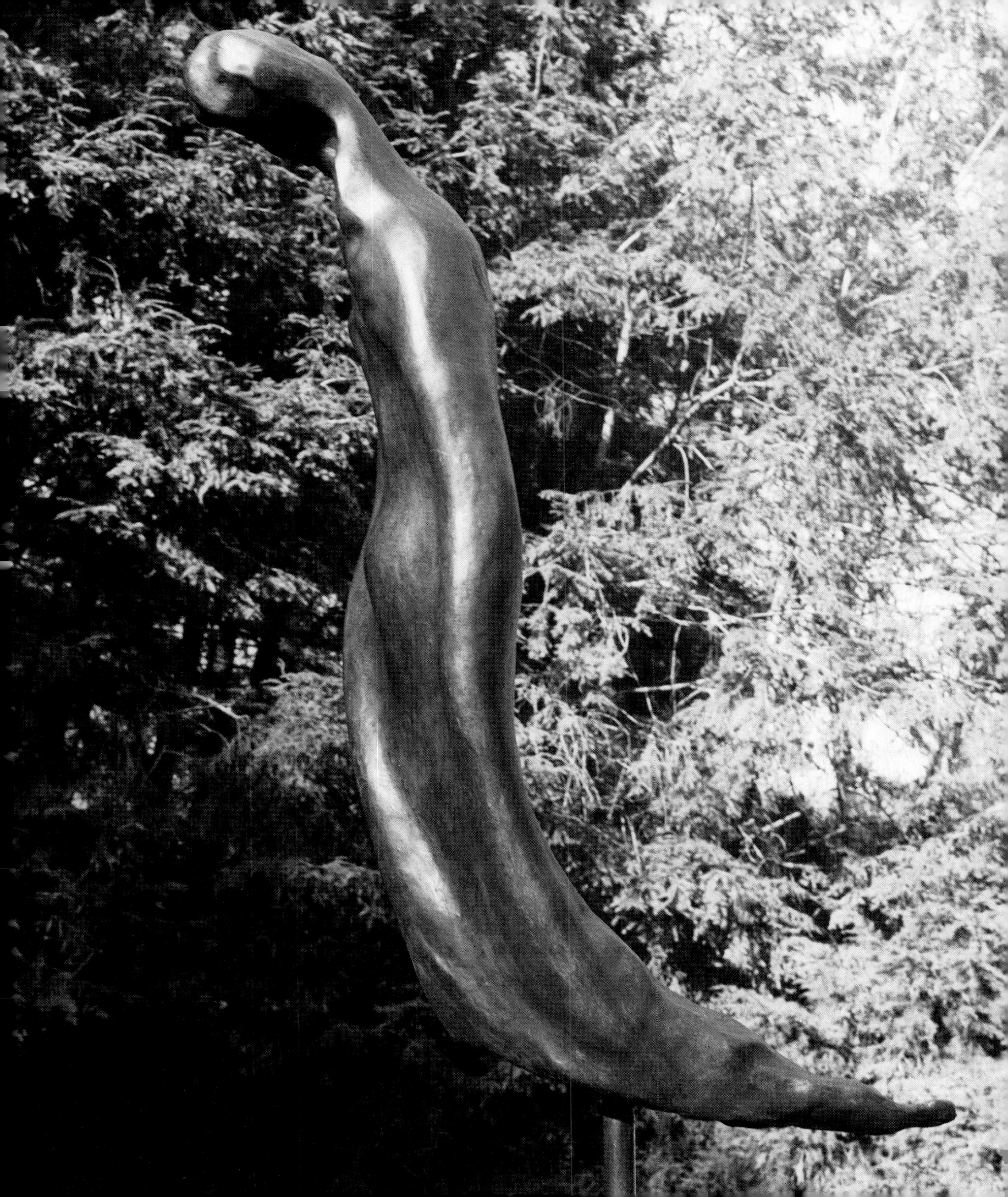

Exodus

The individual depicted in this sculpture seems to be at the last chapter of his biologic life. Therefore the title.

With the Holocaust in mind, one might suggest that this must be an inmate of a concentration camp.

It happens to represent a patient well looked after in a hospital.

I saw him often during those days before he passed on. One might say that he happened to harbor a museum of serious illnesses.

He was a man in his sixties. An old smoker. An old boozer. A fabulous carpenter. And a patient and grateful soul.

His joints in arms and legs bore painful arthritis, which made it impossible for him to move. Every effort to bend or stretch created lightning pain. His back was curved and stiff.

His breathing was labored. He was close to being what the nurses termed a respiratory invalid.

He had generalized hardening of the arteries.

He was in heart failure, thus throwing him into intermittent coughing spells with miserable struggles trying to rid himself of frothy mucous by mouth.

When sitting in bed, he had to keep his head in a hanging-down position so as to permit blood by gravity to reach the respiratory center in the brain.

He would faint if his head was raised to an upright position without oxygen inhalation.

He knew he was in misery.

He knew it was of little use to fight it out. Still he was patient with the nurses, who realized his special, intense need of care, while the fellow himself, as well as the medical staff, knew full well they were up against a dead-end street.

I have not tried to hide in my writing that this sounds more like a patient's hospital record, to be filed in the Record Room. I agree, but if I had been in complete agreement that would have been the end of it—and there would have been no sculpture by my hand entitled *Exodus*.

Through the personal miseries of this person's last few hours, I could sense the heroic aspect of a human mind confronted with adversity—and worse.

I gently whispered to him. He answered. It was like a quiet, sensible conversation over an open grave—not frightening to either, while between the spoken words one heard a stillness filled with human wisdom about something never taught and at blessed moments coming upon us when needed.

I saw him again a few times. It slowly came to me that even in the most calamitous bodily destructions, it seems that the human mind erects a biologic balance and equanimity touching upon heroic monumentality.

That is when I sensed that a sculptural involvement was naturally entering, while medical science had to throw in the sponge.

I am in great awe of the best in both; so rarely can they constructively be seen in the same light.

I have tried to join them here.

Sculpture and medicine as one.

18″ × 25″ × 46″

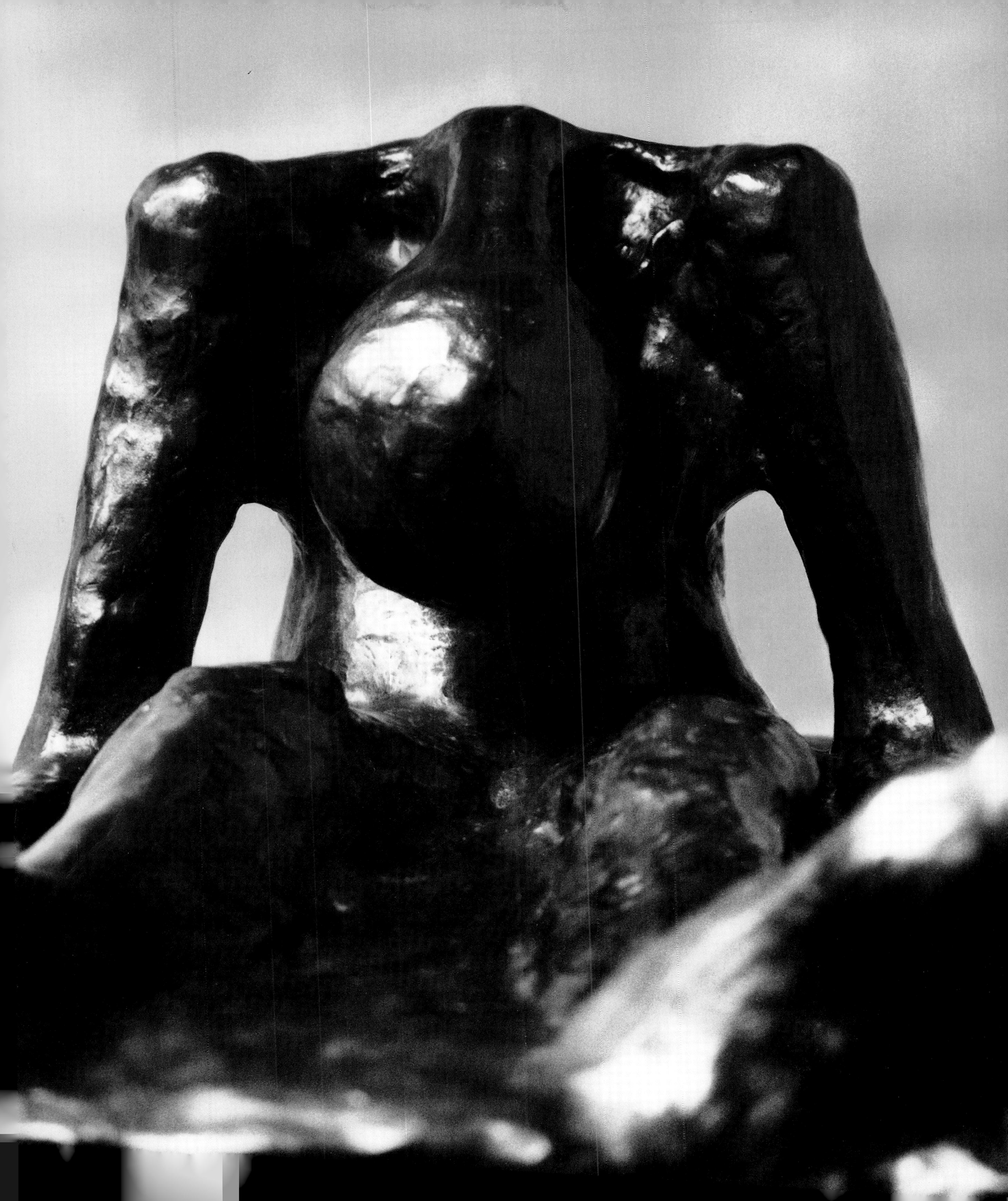

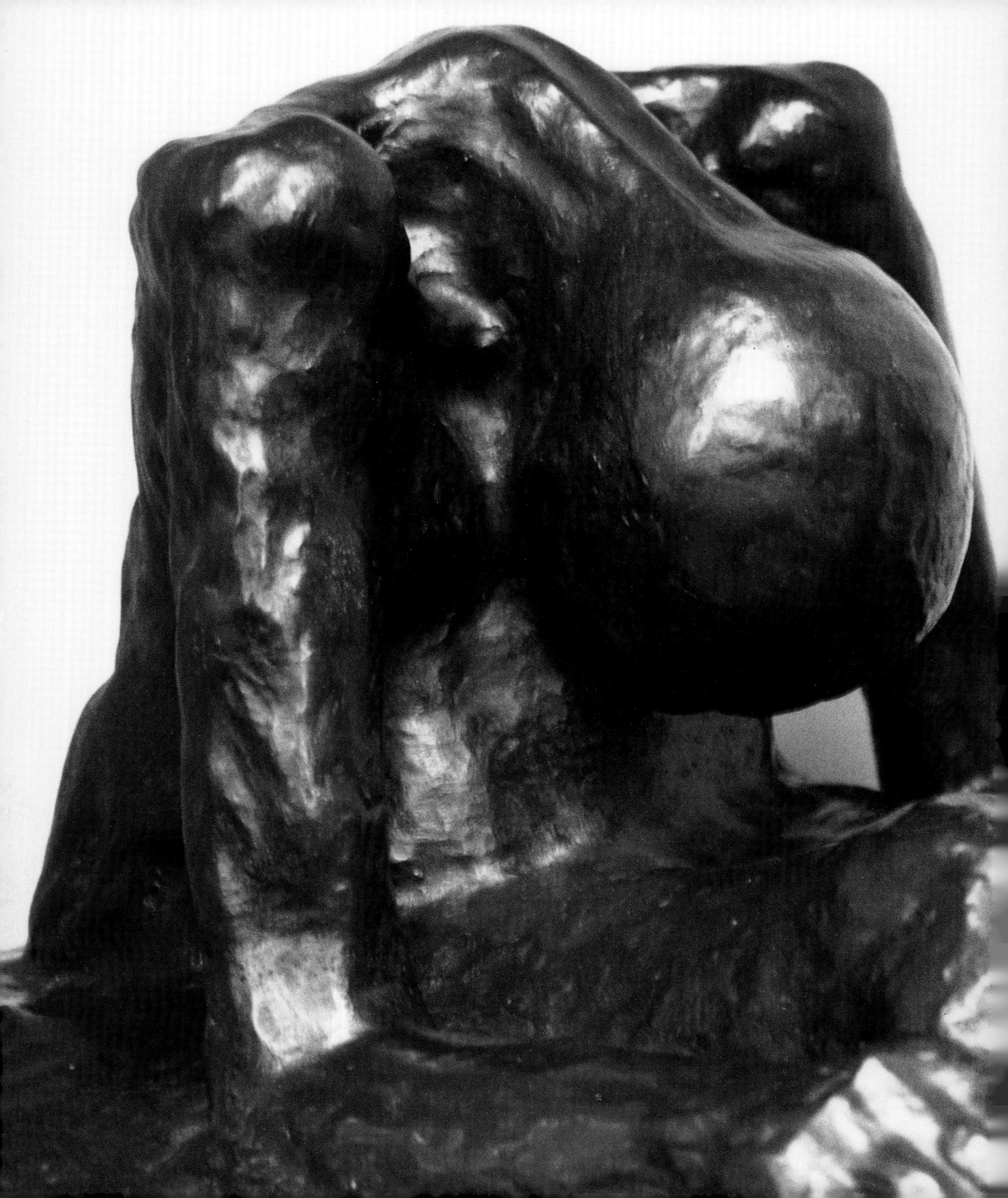

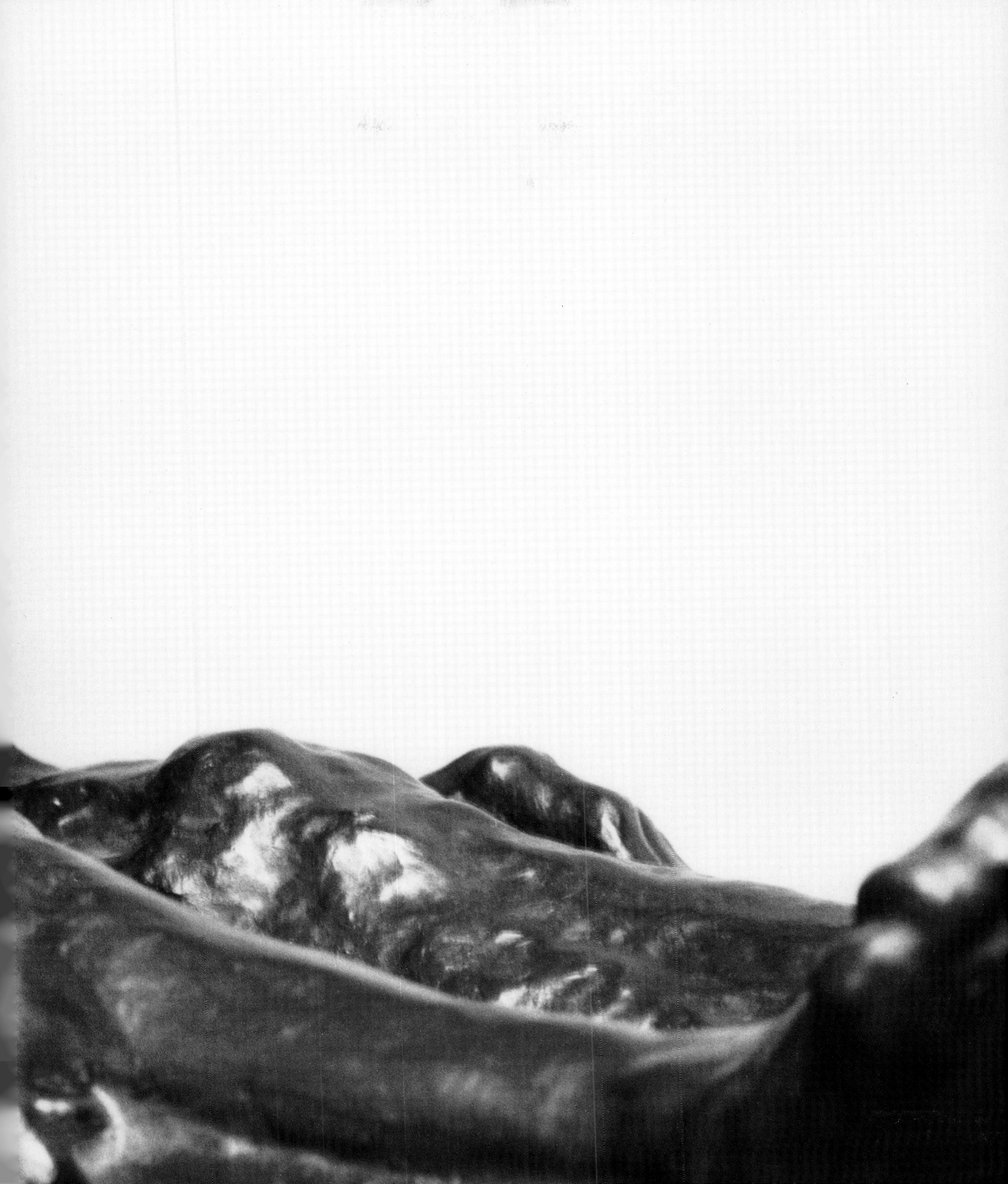

My Friend the Village Idiot
Father of the Village Idiot

It is told about Leonardo da Vinci that on occasions he could be found searching along the streets of Florence for intriguing faces suitable for models. I doubt I should ever be able to do exactly that since I am not particularly interested in faces. At times I am fascinated by the human being behind that face, which I know I shall ultimately learn to grasp by his speech and by his acts.

Take my friend, the village idiot. I learned to know him well. I finally executed a bronze of him—in no small respect and admiration. Yes, he was so-called deformed by nature in limbs and brain. He lived miserably. He managed his daily routine. He did it with a certain dignity. With courage among crazy aberrations.

I did a bust of his father also. He was no less gifted in genetic abnormalities, no less honorable either. What he might have observed in himself might have been a double image of the miserabilia in his offspring.

The faces seemed challenging to me the moment I could smell the souls behind them. From that second on there was a straight way for the brain to tell the hands the warmth of the story, releasing an immediate attack on clay.

21″ × 15″ × 13″

(*page 92*)

23″ × 16″ × 18″

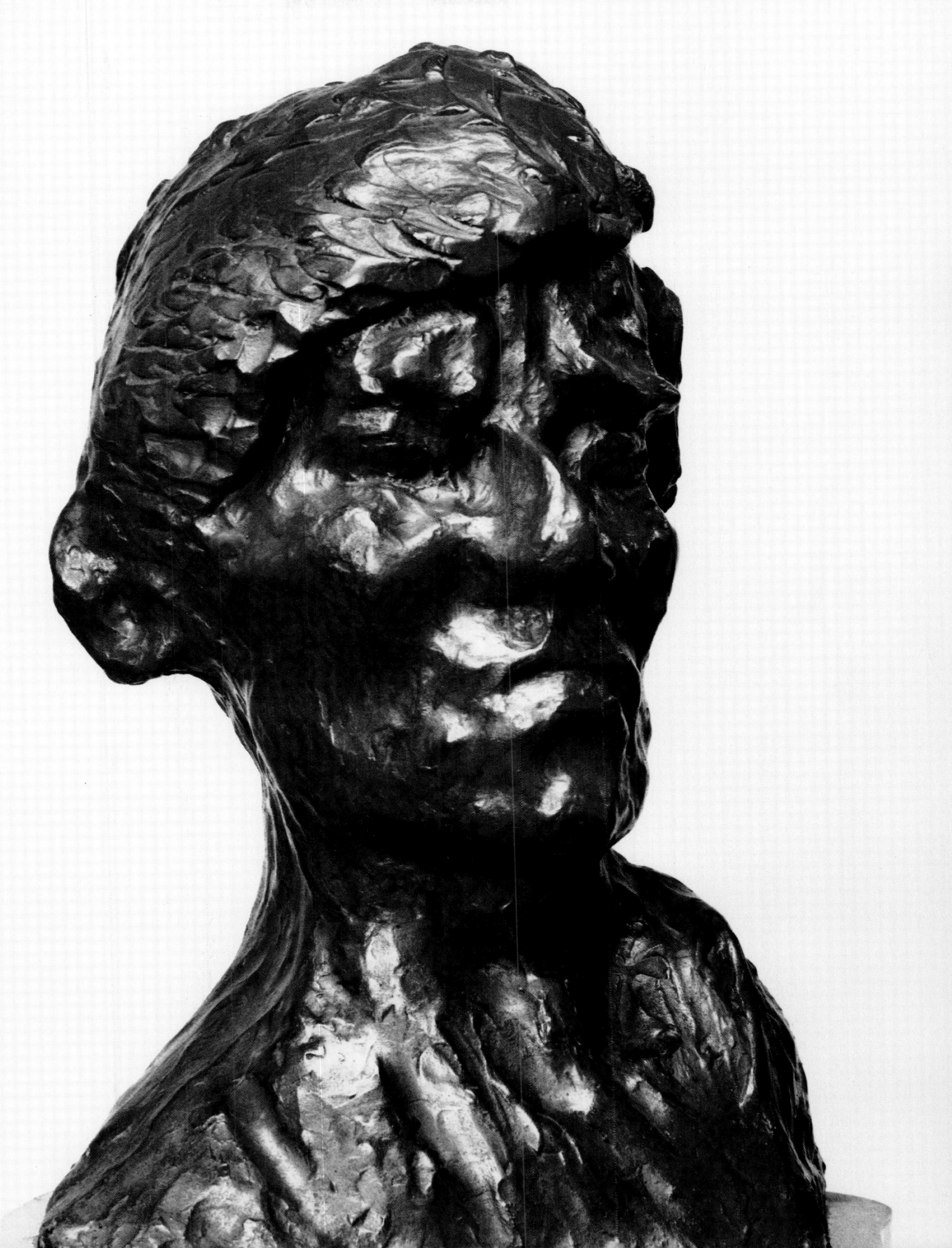

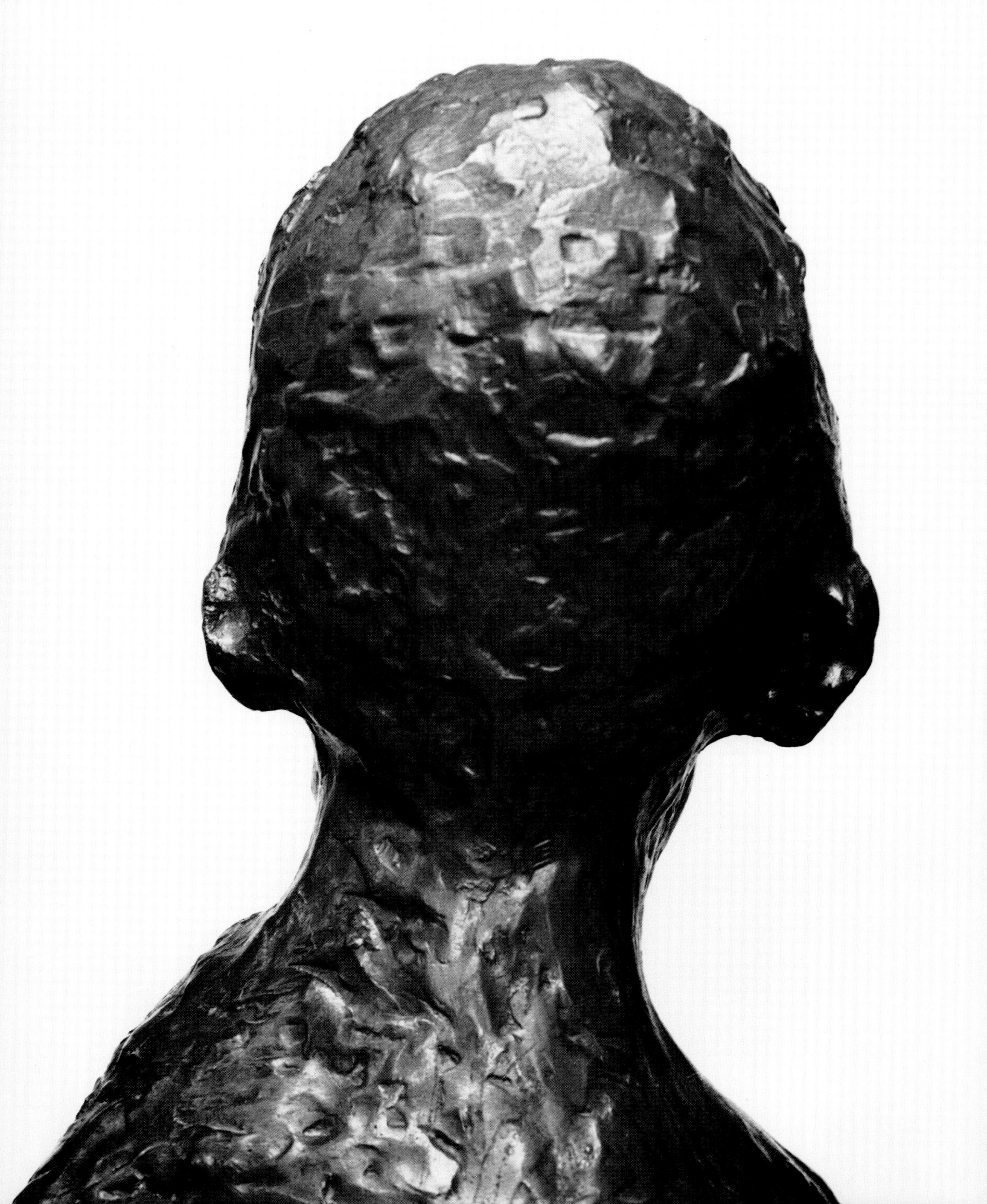

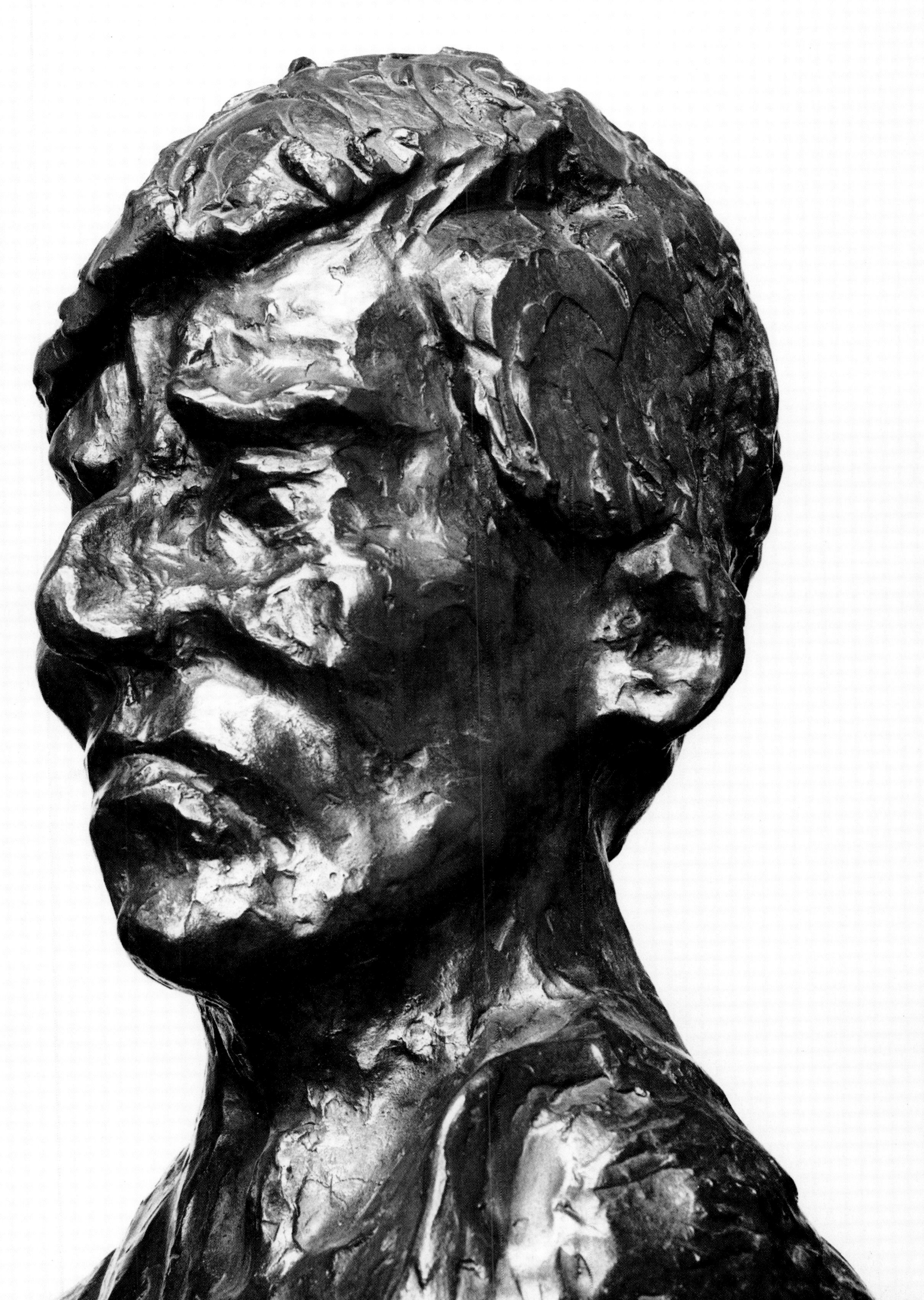

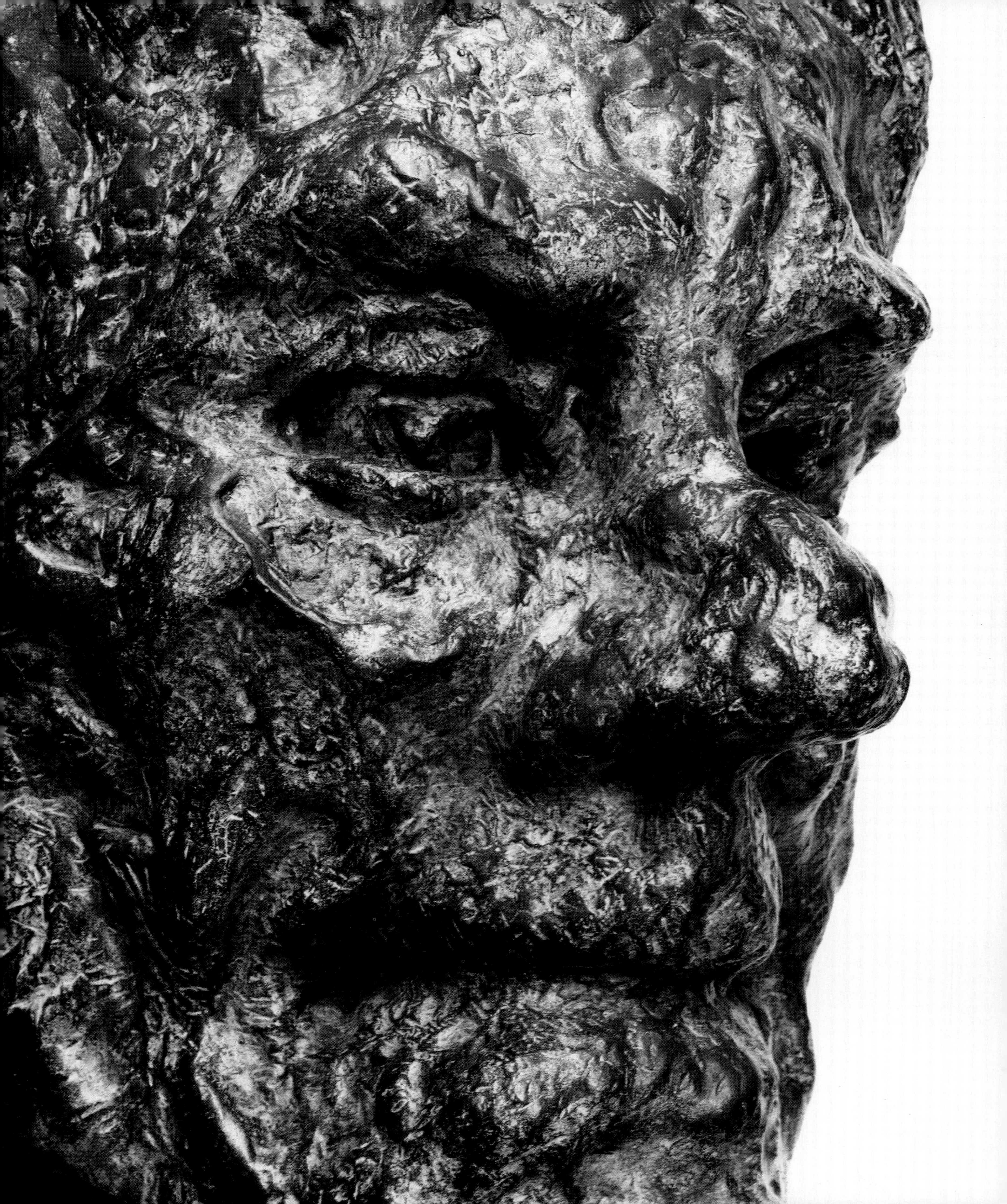

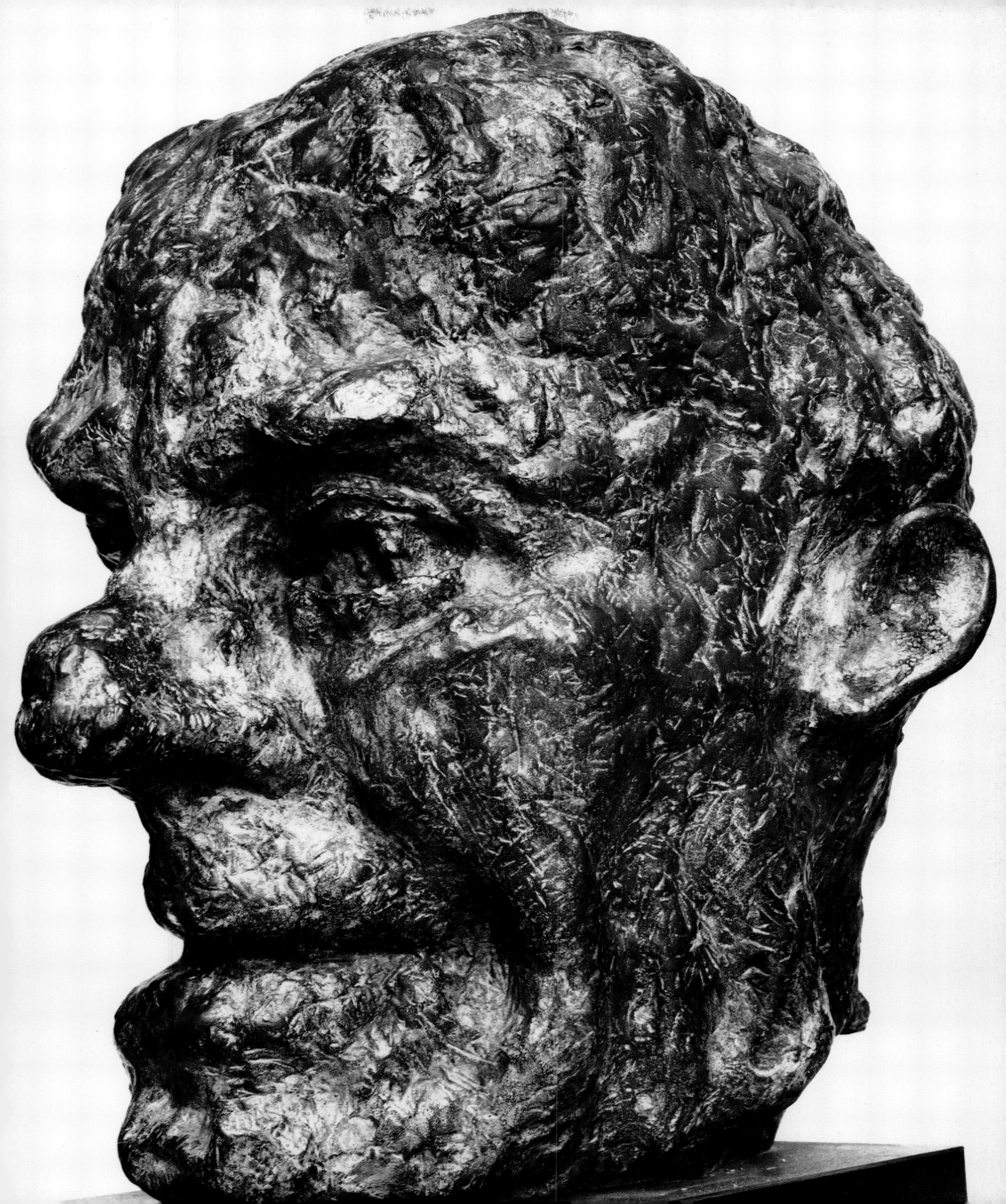

My Friend

I executed this bust many years ago. It has been on exhibit a few times. It has carried the title *My Friend* and I may be justified in giving it that title.

I had operated upon him twice—a gallbladder and later a hernia.

I am a bit proud of not having operated upon him for a serious abdominal inflammation years ago, when his internist screamed at me: "You must understand; you have no moral or medical right to say you feel it advisable to sit tight."

I did. He recovered with no cutting.

I had been closely involved with other personal segments of his life.

Olga called me one morning. "Joe and I are going to get married at noon today. My parents are here—and my two sons. I would be so nice if Ella and you could join us."

From the cellar, I got two bottles of vintage champagne.

Their Round Hill estate in Connecticut was only twenty minutes by car from home.

When we arrived they were happily married.

There was a quiet luncheon. Afterward we walked around outside of the house. We had done that very thing many times before. There were about 50–60 life-sized contemporary sculptures representatively placed on the large green lawn.

The conversation, as often before, centered on the problem of the final placement of Mr. Joseph Hirshhorn's collection of sculptures and paintings, gigantic in numbers.

Mr. Joe had authorized me to bring to Governor Nelson Rockefeller's attention the alternative of seeing the collection placed in Purchase, New York, side by side with the projected Visual Arts College of the State of New York University. The date was 1960-1961.

Olga had stated in July, 1985: "There were many conversations. Joe considered Purchase seriously." This for the record.

The great collection finally found its logical and honorable place in Washington, D.C., as a unique museum in the name of Joseph Hirshhorn, and under the auspices of The Smithsonian Institution.

Mr. Joe and Olga were welcome guests at our home. I enjoyed his lack of diplomacy.

"How many copies are there of this bust of your friend?"

"You have one. I have one. That's all."

"Are you sure? Is that all?"

On occasions he would come back to one and the same thing: "I never had such a neck!"

He was absolutely right. Anatomically speaking, he was never created that way. Competitively, however, he was imbued with mental streaks reeking with ambition, striking with velocity.

He said once: "I was half-naked and hungry many days in my younger years."

He swore that when he grew up it should not happen again.

It did not.

By the grace of our capitalist system, by the constant love and help of his mother, and by his own genes he developed into a successful man and a capitalist in his own right—with a weakness for dollar signs, for color and pictures, for forms and lack of forms, and for art in whatever shape.

For all this I admired Mr. Joe, as I called him.

16″ × 12″ × 12″

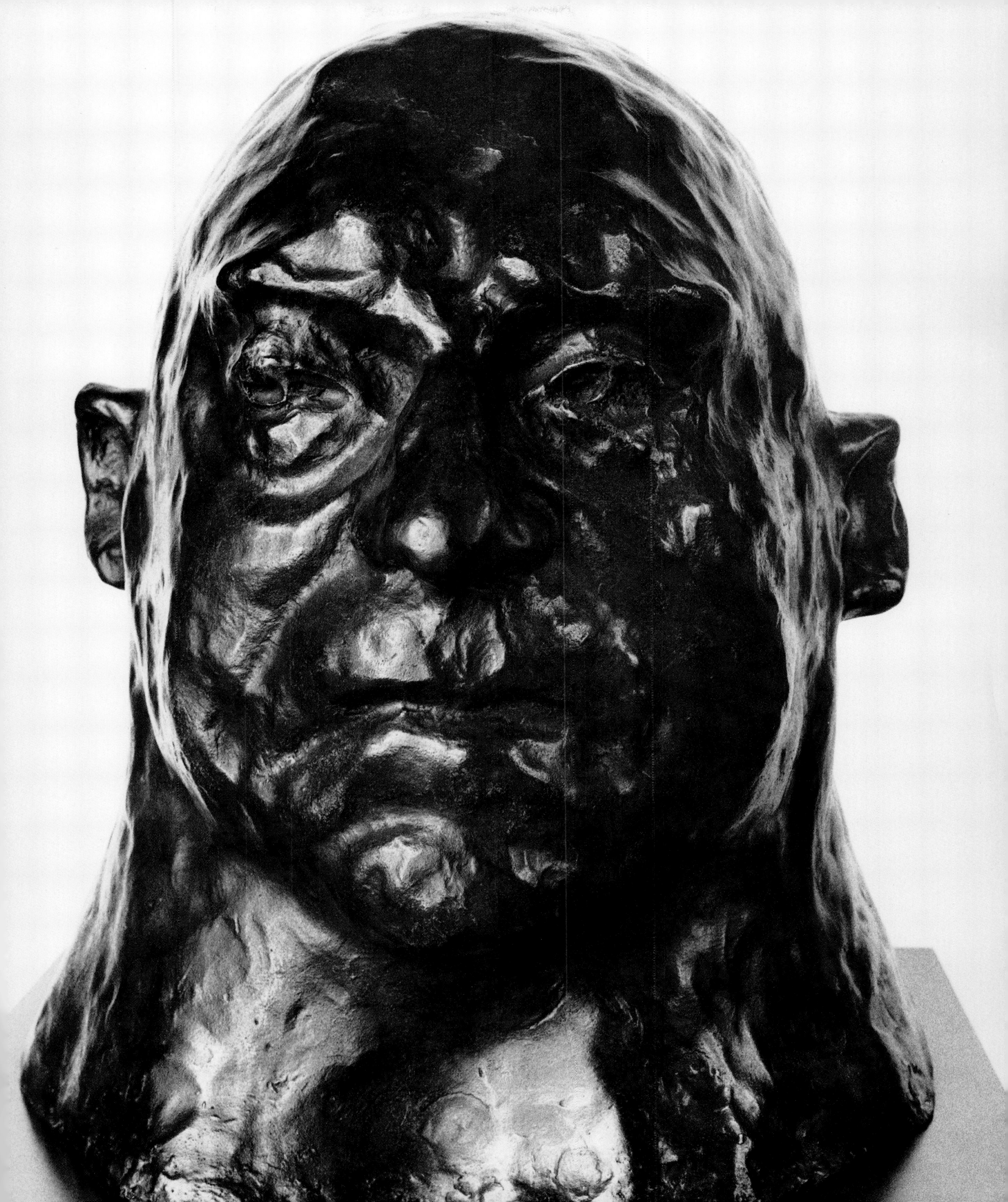

We were both immigrants. He had done very well. I felt we had no competition going between us. He would have won hands down.

He loved the illusion that he was a self-made man. In my world, I sense that no one is ever self-made.

No one ever enters this world naked and alone.

The historical and miraculous biologic process called our birth came about through the functional guarantee of the umbilical cord and the placenta, and through the fighting grace of our mother.

In our subsequent existence, from stage to stage, we grew by the forces and the genes within us. And we grew by the benevolent assistance of family members and good friends, who were fully aware of the respect and responsibility for their own existence and their part in the time and the day when they actively, fully exercised their own benevolent potentials to give a hand when needed. Thus we all get to be part of it, get to be responsible participants in our surroundings and in our own lives.

"Man is a piece of the continent, part of the main" (John Donne).

A self-made man seems to ask for exemption to this common involvement in a common fate.

I am not bearing down on Mr. Joe.

He borrowed the term from an ambitious society galloping along Wall Street with hunger, unaware of the finer growth patterns from birth to maturity, from isolation and loneliness to an organized society.

None of us are self-made.

Mr. Joe neither.

He made himself admirable in so many and better ways.

And in the end—and with the blessing of Olga—he donated to his adopted country the Joseph Hirshhorn Museum and Sculpture Garden.

I am honored if I have earned the right to call this bust *My Friend*.

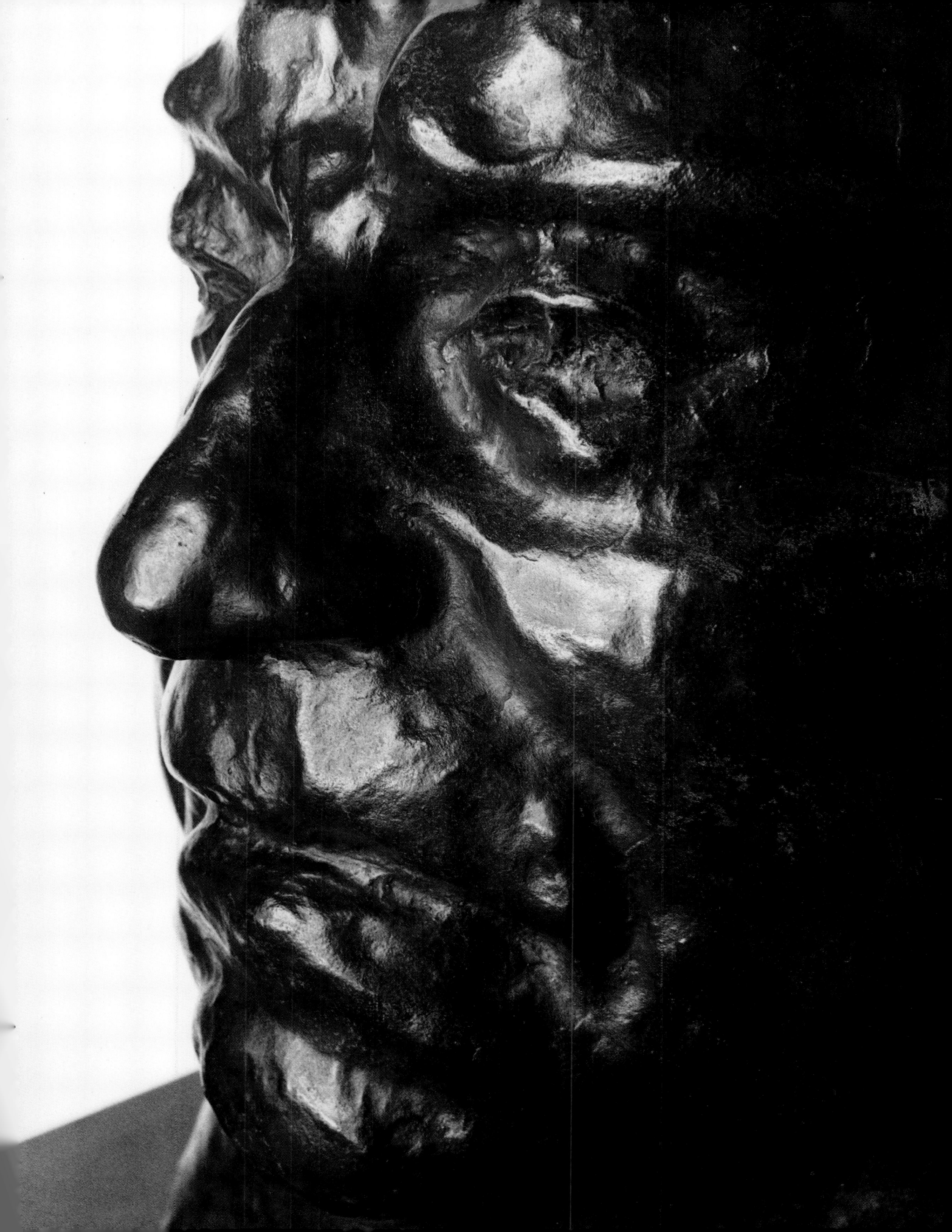

Spirit of the Dance
Dance of the Spirit

There are two absolute abstracts in art: music and ballet.

I am exaltedly beholden to the monumentality of Beethoven's last string quartets—and not less to the sculptural impact in a dance by Martha Graham.

I transformed those abstract movements into bronze, praying it might still embrace the *spirit of the dance*.

It came to be a body in motion, starkly simplified, with minimal human anatomy and maximal emotional vibrations, while still a figure maintaining full physical and mental equilibrium within clearly outlined spaces of air surrounding the moving body on all sides.

Then, in the next fraction of time, the tempo changes, the music moves on, the arms are raised, the dancer moves on—leaving the bronze behind.

While working on this larger figure, I was aware of another moving around in my mind. In this smaller work there is no scrutiny or analysis—only spontaneity.

There is music in the air.
The rhythm urges her on.
Her bosom, her thighs, her arms, her neck swing in uncontrollable joy.
A sensual, musical delight flows through her feminine reverberations.

There is song in my soul.
And rhythm in my joints.
I am moved by a tune.
I am beset by a joy.
I sense not from where.
I am the "Dance of the Spirit."

26″ × 6″ × 21″

(*page 102*)

14″ × 5″ × 14″

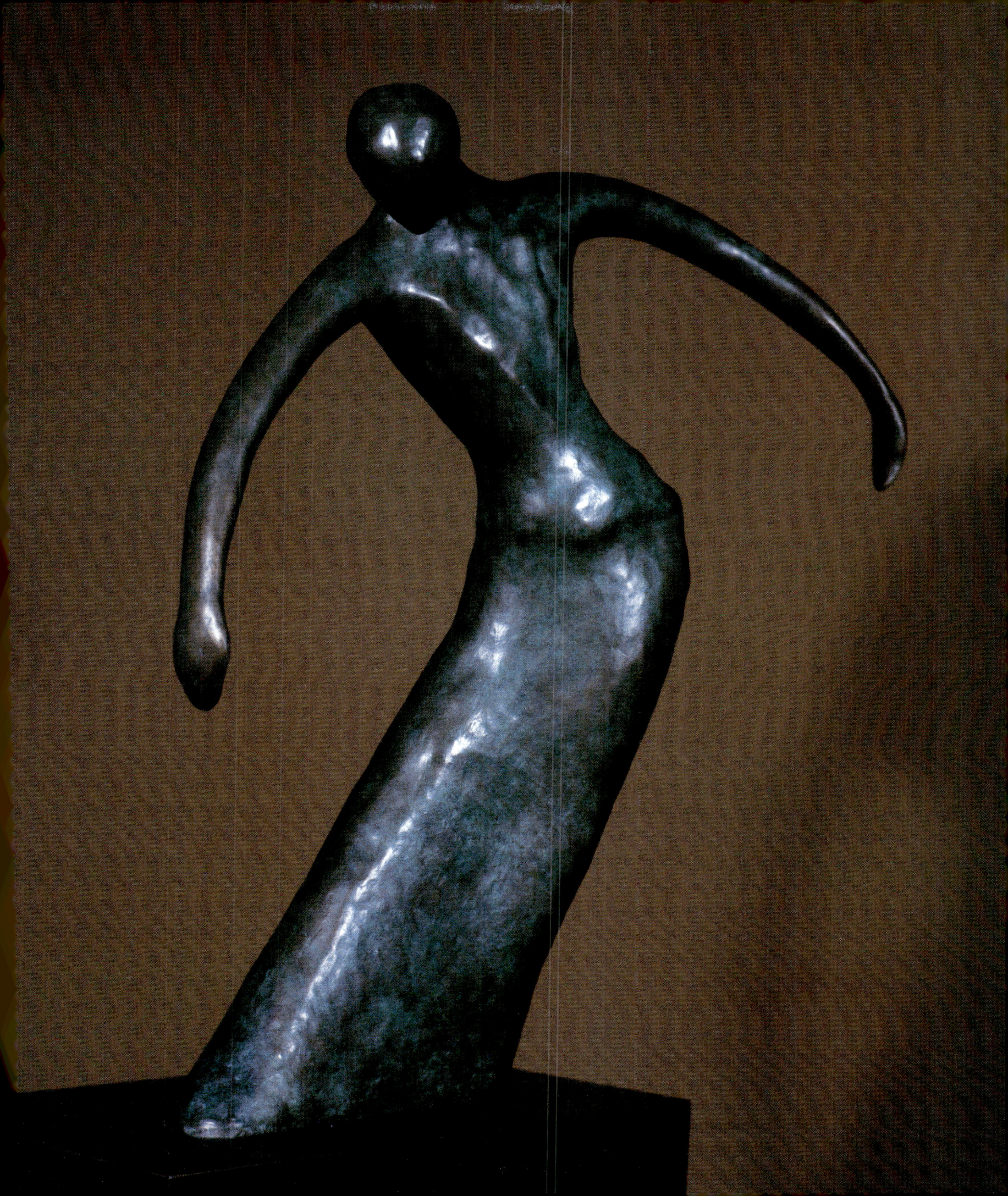

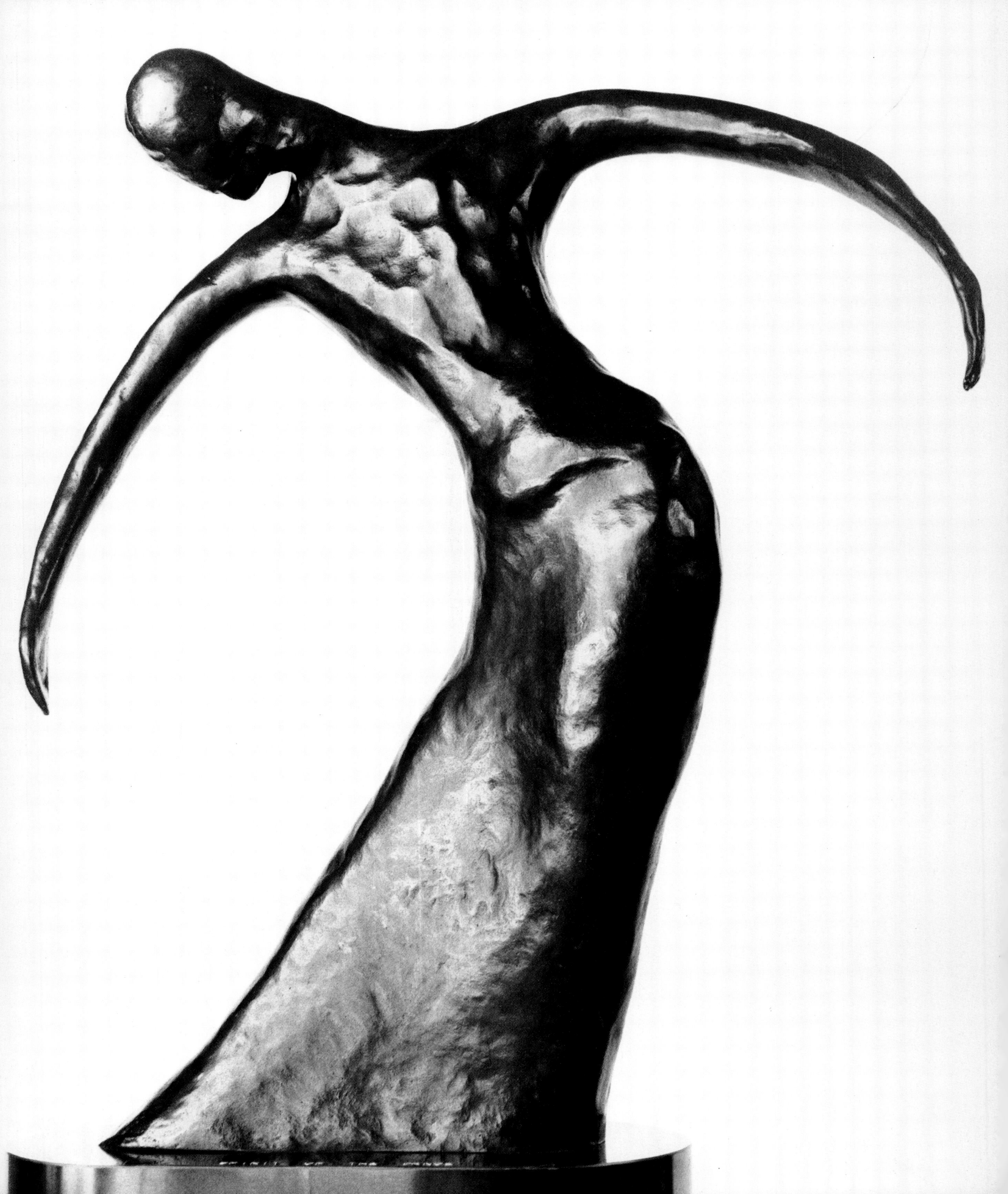

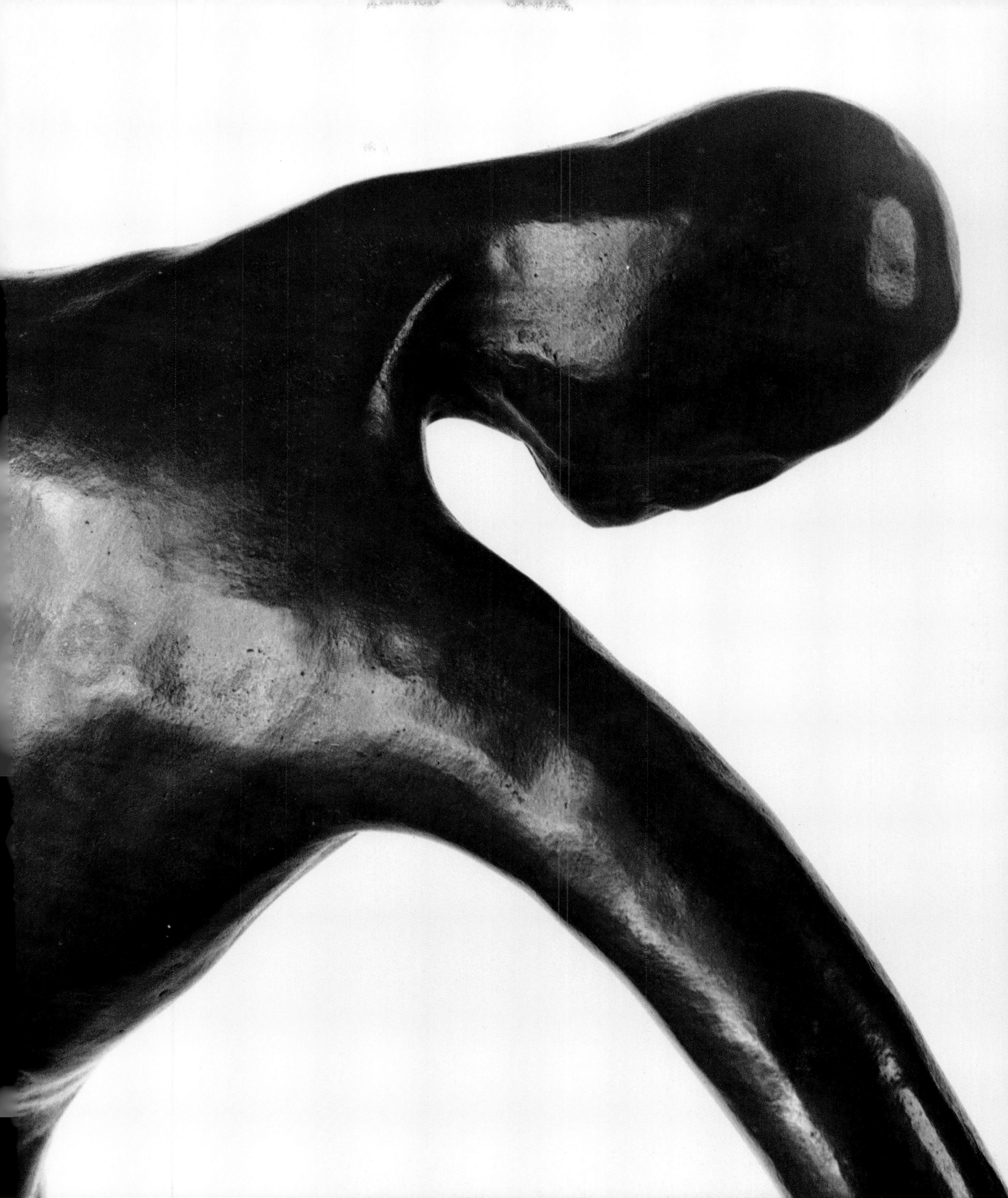

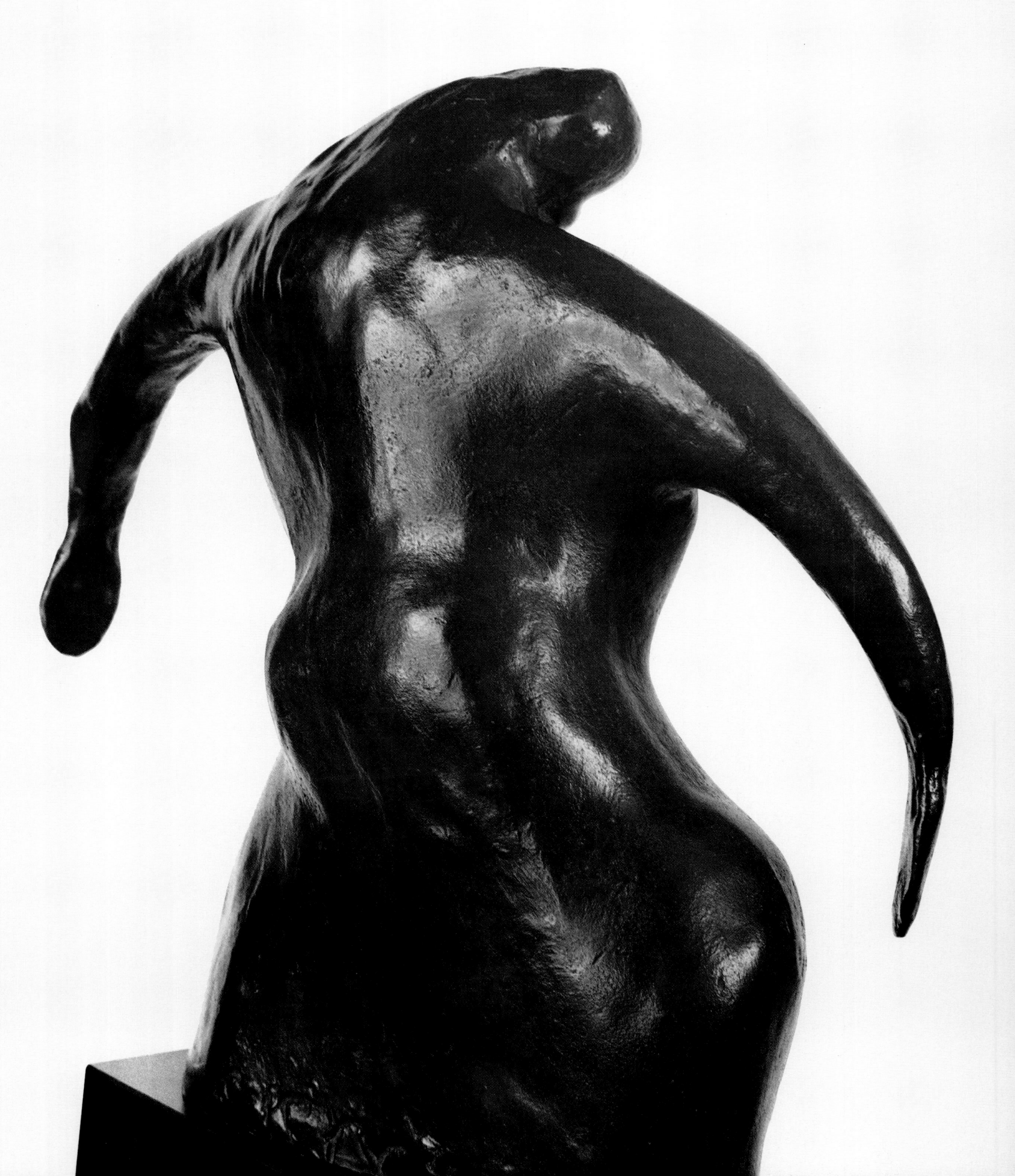

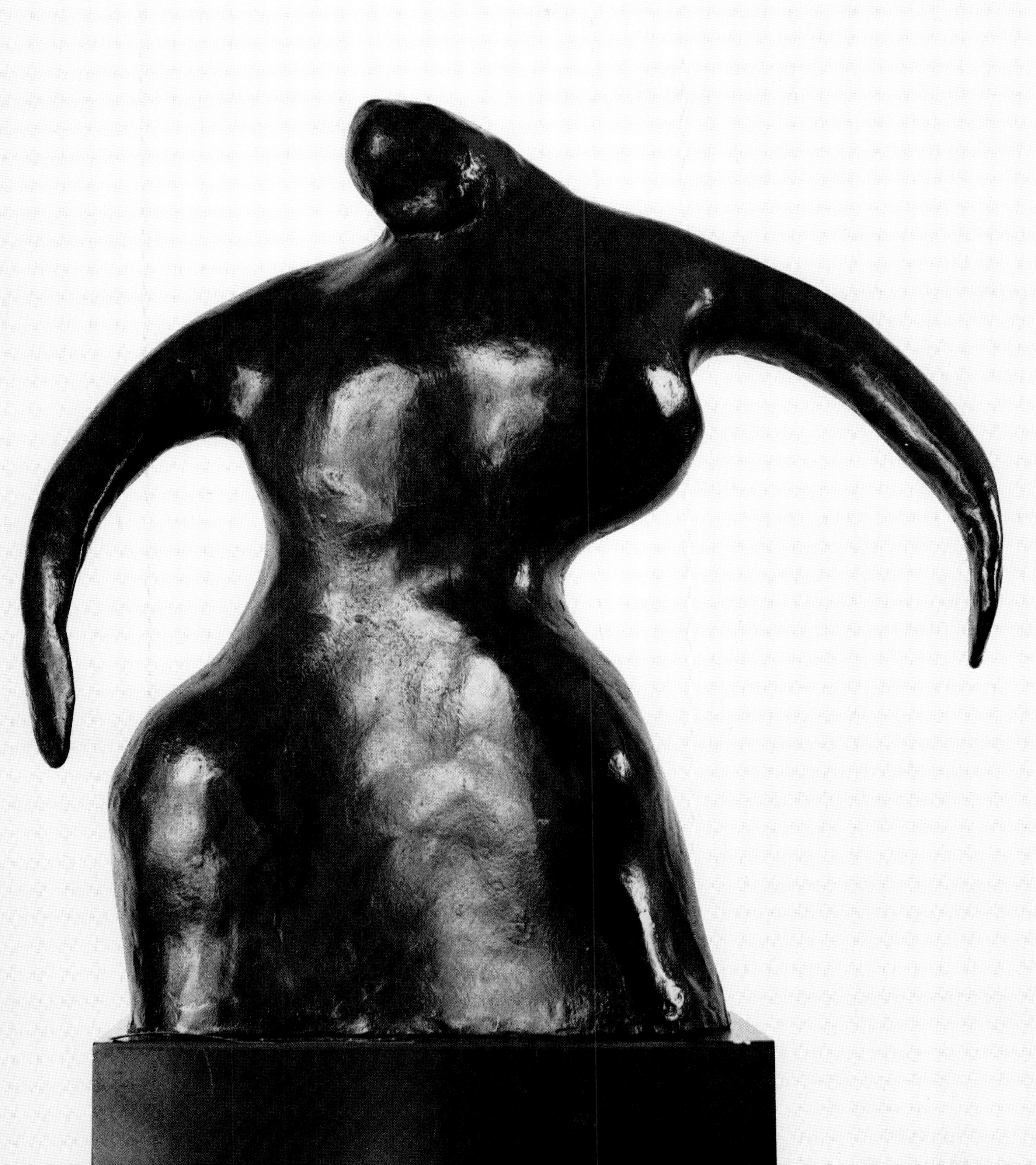

Men Against Man

This bronze group deals with men's cruelty to man.

Is cruelty an inborn characteristic of homo sapiens? From his onset, the history of man seems filled with destructive potentials. We witness in our time violence and cruelty in wars and in our daily life. We seem infested by it and saturated by it. The subject matter for this sculptural group, therefore, should not seem foreign to our present day.

I wonder what came first—the subject matter or the sculptural form.

Even if I had completed it yesterday, I believe I would still be wondering: did my distaste for cruelty drive me to the work or did my need of a certain strict sculptural form haunt me in search for a fitting form and theme?

I cannot answer that satisfactorily. Too many times in my work, as I know it must be in the life of a great number of artists, we cannot get really going before we sense that lucky constellation of form and idea, which flares sparks of light into warm flames lighting the canvas, the marble, or the empty white pages of paper.

Maybe it is that particular, blessed coincidence that we call inspiration.

Men Against Man can be an example.

For a long time I had been occupied with a simple notion: what, if anything, can be made out of a heavy slab of stone shaped into a gigantic cube? The vast rough plane of its walls! The sharp, cutting corners! The very heaviness of the giant, dragging into the ground onto which it is heavily set!

At the very same time, the cube, in all its simplicity, commands respect and exerts monumentality!

Could nature's raw and brutal beauty still be preserved? Could I sparingly cut into its four sides and its top surface and, within that hard material, release a group of men from its stony prison?

In art, the creator never succeeds completely.

The image of the potential creation burns too intensely in his mind ever to be fully or convincingly realized by material means, be it pigment or marble, be it words, be it tunes.

Still, he dares to think, to struggle, and to strain to bring the medium so close to the flame of creation that he can smell the singeing of his hair.

Thus he might have to leave every fragment of his work, always incomplete, never quite finished, while still sparkling in unfinished beauty.

In its own way, *Men Against Man* has tried that.

It has forced six uniformed Nazis surrounding one defenseless creature into a compact group of militant anti-humanitarians who, in a heavy slab of metal, hover over the demeaning act of men's disrespect for man.

64″ × 54″ × 54″

(*pages 108–111*)

Men Against Ma[n]
Uncompleted
Plasteline for
Bronze Version,
1986
28″ × 27″ × 24″

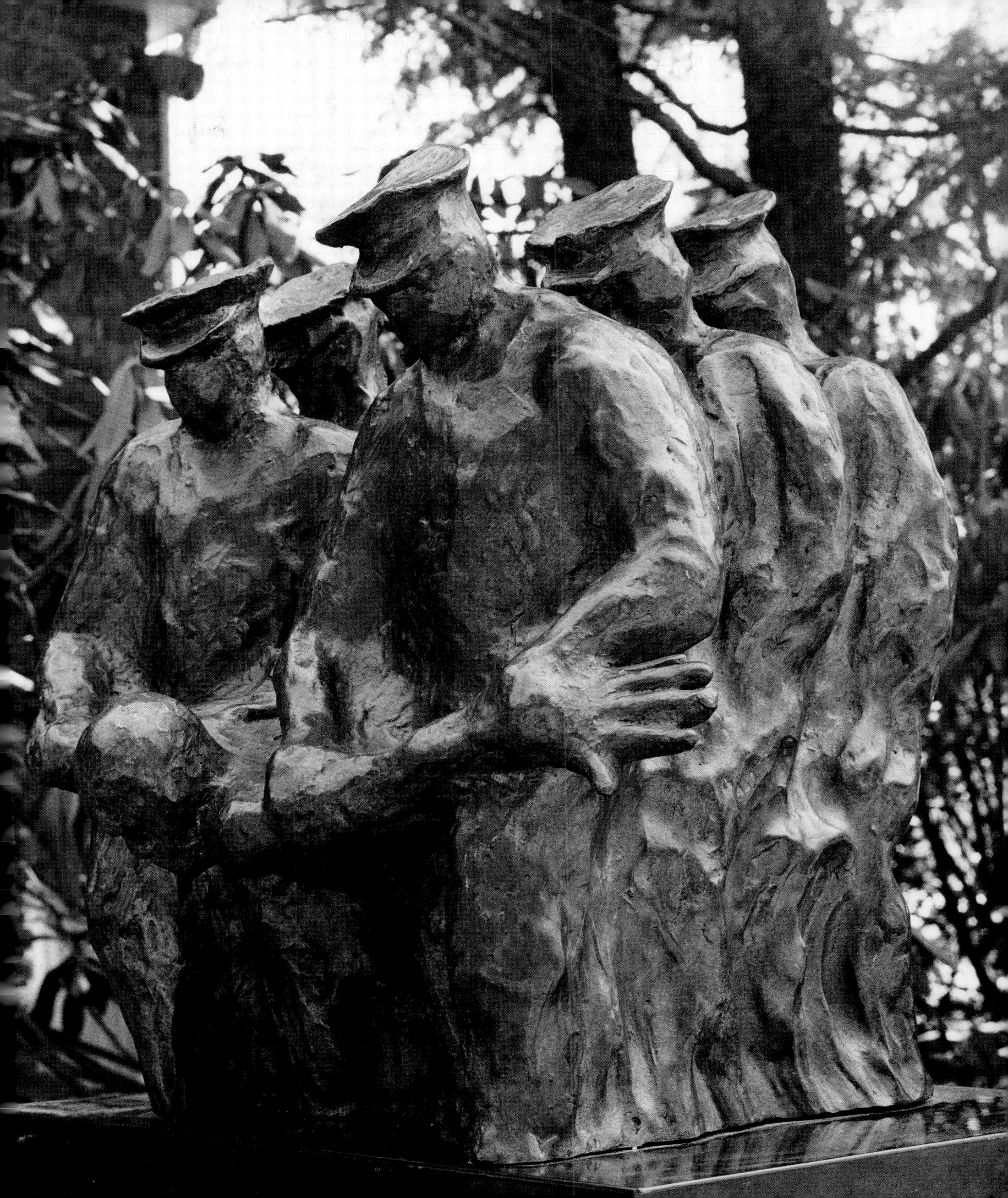

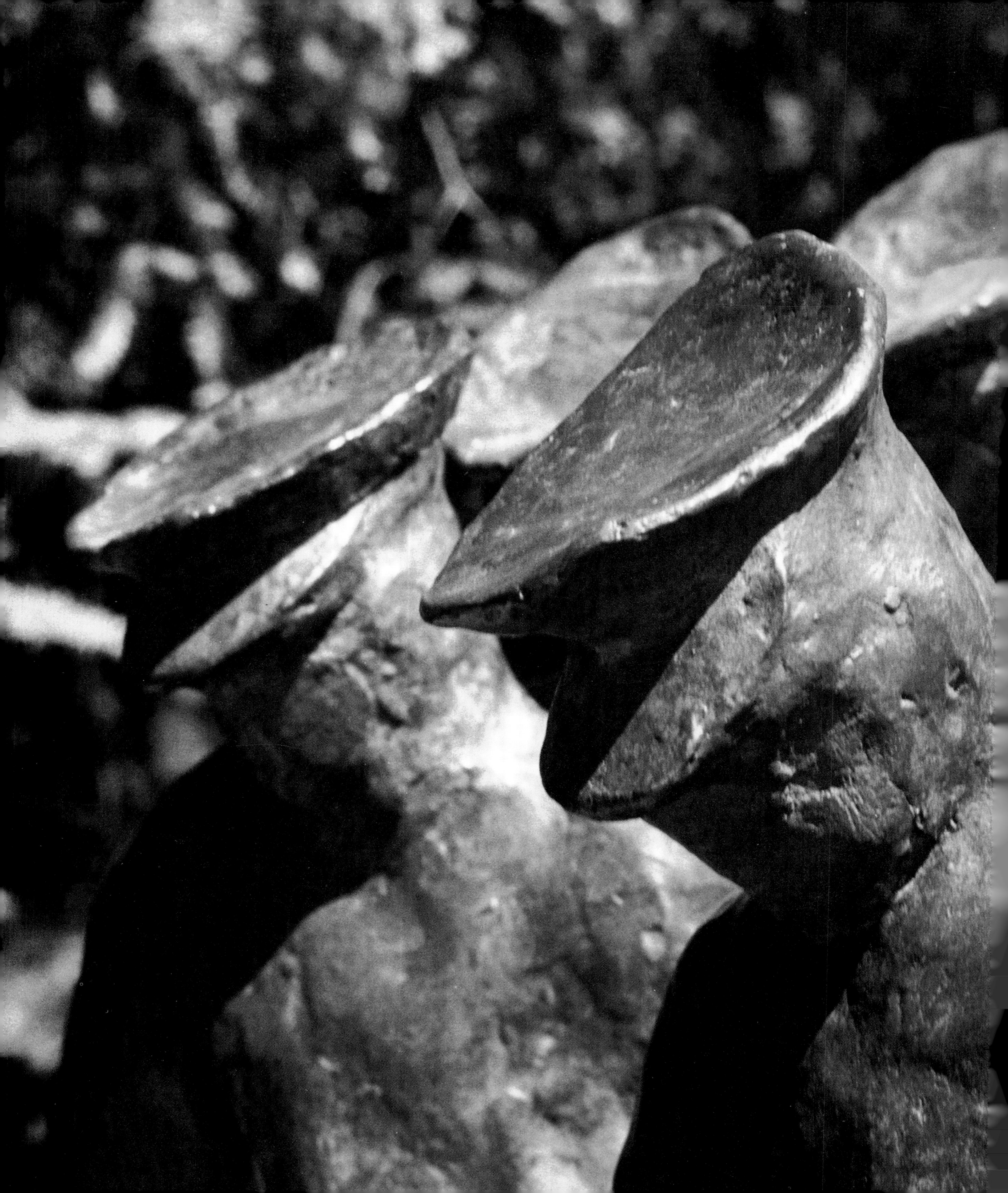

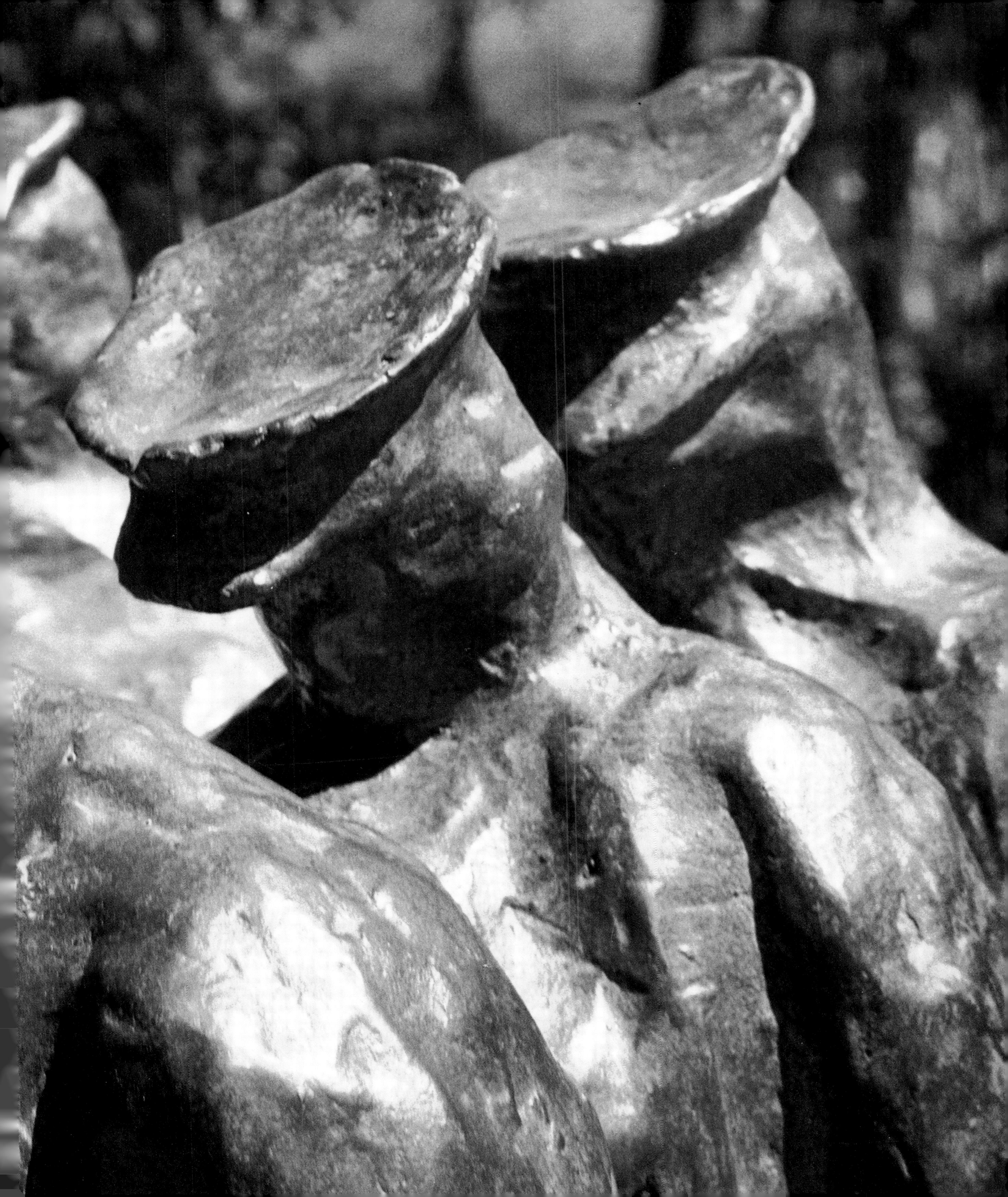

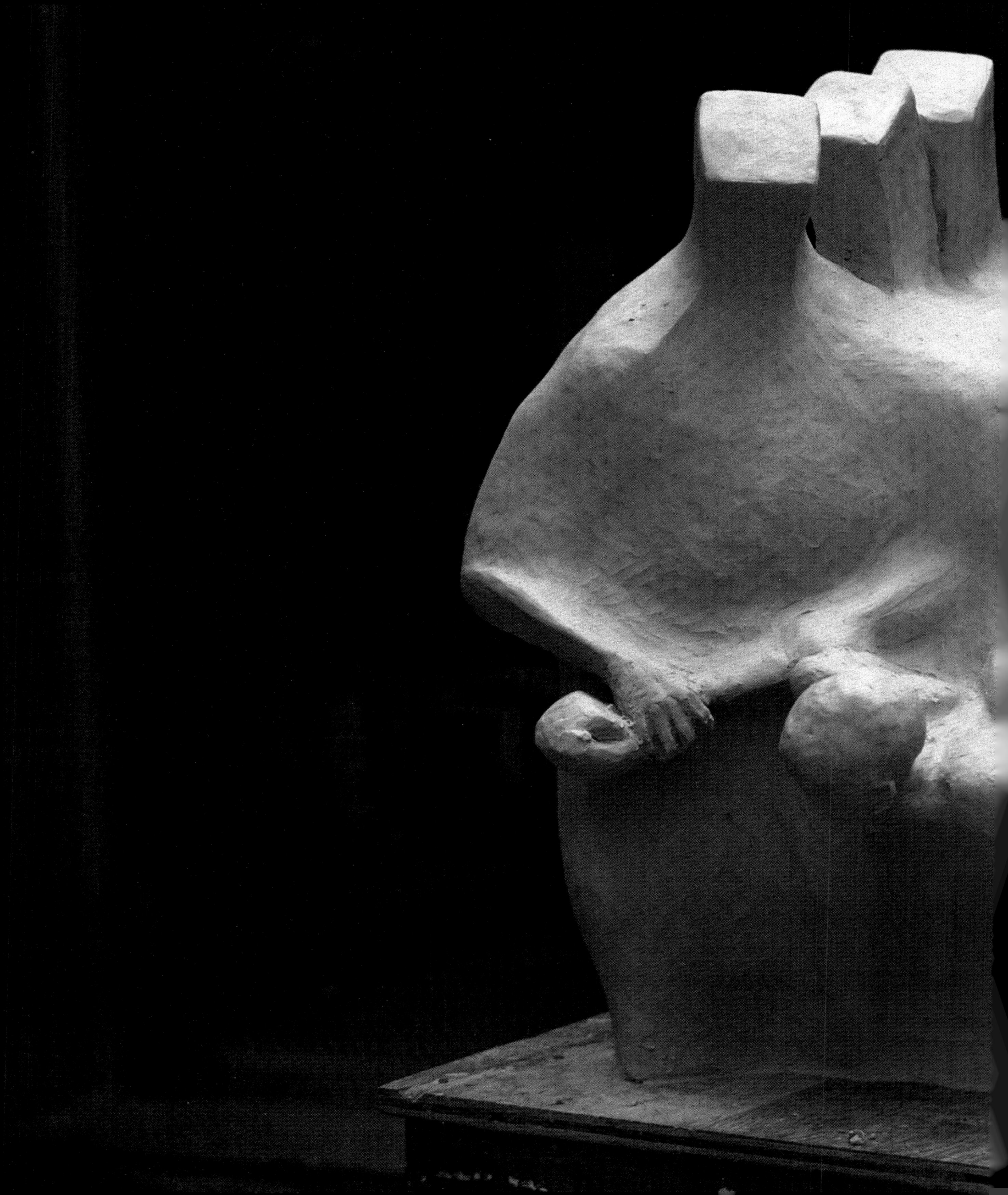

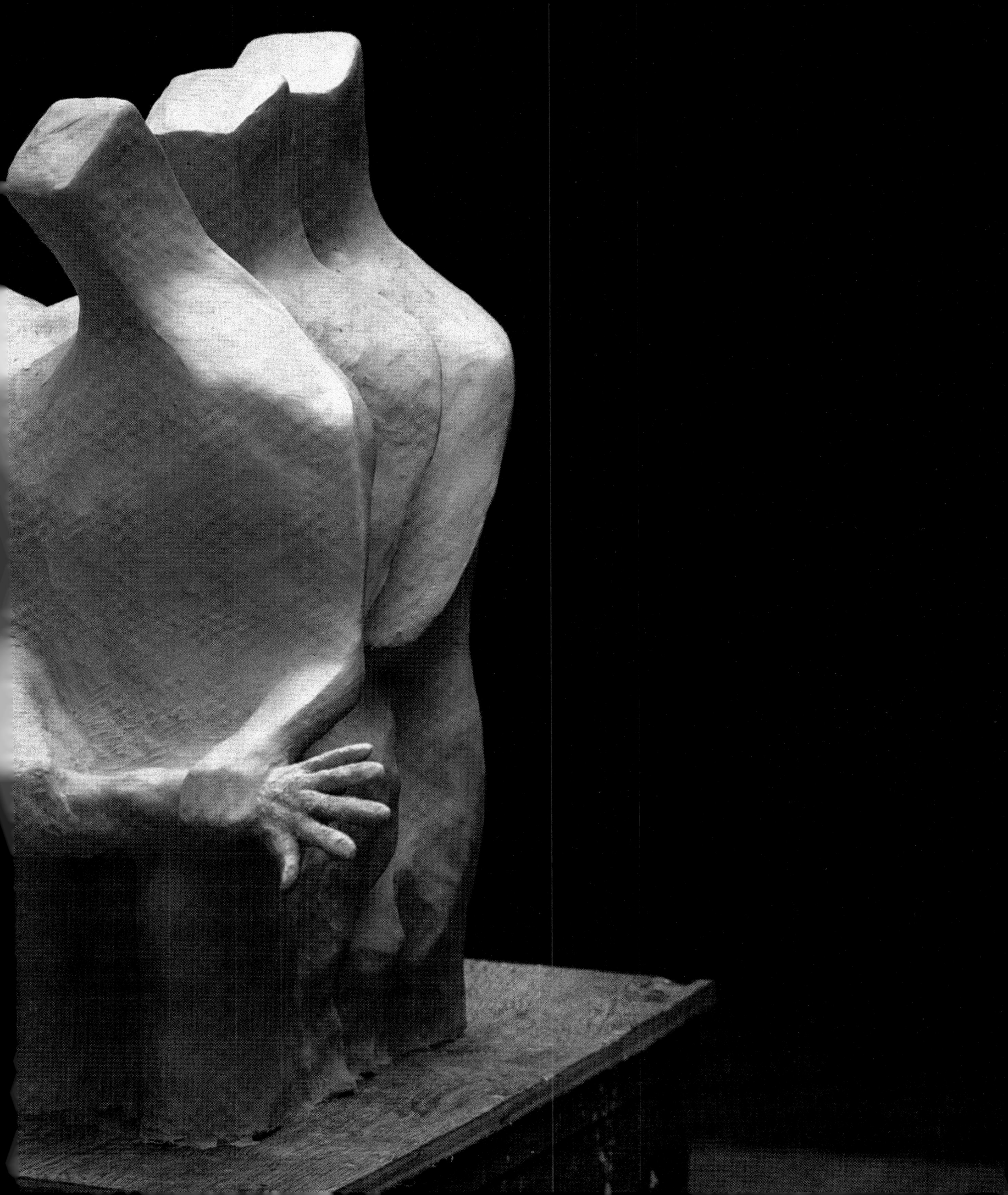

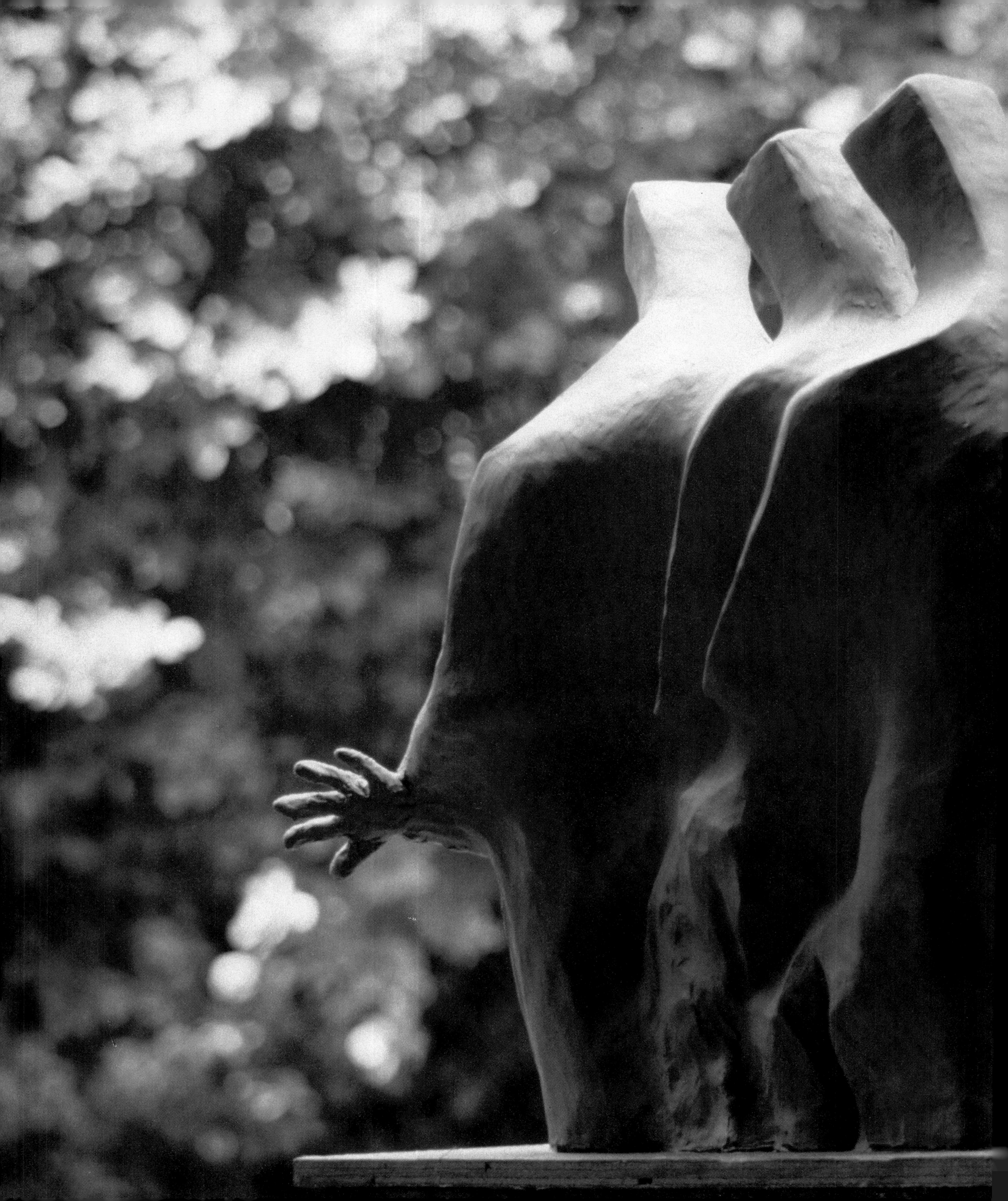

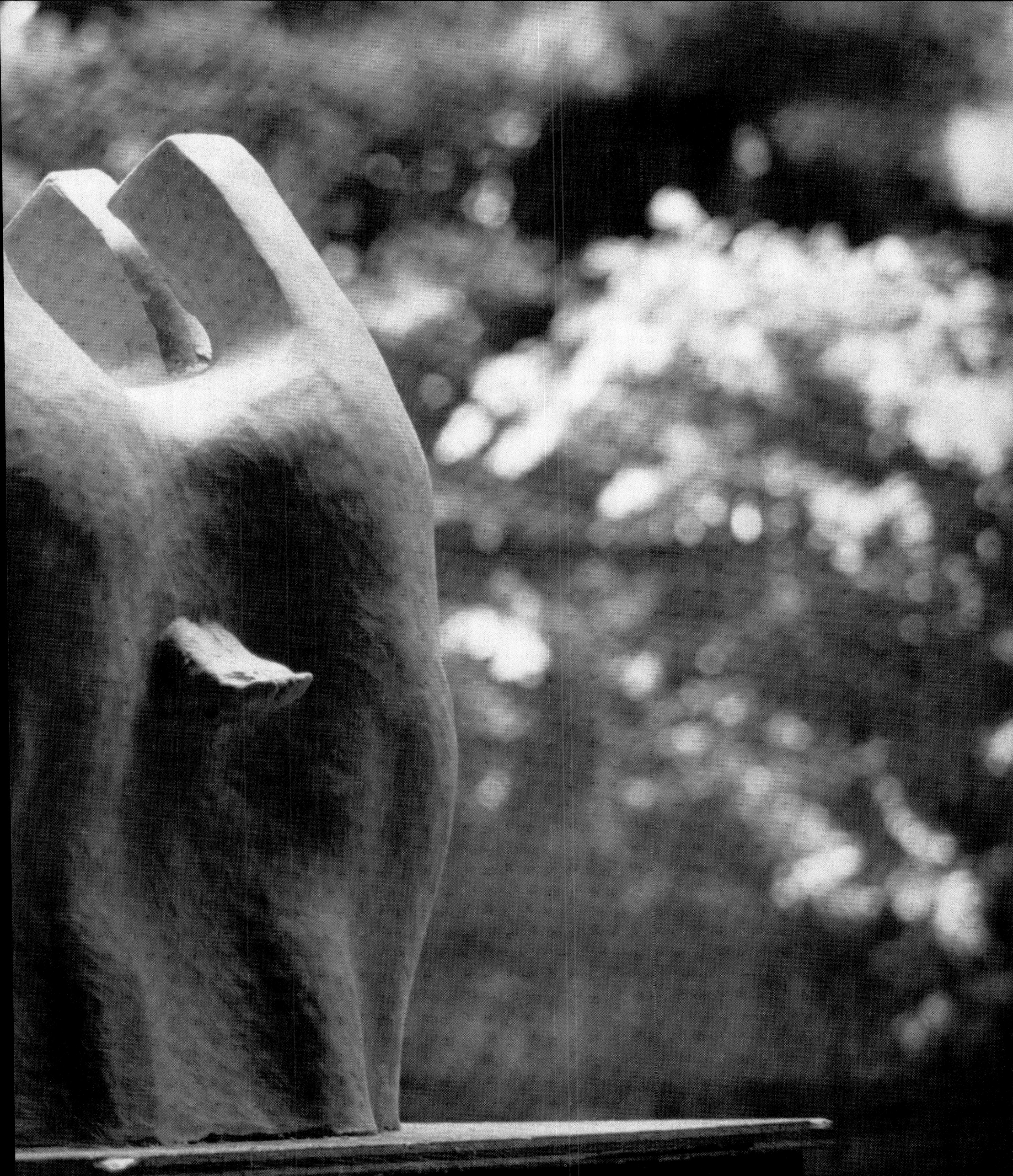

The Refugees

I completed this statue in the early sixties. It did not have a definite title. It could have been *The Chicago Fire* or *Hiroshima*, or something like that.

In the spring of 1970 I learned about the philatelic competition for a United Nation's commemorative stamp on the theme "International Support for Refugees."

A subsequent lithograph was produced and the design submitted to U.N. It was found acceptable by the committee.

I cannot honestly answer the question, what goes on in one's mind during execution of works of this subject matter.

I can readily confess, however, that the theme of the refugees has concerned me as a plain human being since the end of the First World War. It was at that crucial time when the League of Nations authorized the Norwegian diplomat and polar explorer, Fridtjof Nansen, to organize in Europe an international drive to assist millions of refugees and denationalized people. An essential part of this humanitarian effort was to extend to these homeless and not defined national groups the so-called Nansen Passport, which granted them an immediate international identity; this was the first and an important step to a much needed rehabilitation.

The magnitude and complexity of Nansen's efforts were not less staggering and heart rending than those repeated after the Second World War by other international leaders.

Thus our minds in the present century have been forced to involve themselves in the constant plight and misery of uprooted people, who have lost their nationality, been deprived of their livelihood, suffered hunger, and been exposed to diseases. The tragedy is still with us.

We have all suffered.

If not personally, we have all suffered on behalf of humanity, which is always the greater loser.

This is the way the theme of refugees has occupied me for years. It still does.

It has lost none of its intensity by my executing a bronze and a stamp.

I shall not use a tempting cliché by saying that I have myself not been a refugee, by the grace of God.

For we are all involved in this plight by what we might have done—or what we might *not* have done.

In a greater sense, we are all refugees. We are all in flight from the past into a future not known to us.

In flight from childhood into hoped-for maturity. From stabilization into insecurity. From safety into revolt.

From a society of norms into one of seeming abnormality. In this sense we are all involved.

In this sense we are all refugees.

And should I add that a flight from something might also naturally harbor the constructive hope of flight into something better.

Such might be some of the thoughts going into the creation of this bronze group.

54″ × 44″ × 59″

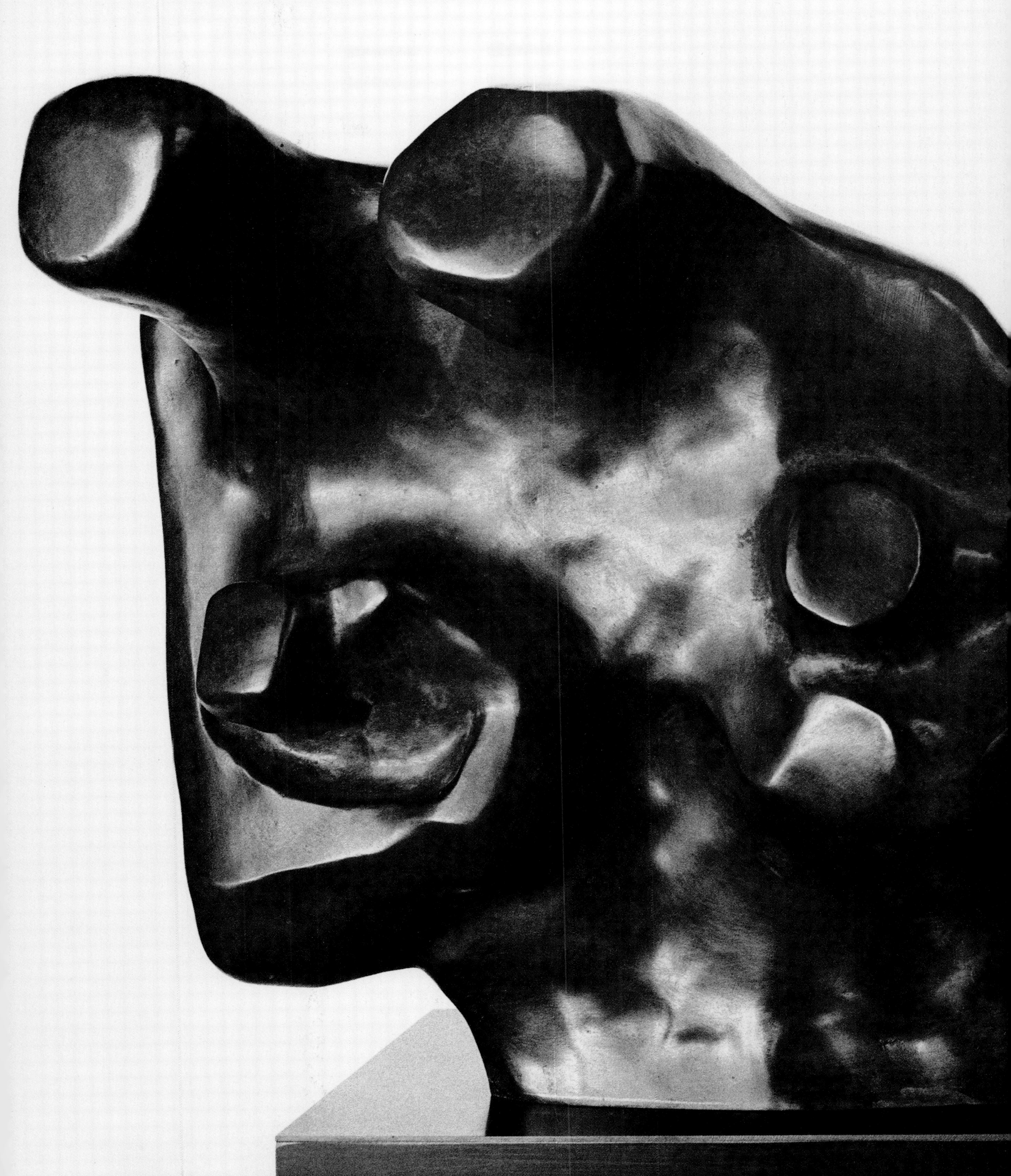

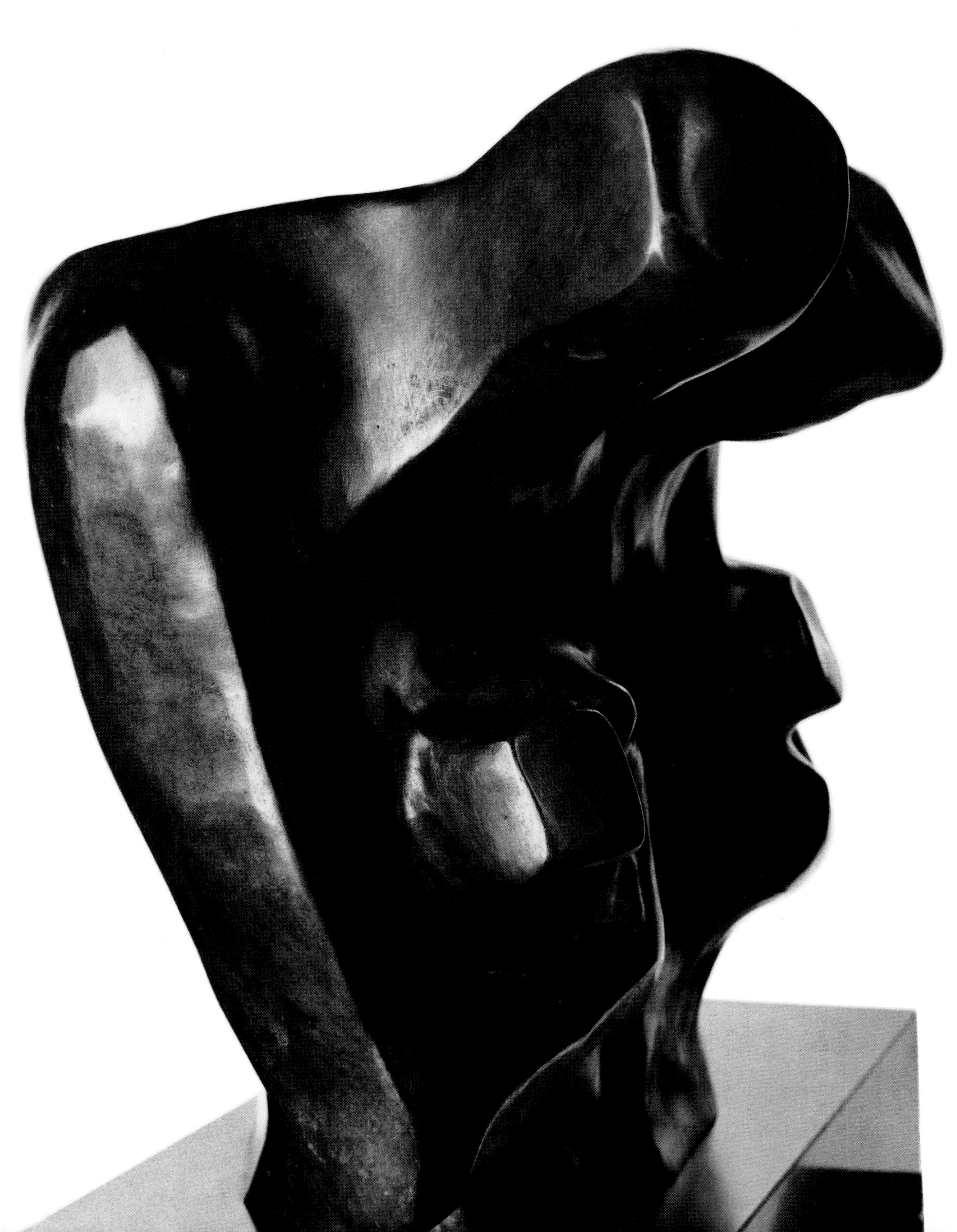

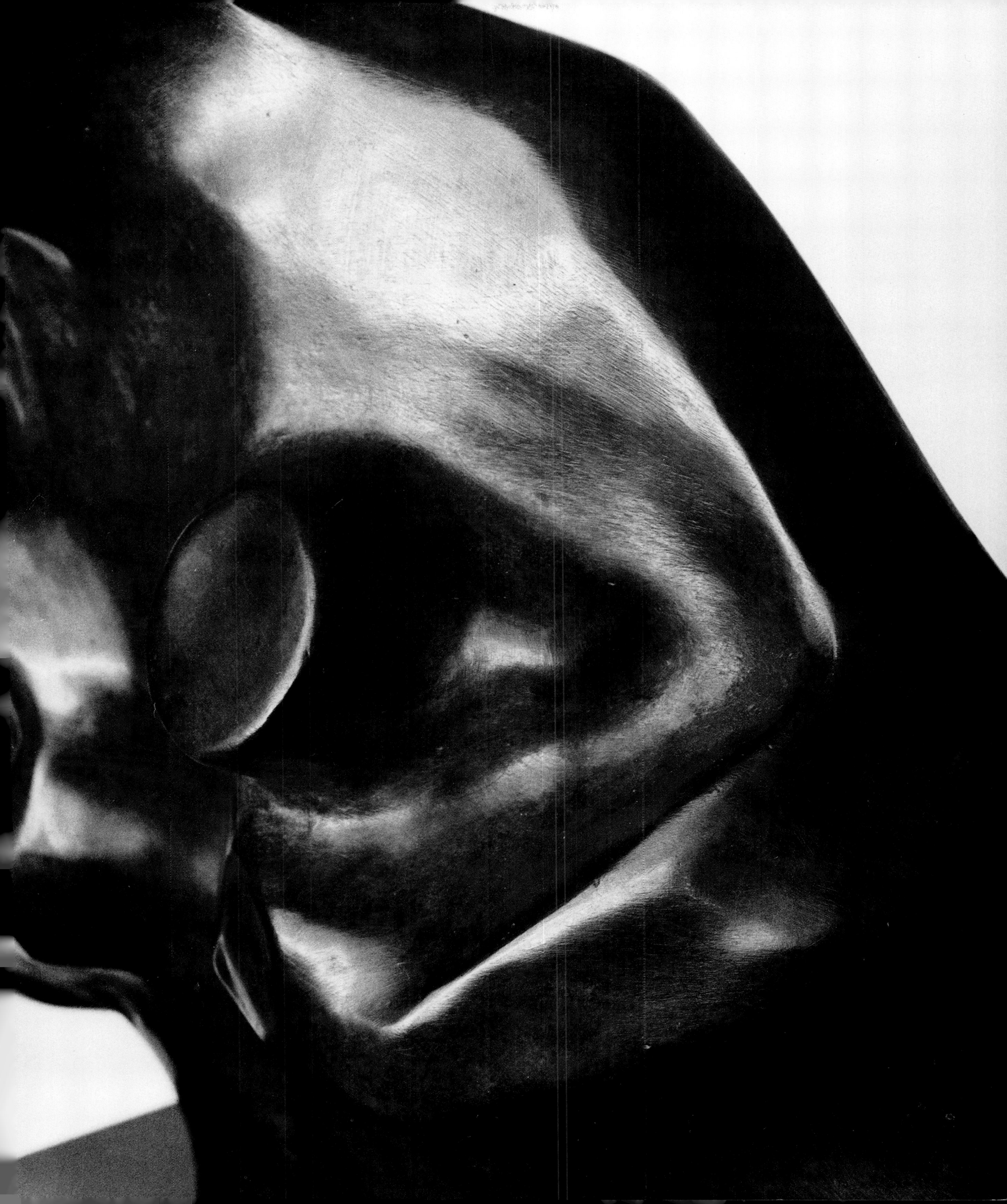

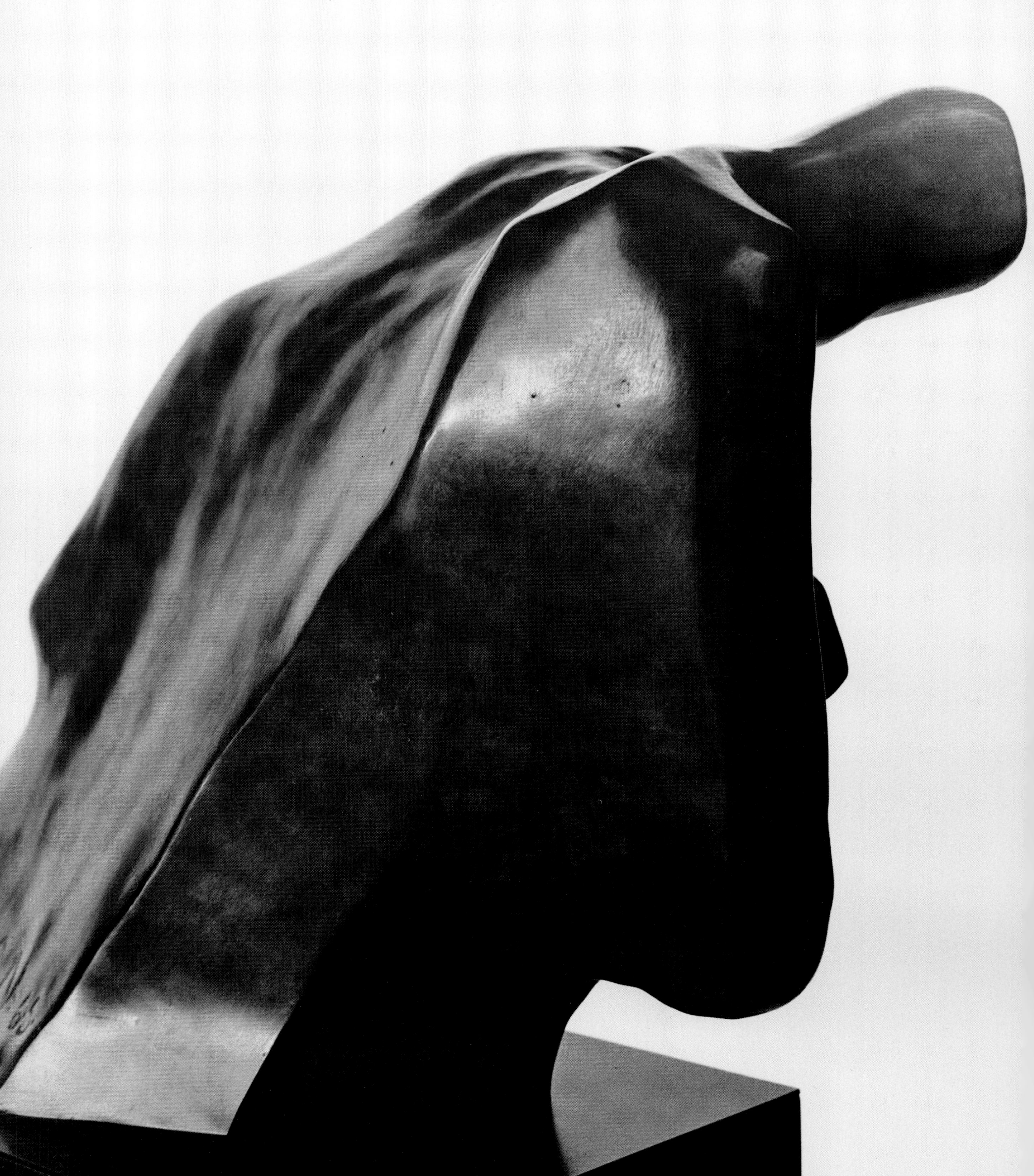

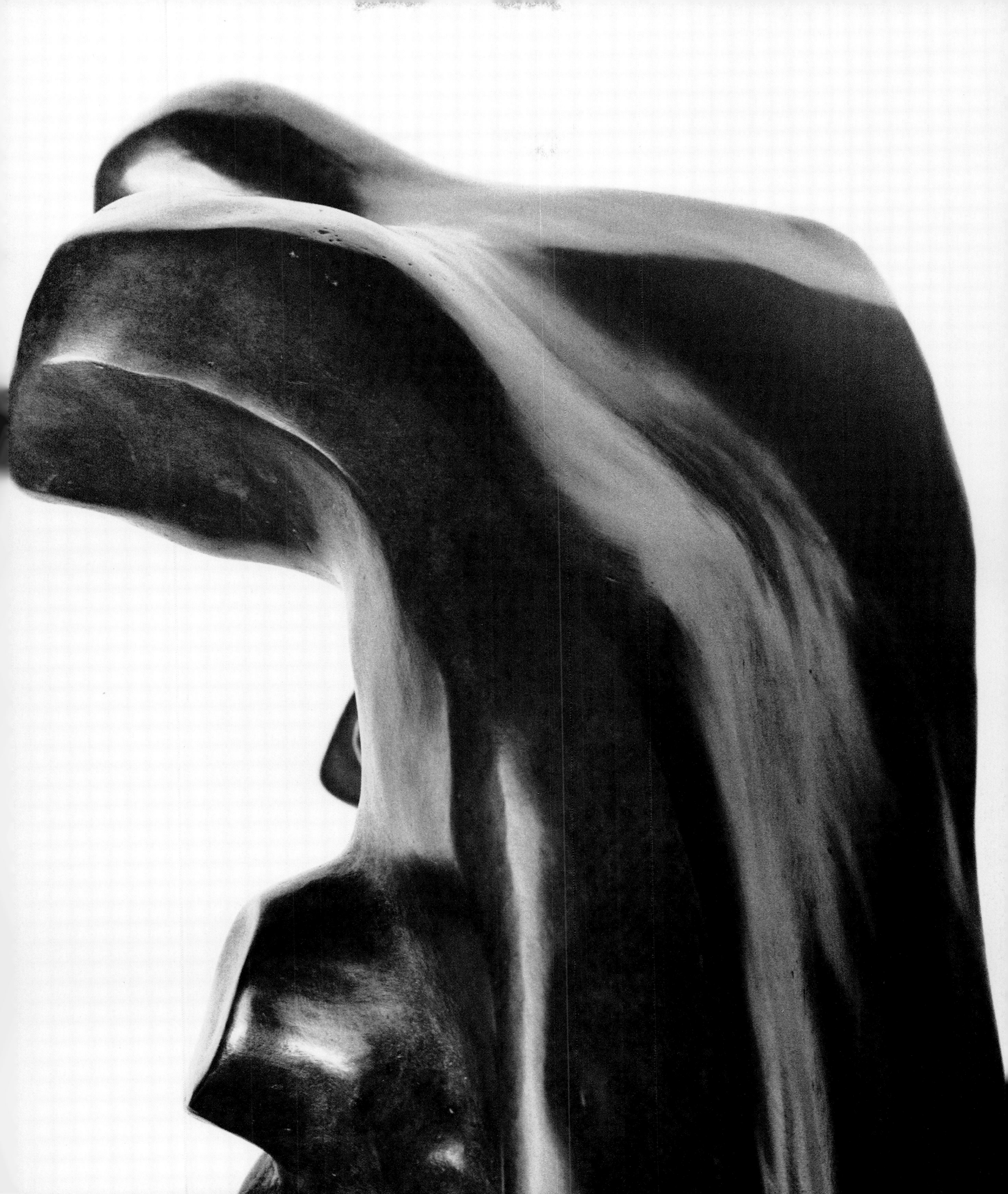

The Drinking Horse

No sculptor shall ever succeed in making the horse as spontaneously alive as did the ancient Greek artists. The Greeks lived with horses. Or the Greek horse lived with people all around him.

In our time the engine has taken over, filled with horsepower. Fortunately not completely. As yet, the species is not considered close to extinction.

Going back in memory to my youngest days, I see horses all over the place. Grandmother worried—I was so small; the animals were so big.

With grandmother's help I learned to ride an Icelandic pony when I was four. He was the size of a Great Dane.

Since then horses have been close to me. It has been natural for me to keep horses in mind when working in clay. Like this drinking horse. I at first conceived him as a centerpiece in a fountain. Given more time, I might still be able to return to that charming blueprint.

After he had the head cast in bronze, my good collaborator at the foundry mounted the neck of the horse at a drastic angle and welded the horse's upper lip to the base.

This is the way I have learned to love that horse. In my living room, he is eagerly stretching his neck downward to quench his thirst or to satiate his hunger on the lush green.

I don't mind if you prefer the water to be grass or vice versa.

To me this horse is a bit of an understatement.

He is like his contemporary, homo sapiens.

When they are in need, they go all out, ready to stretch and to struggle for the liquids of vitality and the means of existence.

The forceful motions might embrace a concept of beauty as well.

But beauty fades into insignificance when grass fades and water evaporates into desert land. This is the way I read this horse.

31″ × 7½″ × 20″

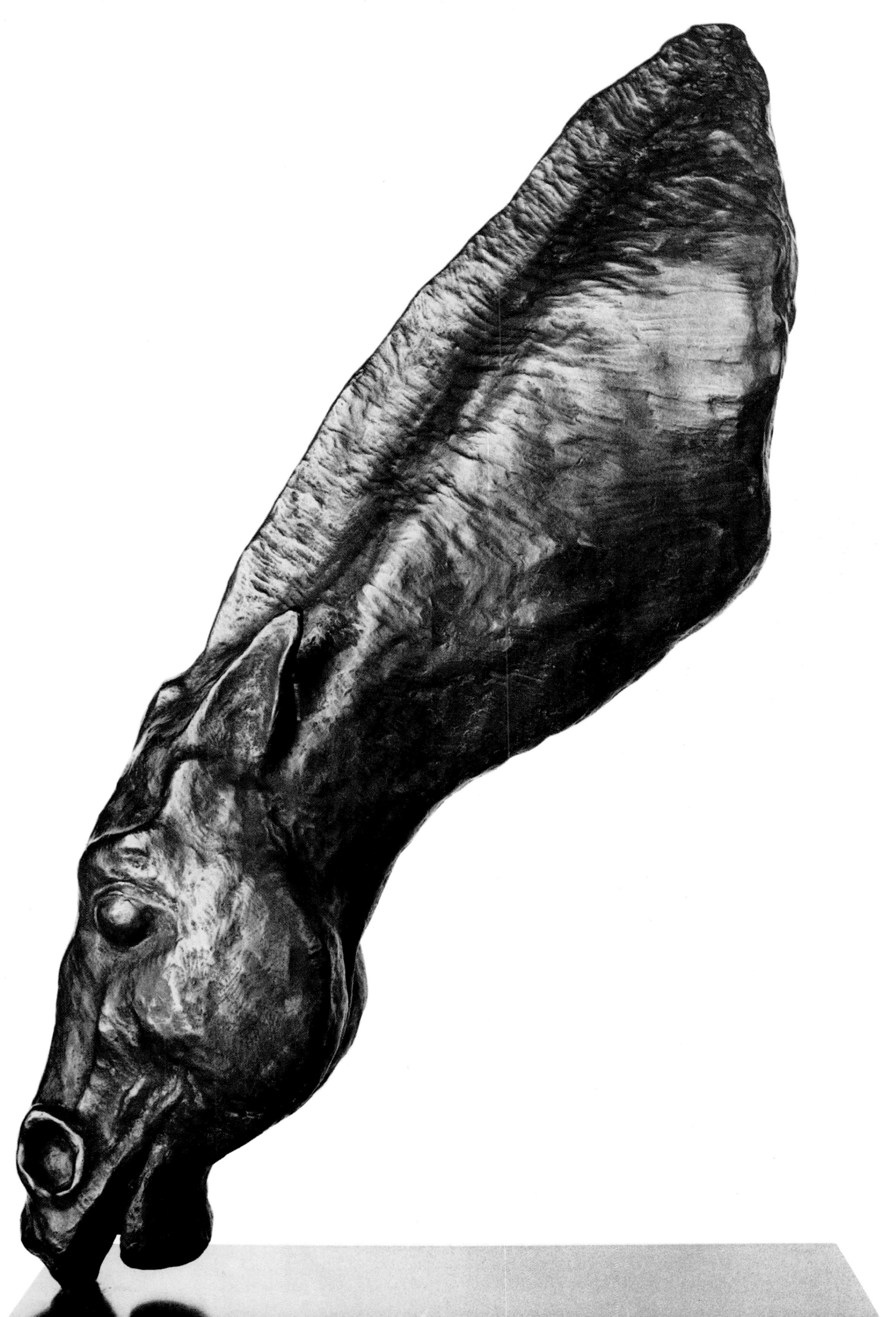

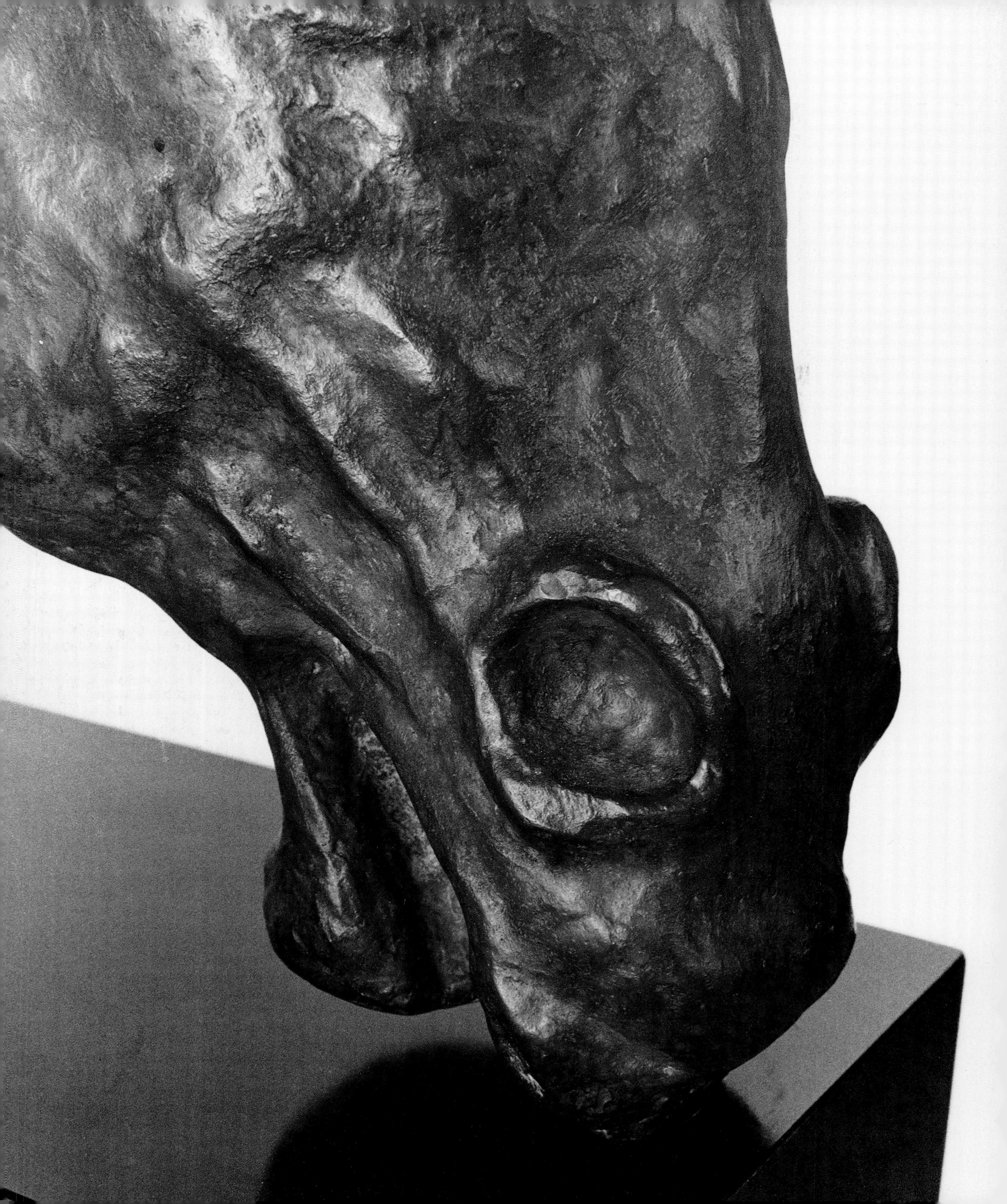

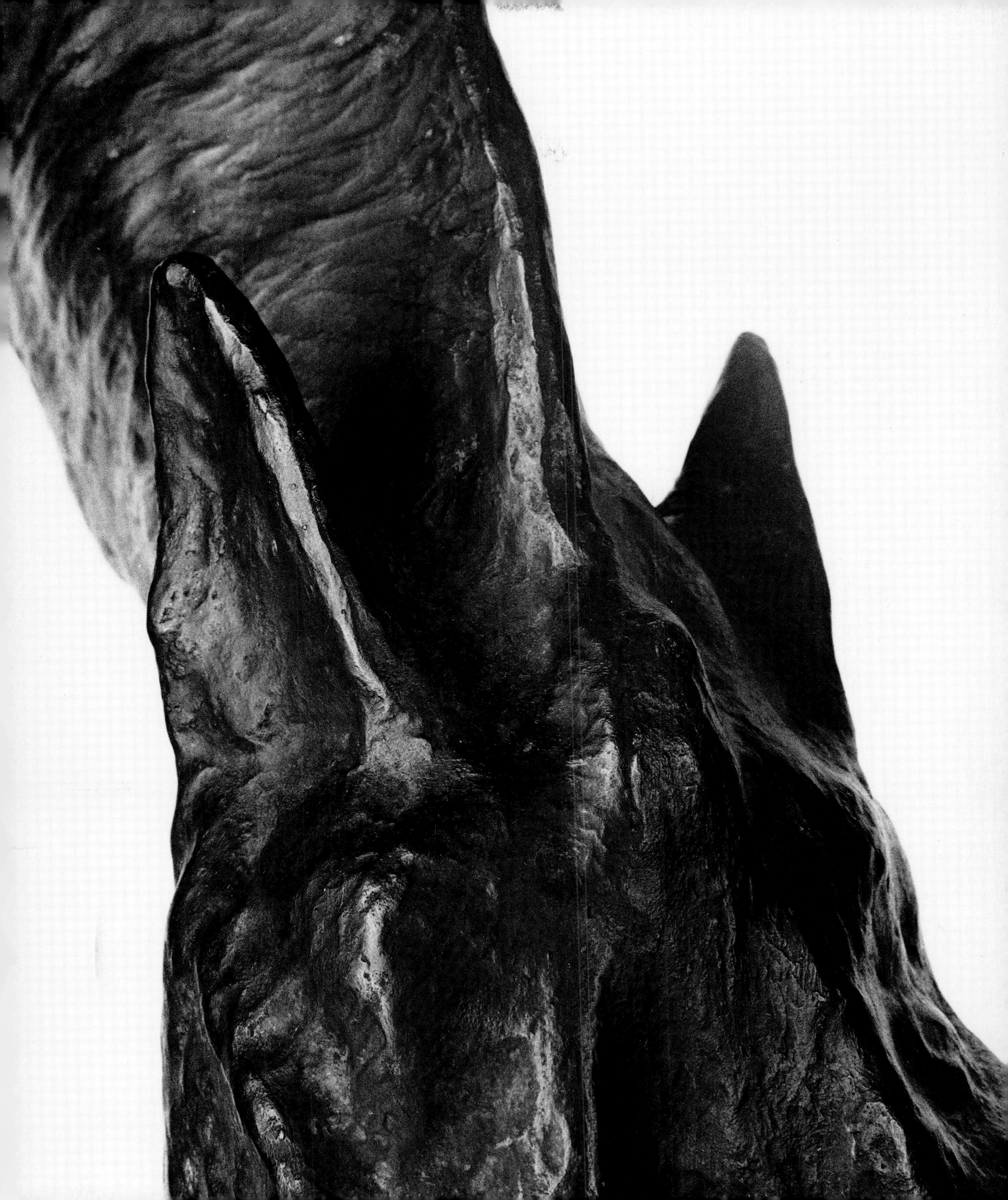

Girl With Cap

In hospital halls I hear the often repeated claim of finding and executing the much longed for dignity in death—if such is possible.

In our days, however, there seems to be no pressing need for dignity in art.

And dignity in life seems a bit foreign to our vocabulary.

In my professional work I have been rewarded through the courage and the equanimity of humans in my care. I have witnessed dignity in their hope for life and in their struggle to remain among the living.

Dignity in life exists.

It is a precious pillar deep inside our existence.

I saw it in the face of the young girl putting on an embroidered tight-fitting cap to go out and meet her *only* and *last* midsummer-night festival.

She had leukemia.

I am not announcing a program for the arts.

I am confessing; working with a struggling mass of human beings, and learning the devastating demolition of the minds and bodies of friends, neighbors, and anyone —such work creates images.

They shall not ask for an absolution if those impregnations ask for an outlet.

16″ × 10″ × 10″

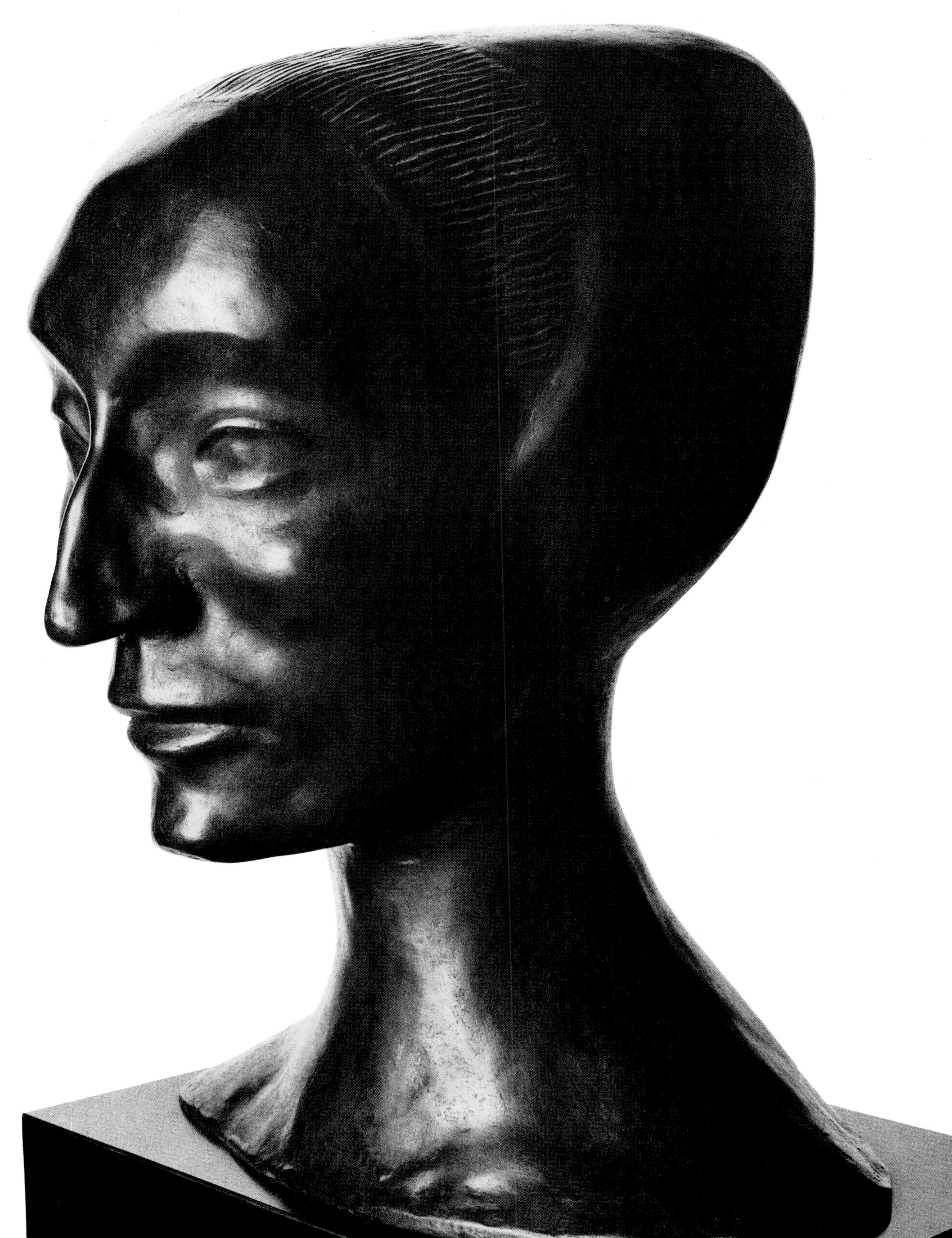

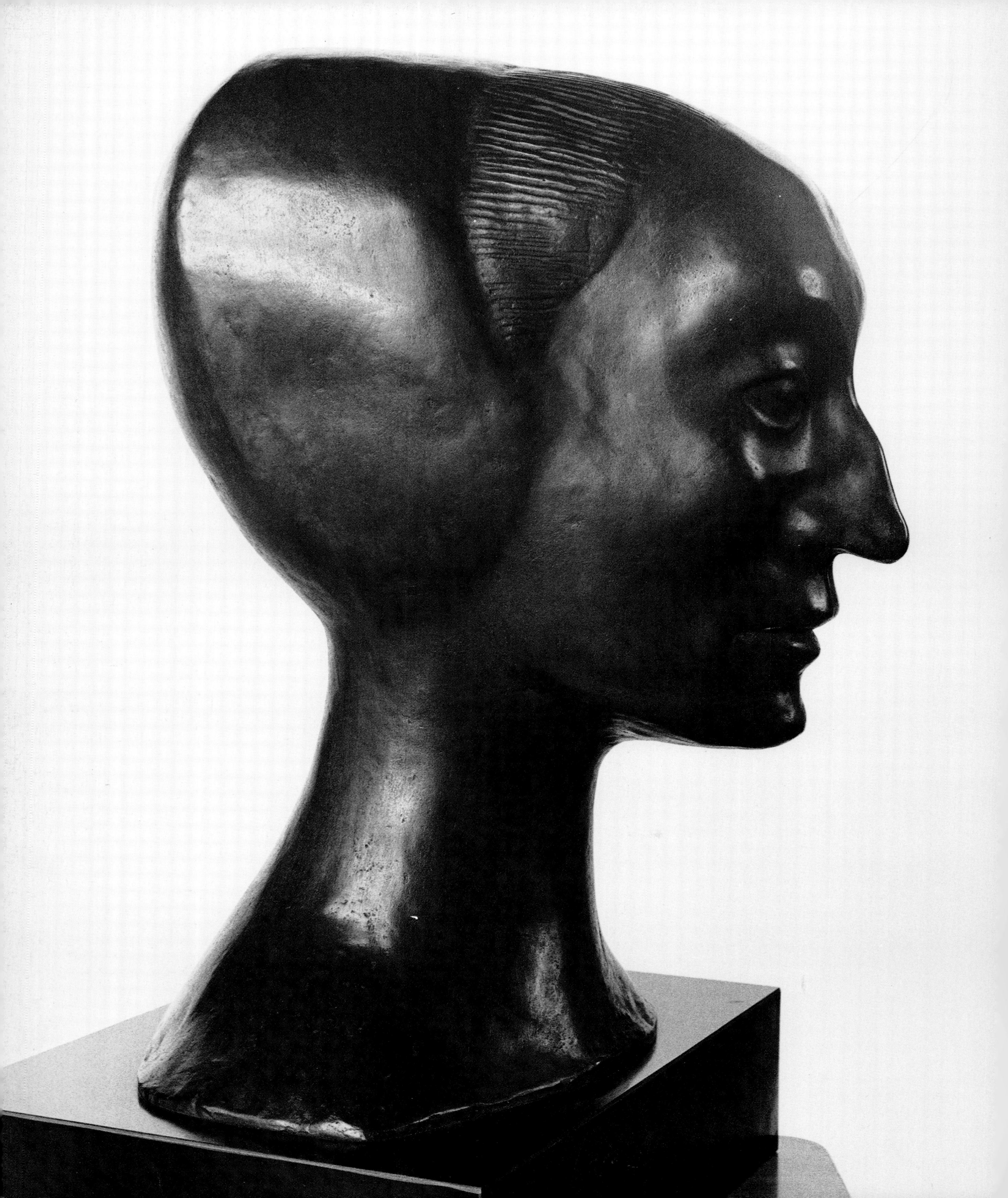

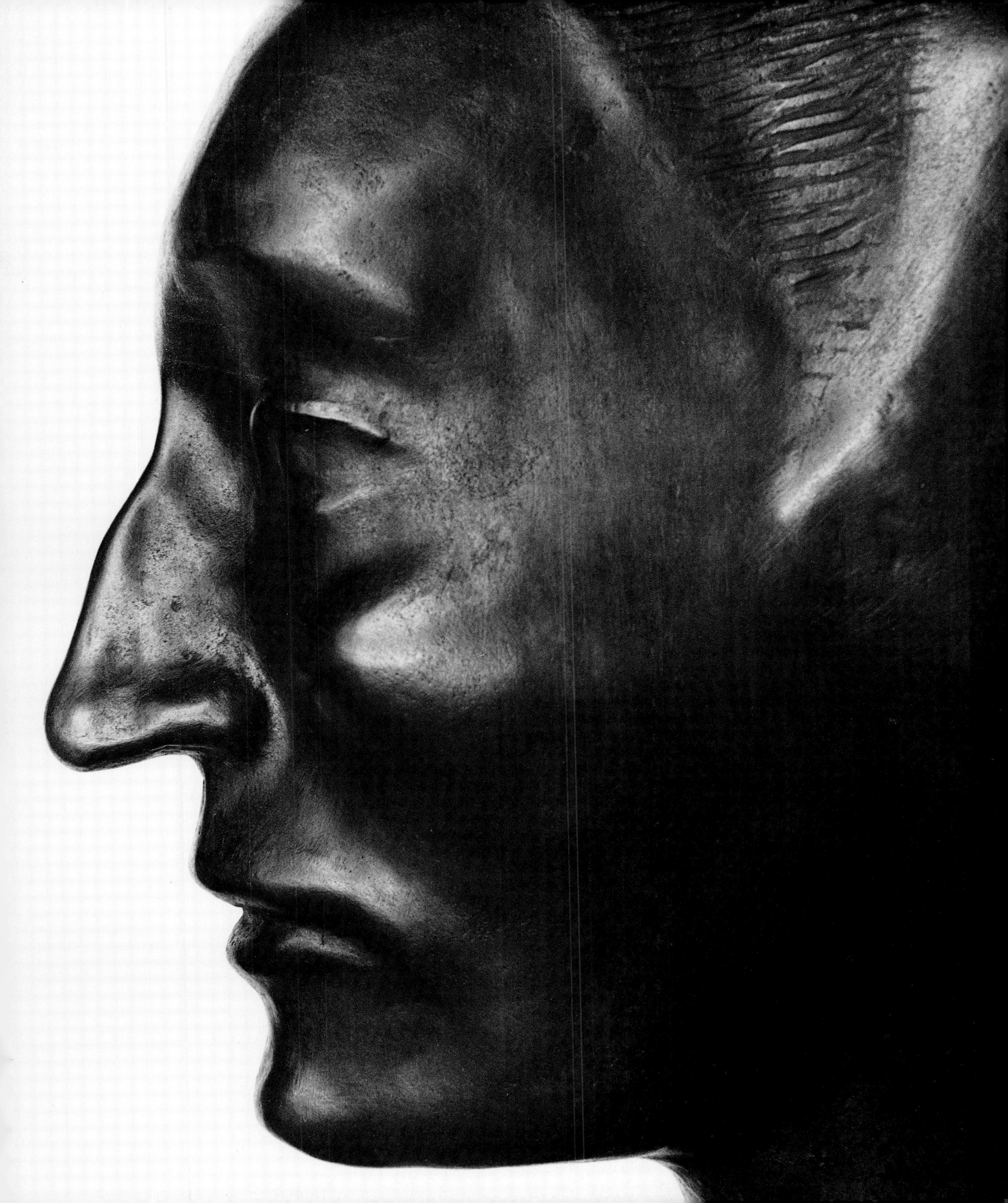

The Little Horse

I am puzzled at times when walking around here at home and looking at bronzes. What gave me the idea for this or that work? Often I don't know or I don't remember. What I always shall remember is this: a blank piece of paper can appear frighteningly white and forbiddingly virginal; thirty pounds of clay can look insultingly immobile, inert, and offensively stupid until a sudden strike of an idea can bring on a frenzied attack on the willing material.

Thus I remember *The Little Horse* from the very onset. But that beginning did not occur in my brain but in that of my wife's. And here is the dialogue, word for word. Ella: "We have so many nice bronzes of yours in our home. But many are really serious and serene. Please, can I ask you a favor? Make one little happy something for me personally."

I: "As for instance?"

Ella: "Oh, I don't know. Something happy. A little horse—or something."

I: "O.K. I will do."

This proved to be an easy commission. Ella had outlined the subject matter. In addition, it was supposed to be a *happy* horse. She appeared delighted when I brought her the finished work. "That one I like," she said.

I don't recall the few steps required to shape the animal except the tenacity with which you have to hang on to the simple—or not so simple—image around which the clay and the horse eagerly join in a frolicking stance.

16″ × 9″ × 4½″

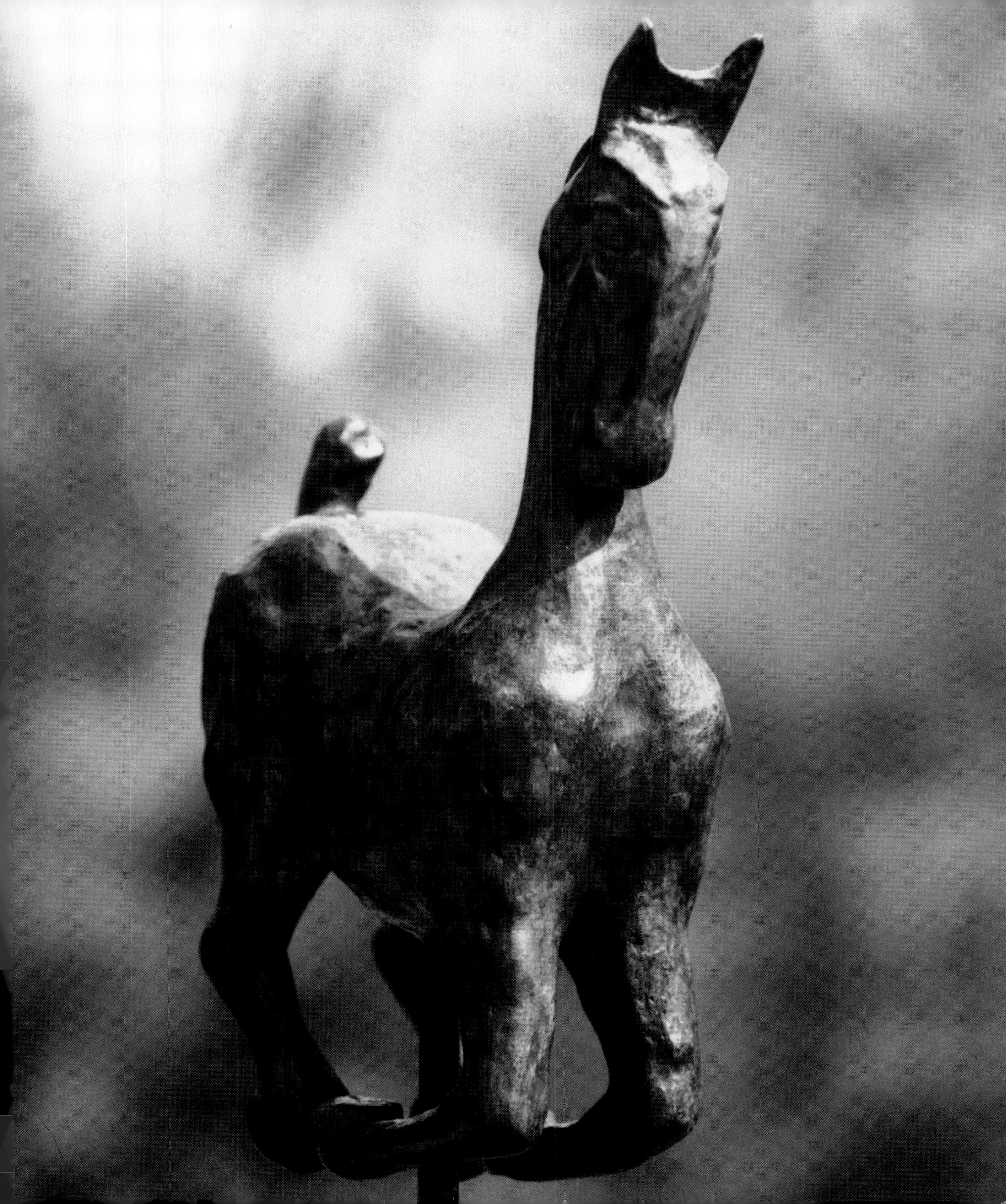

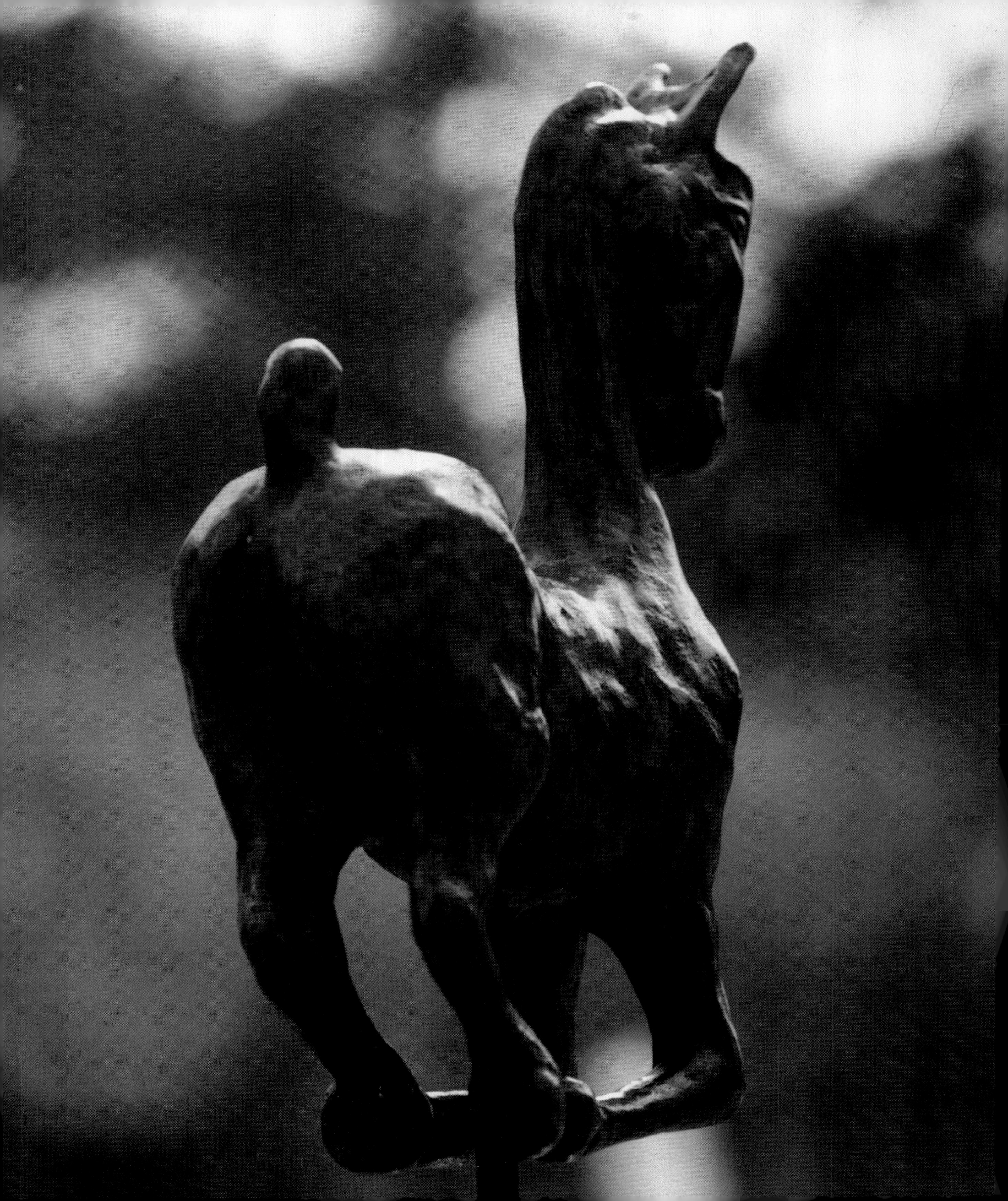

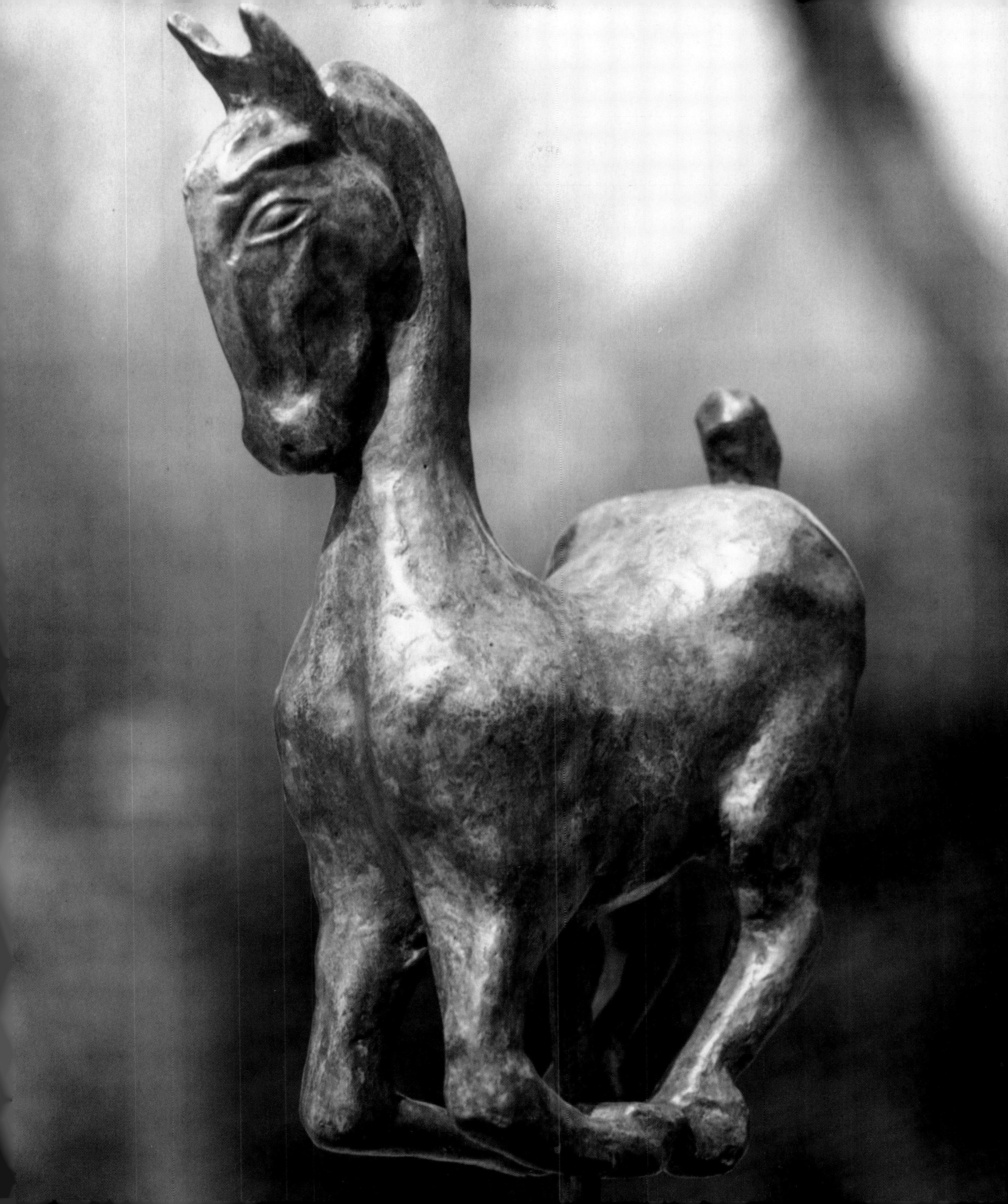

Seated Lady with Cap

I have never made a bust of Ella.

I know for sure.

The spirit of the woman who was my wife for forty-three years, that spirit must have found its way into this sculpture.

The seated arrangement is somewhat formal and touched with dignity.

The lines are clear and feminine.

There is a quiet equanimity emanating from the bronze.

In the right light she is living.

In those seconds I again learn to know more than beauty.

She was a good woman.

She was of a rare humane dimension.

24½″ × 10″ × 10

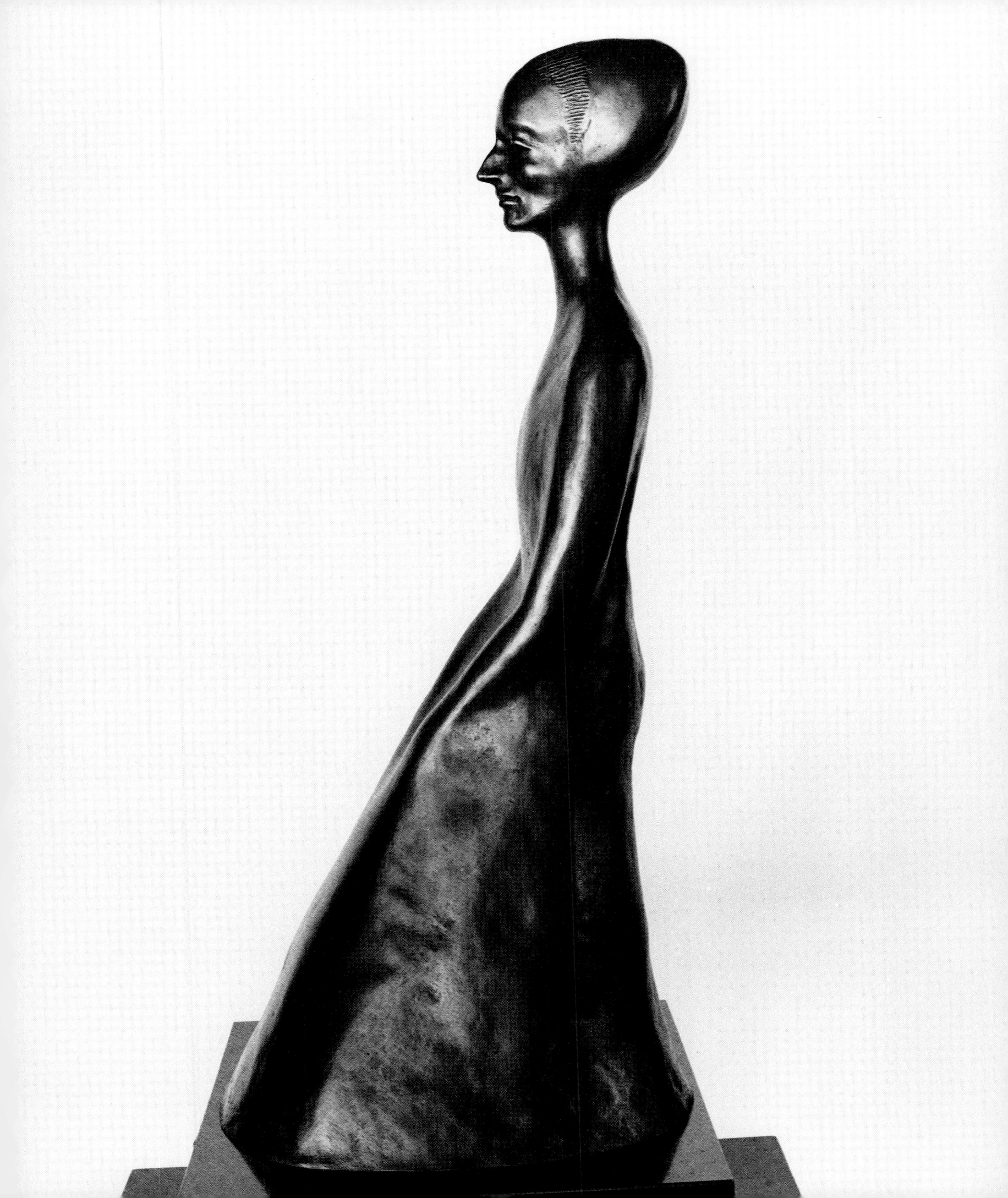

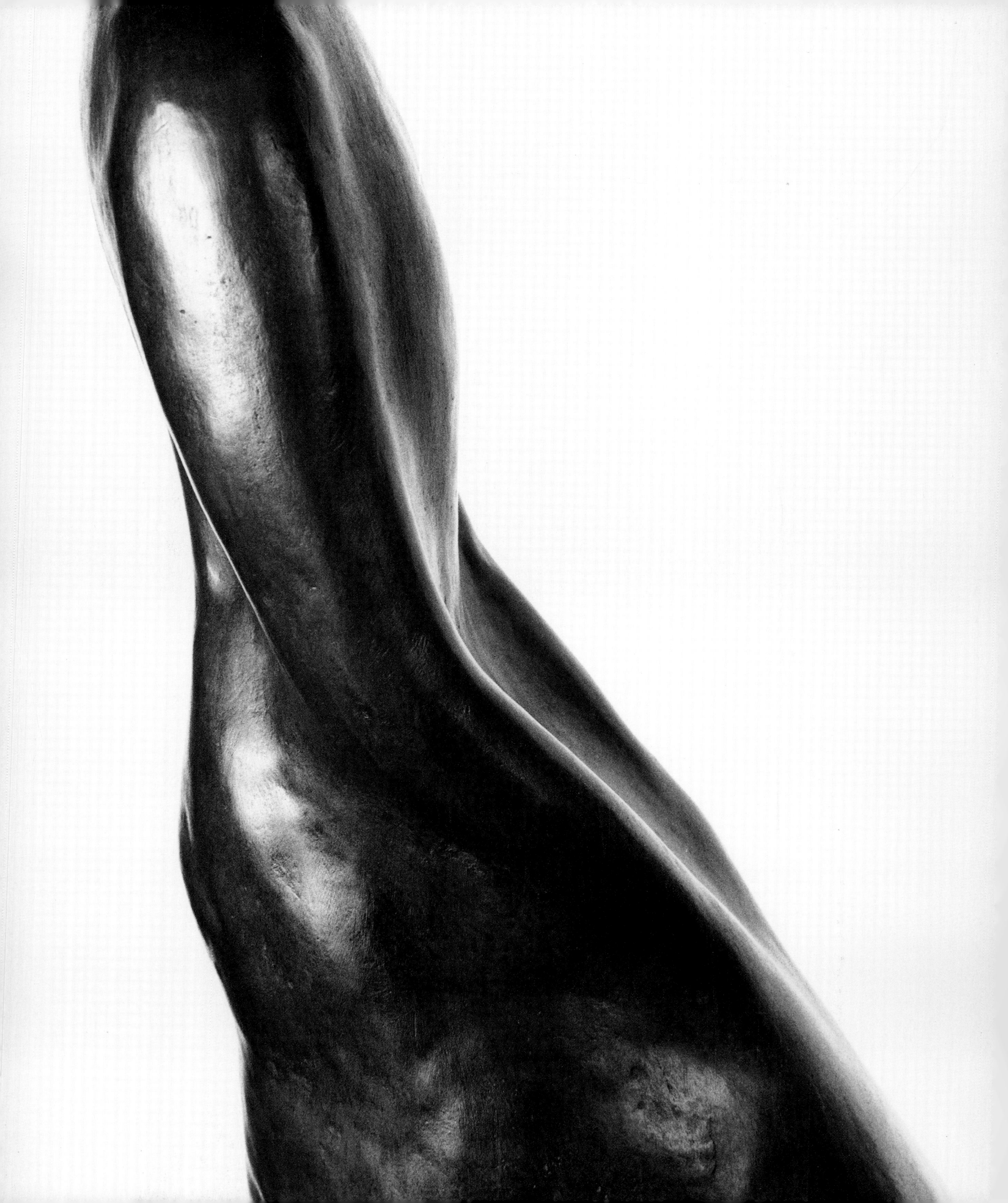

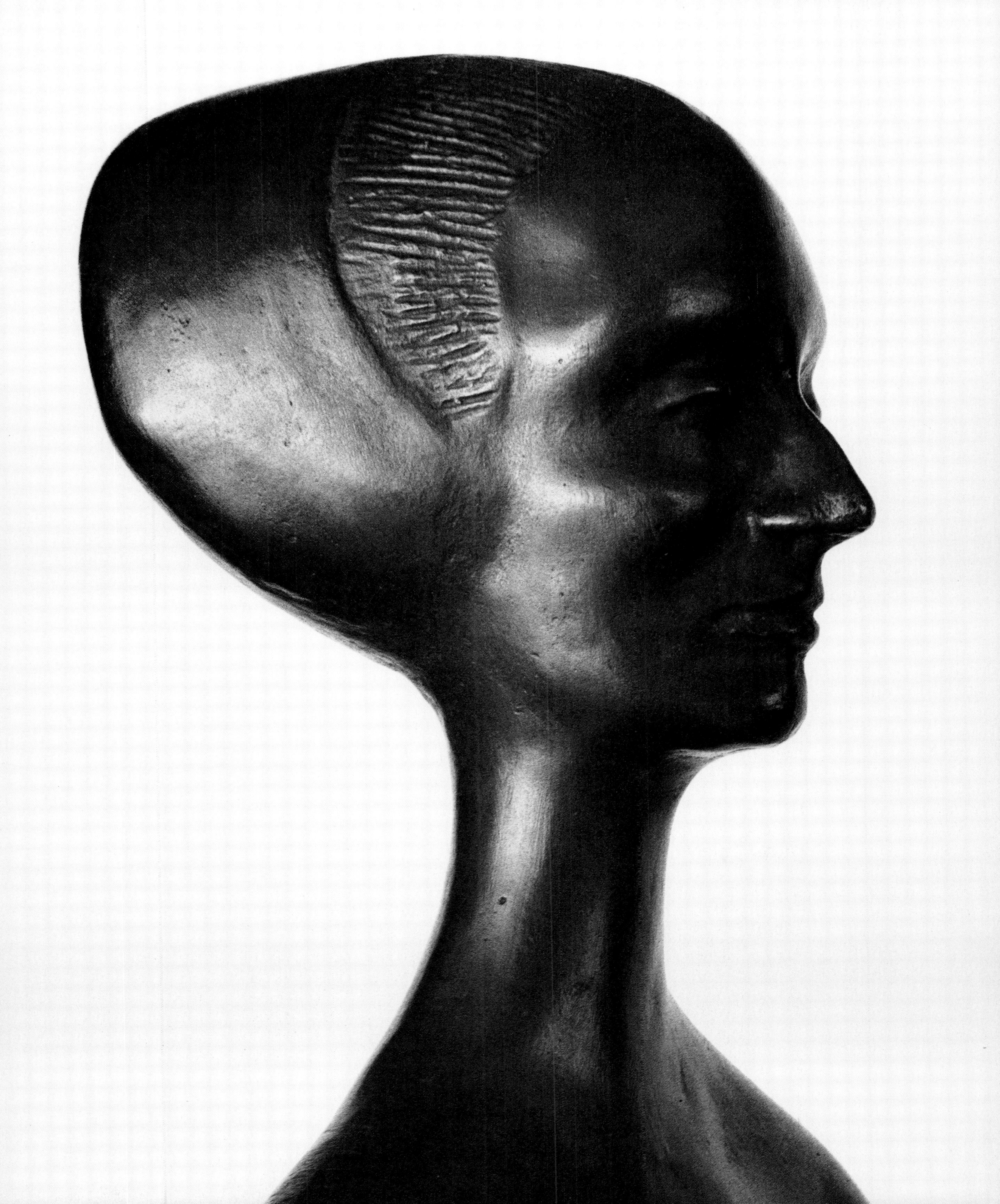

Dr. Ben Colcock

In my sculpture collection there are busts of men and women. I have not been commissioned to do them. They have all come out of my personal interest in the challenge.

I should add: the challenge might be provocative and demand action. Long ago I have found a natural and happy compromise between what I would *like to do* and what I *can do*.

I know my priorities by now. There has been no ongoing fight between my daily duties in the operating room and my urgency to get to the studio. Both places have felt like a natural habitat for me.

I have been aware that I, by training and makeup, belong in either place and sense no competition between them.

Rather, it would be like two supplementary and complementary locations where it is my privilege to work out the requirements of the day and the night.

The operating room should be a quiet, well-organized working unit, where mature, sound people with years of training meet, on behalf of their fellow men under their care, the challenges of the surgical problems presented to them.

The work must be done. It must be carried out to safeguard our patients' continued worthwhile existence.

All constructive things must come together in that room and in your mind. You are there to serve and help.

On occasions a warm trickle comes into your heart after a trying procedure. You may see her in the recovery room. Her voice is clear. The symmetry of her face muscles is perfect.

You need no further reward.

In the studio I can confess to a similar and rare sensation of warmth briefly diffusing in my inners. It might come after weeks of struggling with a resistant image, which suddenly seems to free itself and is coming at me like a child I have never seen before. That was the way Dr. Ben Colcock finally emerged.

He was an outstanding surgeon at the Lahey Clinic in Boston. We were both early members of the Surgeon's Travel Club.

I was first struck by his character—a genuine surgeon with a wealth of know-how and a gentle strength that serves us all well in our work. I sensed he had a face that he well deserved.

I saw him at least once a year.

One day I felt secure.

Without him ever sitting for me, I got to the clay with urgency.

After the bust appeared in bronze, his wife, Grace, exclaimed: "That is my husband."

I have been comfortable with the bust around me here at home. On occasions it has occurred to me that some meaningful bust might somehow also borrow aspirations and hopes from the executor, to be gently placed within the features of a human creature, seemingly possessing it all.

21½″ × 21″ × 15″

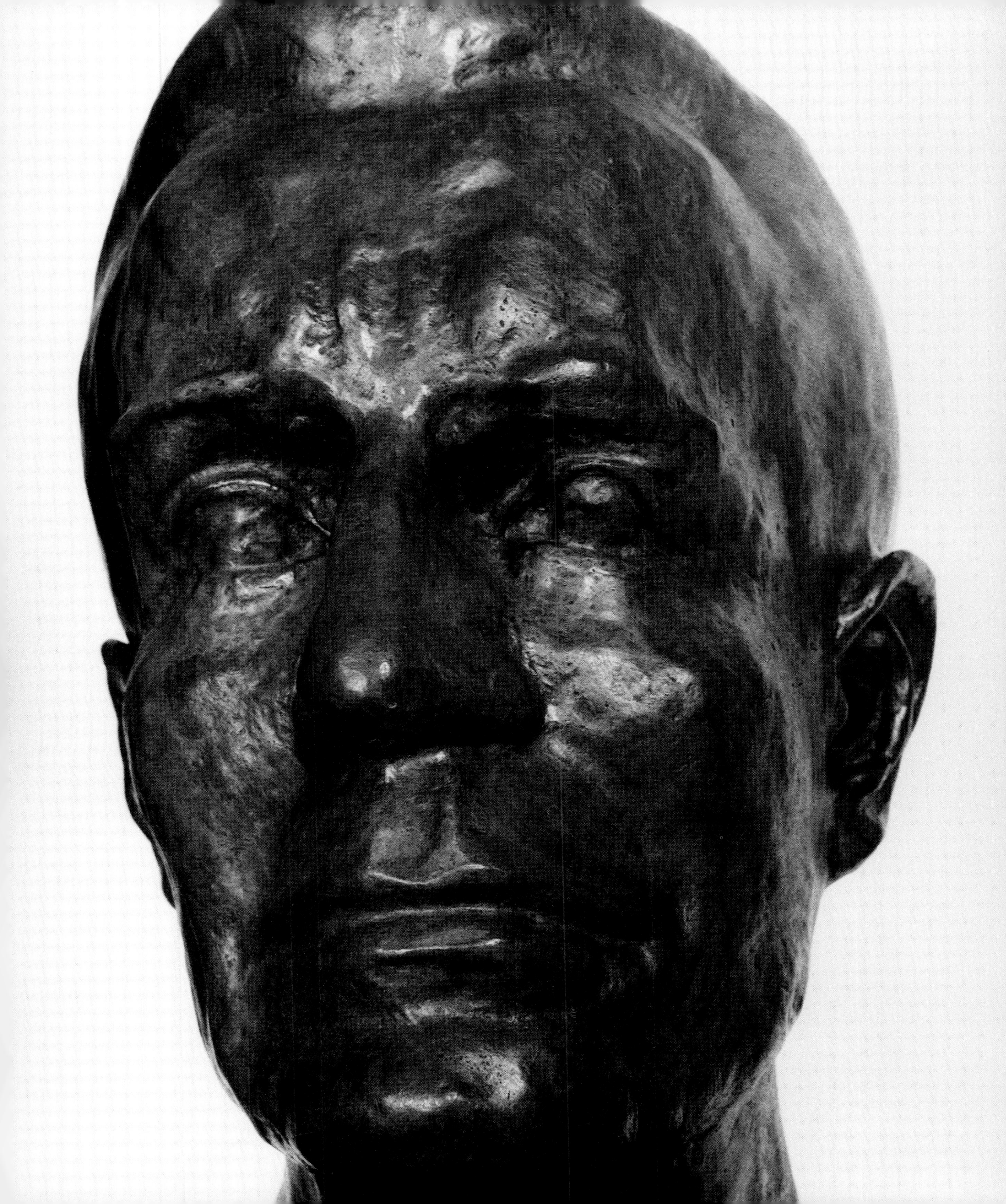

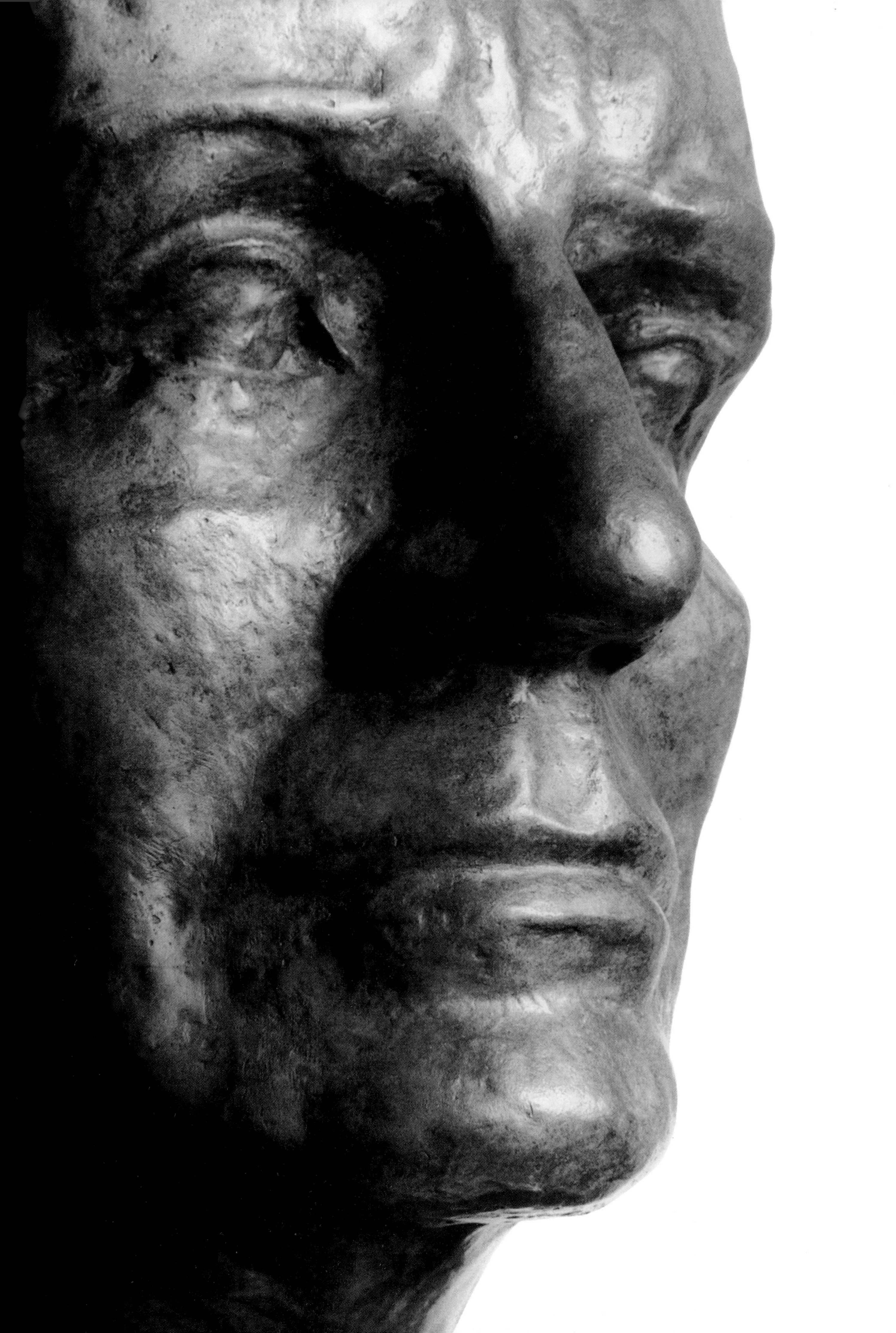

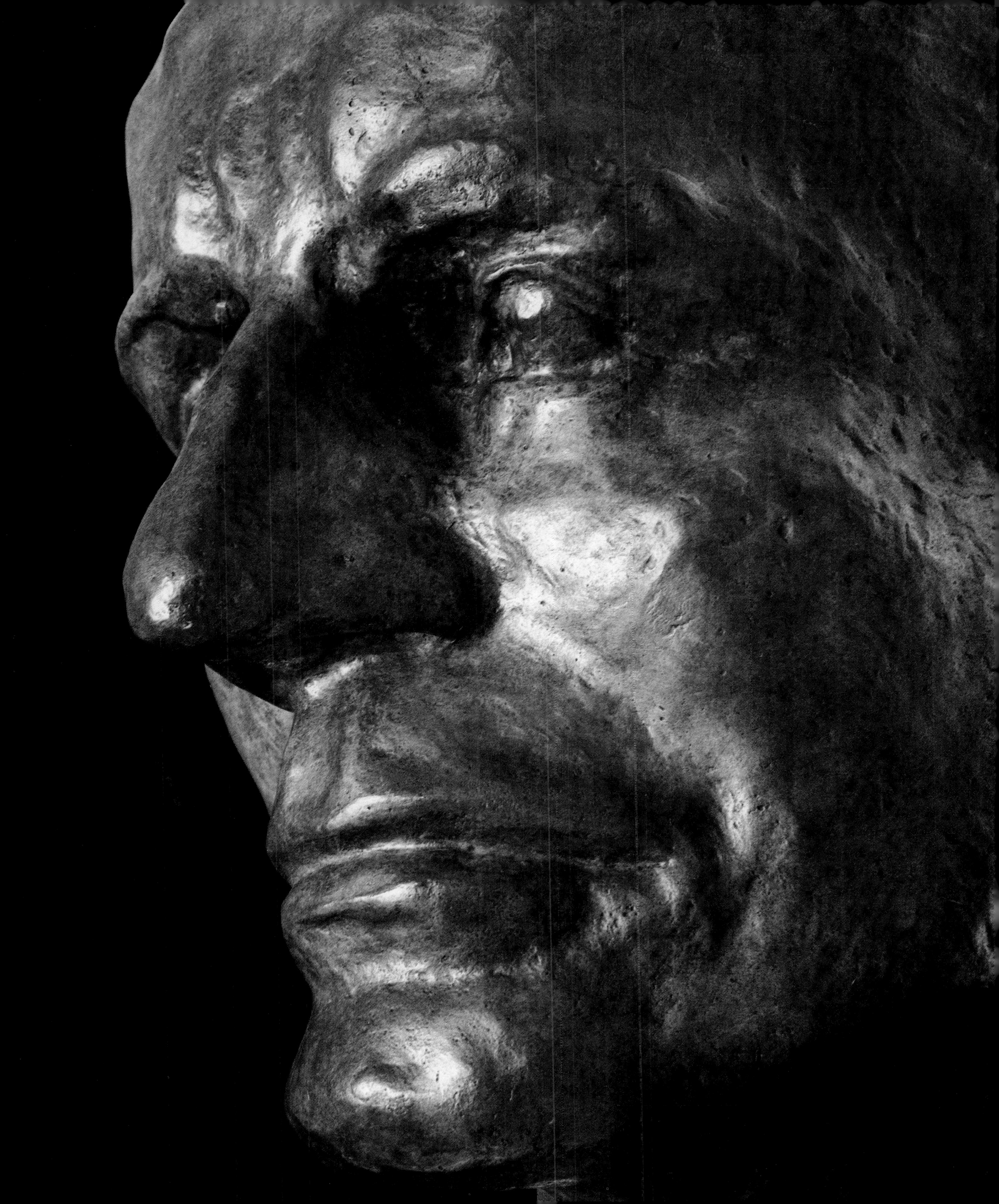

Percy Grainger *(1882–1961)*

In June, 1985, I was invited by the University of Melbourne, Australia, and the Percy Grainger Museum to give the tenth Percy Grainger Oration in Melbourne. The title of the lecture was "Percy Grainger and His Surgeon. A Psychologic Study."

I accepted the invitation in gratitude. Percy had been my friend. I learned to know him and to admire him. He was a genuine soul. I learned to defend him against subtracters and detracters; to explain him to benevolently listening individuals impressed by his so-called eccentricities; to carry, on Percy's behalf, his surgeon's view to a greater audience of a rare human being, who, in spite of grave difficulties, developed into a famous composer, brilliant performer and pianist, and visionary in creating his so-called Free Music. And above all, maturing into a convincingly alive and humane human being, in spite of it all.

There was a concert by Percy Grainger at Lillehammer, my home town in Norway. The year was 1913. I was nine years old. My mother took me to the concert. She thought I had been doing quite well practicing the piano.

I don't remember the program, but I am still aware of the excitement of the evening. That tall young Australian playing like a wild Pan and leaping onto the podium and off again, with his golden hair flowing about his impressive head.

After ten years of postgraduate surgical training, mainly in the Middle West, I came to White Plains, New York, in 1940. I have been there ever since. And, strangely enough, Percy Grainger and his mother had since 1923 a home in White Plains only two blocks from the White Plains Hospital.

Percy was still physically overactive. He was still leaping like a leopard. I learned many more valuable characteristics that I felt attached to.

During the last eight years of his life I was closer attached to him as his surgeon.

It is said that during sickness the true nature of a human being is revealed.

It is also said that a surgeon's life is bloody and rough.

It is not always understood that his activities represent a two-way street.

It is his duty to give—and to give his best. Much is given him in return. It is like living with another person who may be writing the last chapter of his life. It is like participating in a dress rehearsal before the final curtain falls.

Thus I lived Percy's life with him during the last eight of his seventy-nine years. We became friends.

At years intervals I have done three busts of Percy. I did not ask him to sit for me.

Percy Grainger was a many-faceted man. I did not fancy that I should be able to grasp more than glimpses of this highly gifted human creature.

I was reminded of Rodin executing a commissioned work in respect and admiration for the "art of the thousand profiles."

While working with the three busts of Percy, I was in a similar way centering on the myriads of impressions Percy had impregnated on my mind with his life, his music, and his sickness.

I recall his expression when I had finished the last of the three busts, where I had intentionally aimed at a heroic posture.

Percy: "This is the way I like to be!"

I knew what he meant to say.

His life in his opinion had been far from heroic, while still not ruling out the hope that he could have been a much more courageous being.

To me, he had been more courageous than most. He had taken his beatings and suffered intensely. I shall not enter those chapters. They would require a sculpture garden and a monograph.

9″ × 16″ × 8″

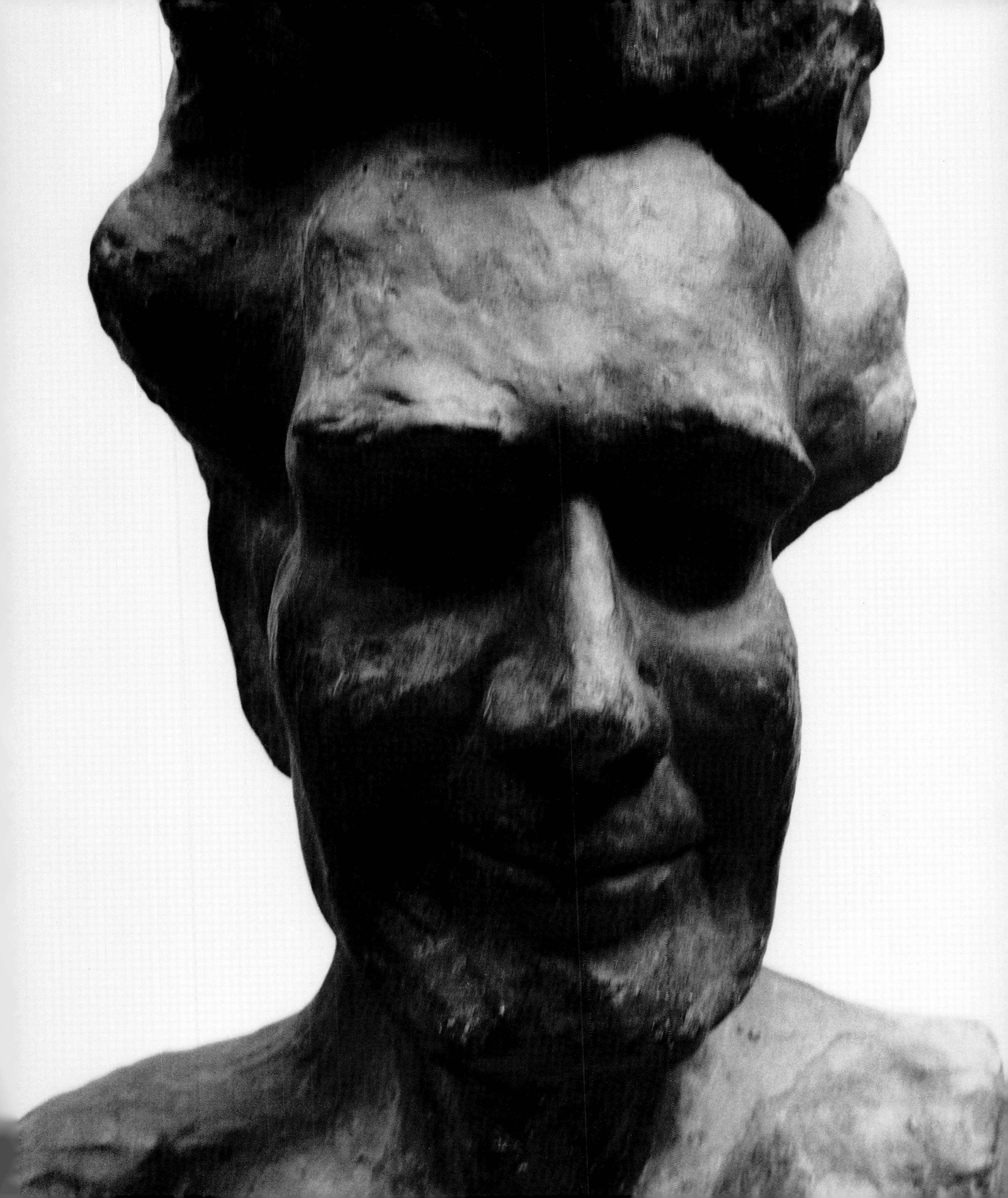

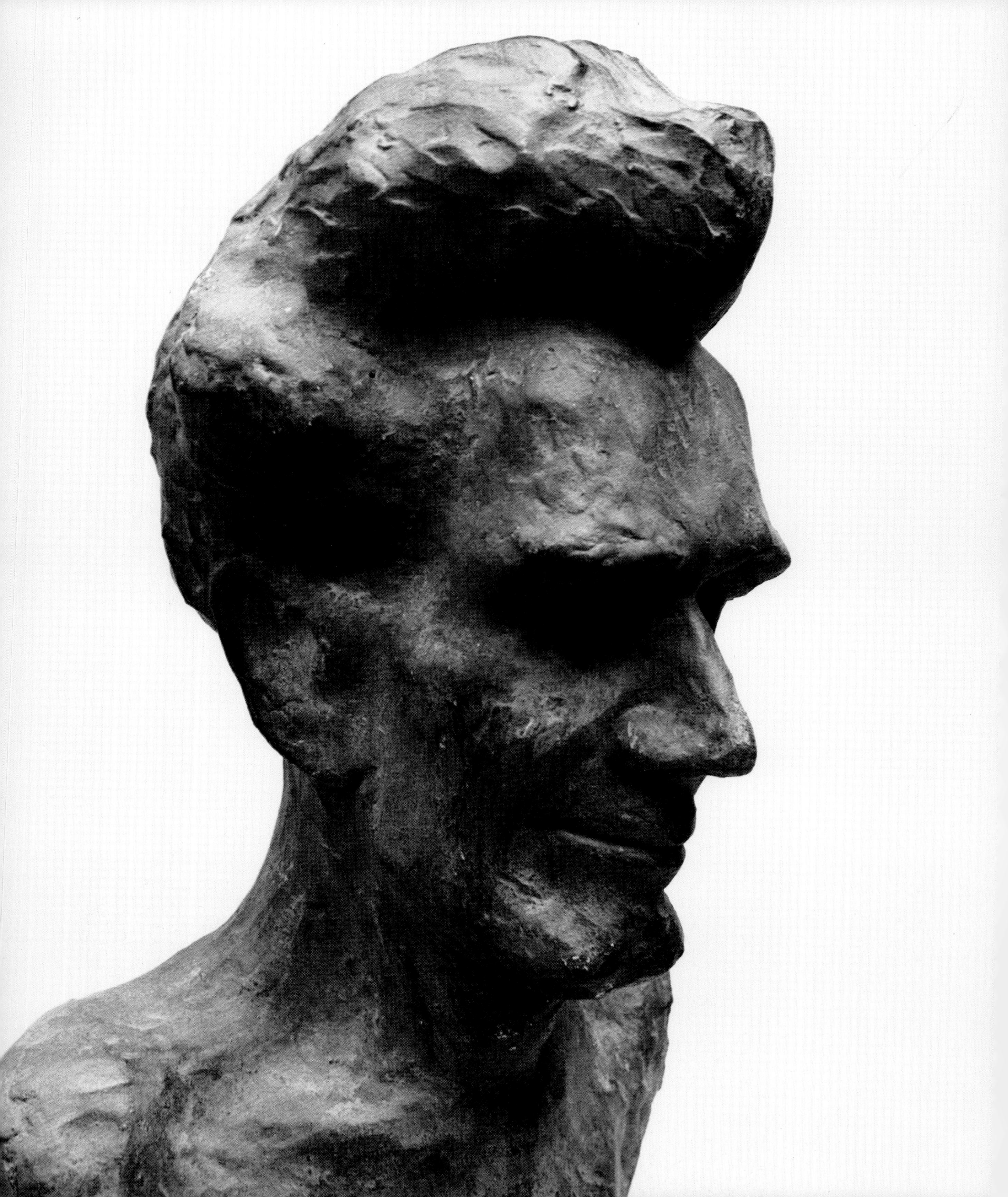

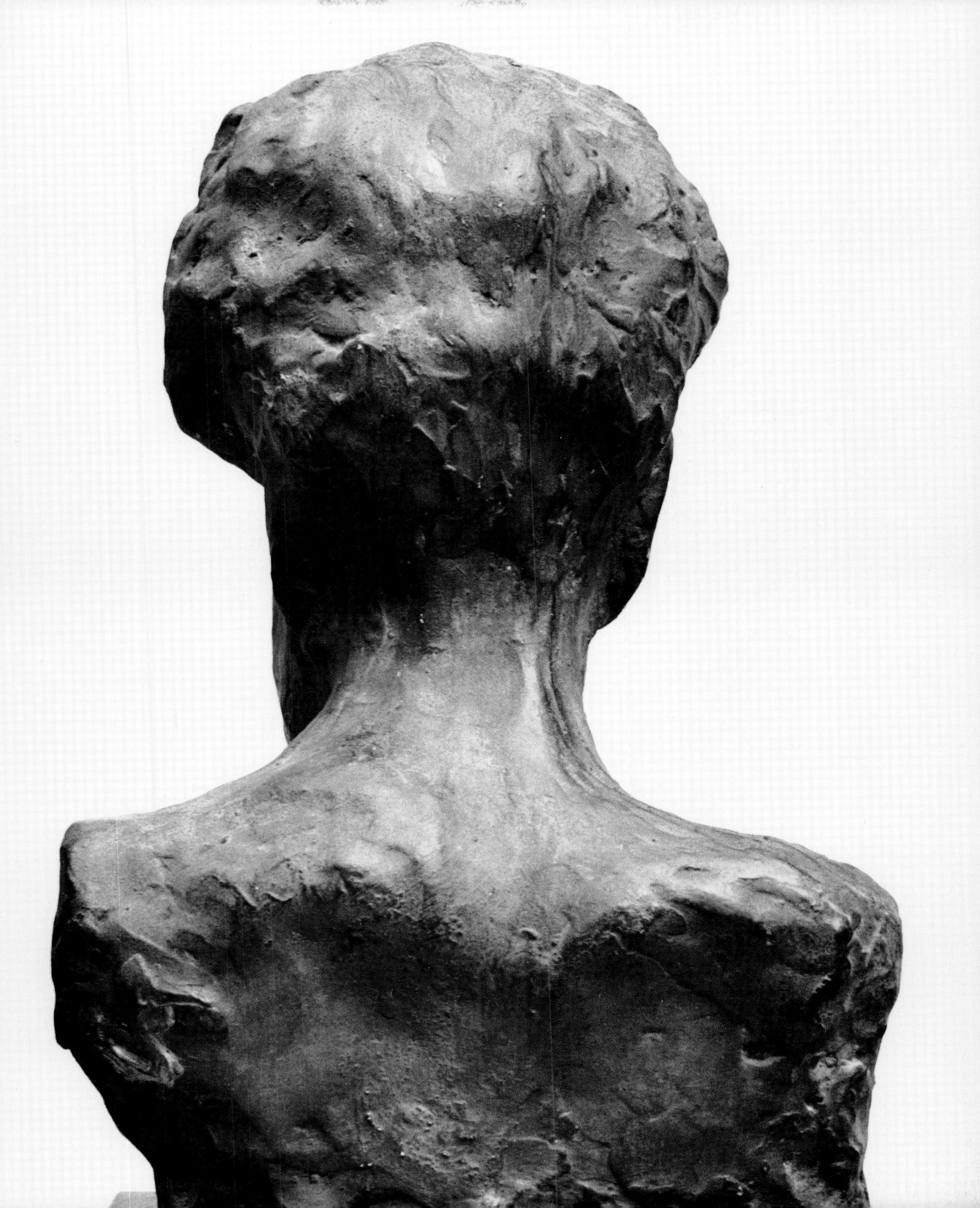

"Nature is not *only* that visible to the eye—
it also presents the inner picture of the soul—
the pictures on the reverse side of the eye."

EDVARD MUNCH

Edvard Munch

At the age of twenty-nine, in 1892, Edvard Munch was invited to exhibit in Germany at the Verein Berliner Künstler (the Union of Berlin Artists).

The exhibit resulted in creating an uproar. It split the art society in two. It lasted only one week.

That exhibit is considered to be the beginning of Expressionism in painting. Munch is considered its originator and father.

That accolade must have seemed strange and ironical to Munch. His shy nature was not made for a soapbox, nor for proclamations or wild dialectics.

In many ways Munch was a subdued man. Due to his sensitive mind he was never unaware of his family's tendency to mental disorders, while still proud of his ancestors' cultural achievements in Norway.

He was also always aware that some of them had been cut down in young life by tuberculosis. His mother succumbed to the disease when Edvard was five years old; his sister, Sophie, died when he was fourteen.

His father, a physician, tried to drown his sorrows in a pietistic life devoted to the poor and the sick in need of his professional attention.

Edvard slowly grew into an artist.

In his misery, he found ways and means to let some of it exude from his boiling inners. The brain and the heart know places for solace and for peace, to be searched for in colors, forms, and figures.

In my student days in Oslo I saw him not infrequently in the streets adjacent to the university.

He was a good-looking man. Tall. Proud bearing. There was something stately about him. His face not unlike Leonardo da Vinci's. His chin made a promontory fit for a field marshal.

His locomotion gave him away.

When on the sidewalk, he gave the impression that he was not sure whether he should be there or in a safer place, or out in the street, or back again up on the sidewalk. He seemed clearly not comfortable with all the people around him.

This was his life style. Never quite at ease. Never quite securely at home any place.

Vulnerable genetic traits had dug deeply into this hypersensitive mind and created an ever-recurring insecurity and ambivalence to life for which he seemed otherwise to have been so generously fortified.

In spite of it all, he kept on working, painting, and creating throughout a long and fertile life.

He learned to know that his was not a voice in the desert.

He knew he was a main actor on the world stage of visual art.

It must have been no surprise (or defeat) for him in 1936 to learn that by a decree of Hitler's, for the second time in his life, in Germany, his art was considered "degenerate" and unfit for exposure. His paintings were removed from the prestigious art museums throughout the Reich.

During the Second World War Hitler invaded Norway during the night of April 9, 1940.

During those subsequent five years of occupational warfare, bombardments, fires, spying, and

Head
19″ × 8″ × 10″

(*page 145*)

After Self-Portrait
20″ × 12″ × 7″

(*page 146*)

Ambivalence
20″ × 12″ × 11″

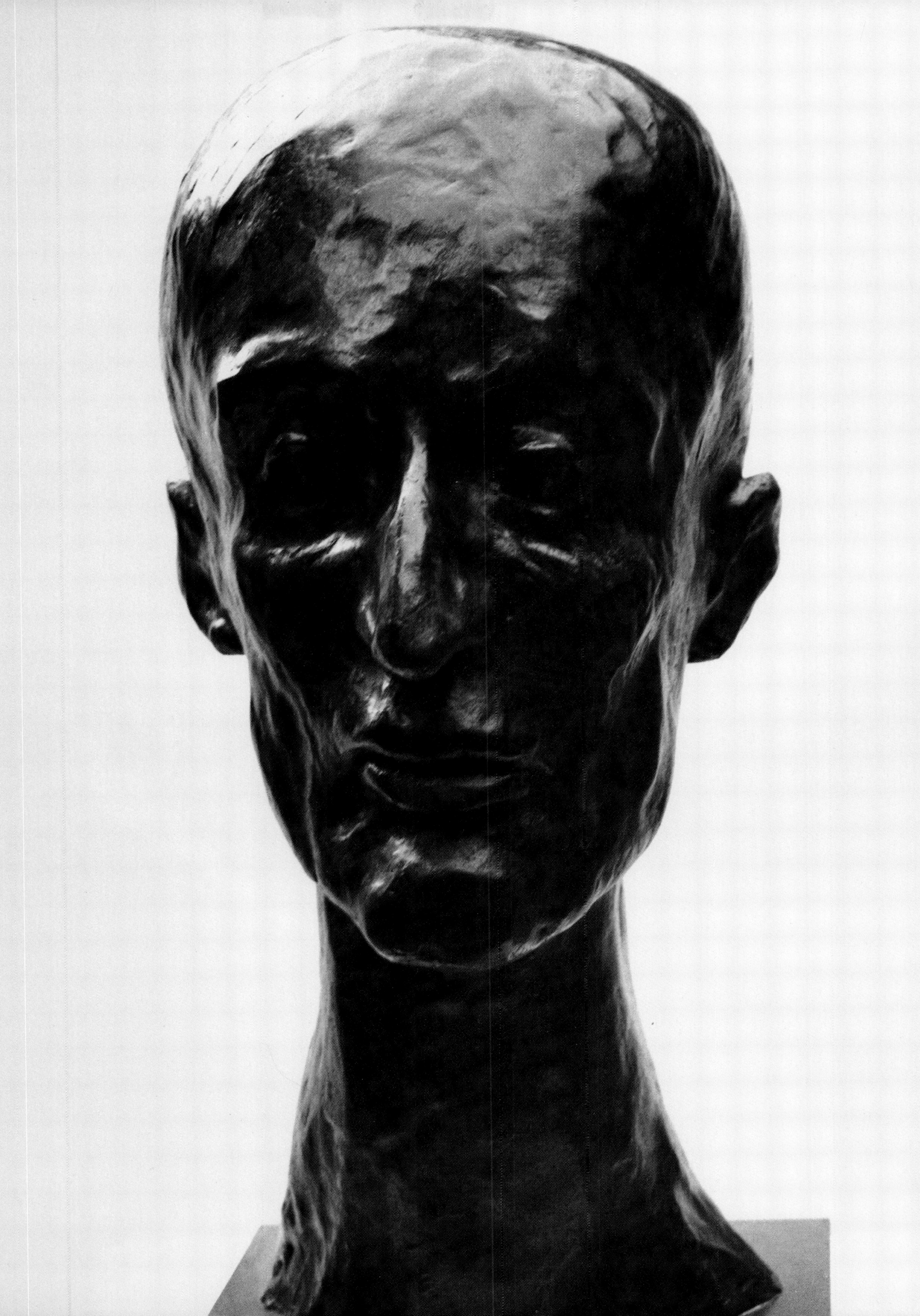

Nazi brutalities, Oslo inhabitants went to bed never quite convinced that there would be another day tomorrow.

Fellows grown to manhood knew that there was no greater value in the world to hope for than living one day at a time, even if miserably so.

Life was to be saved, if feasible.

Death to be accepted, if required.

It was in that strangulated city that Edvard Munch was forced to remain incarcerated for the remaining four years of his life.

He was living alone on his estate with many barking dogs. Intermittently a housekeeper was his closest alliance. Once in a while he would call a friend by phone. It meant the friend would come and visit with Munch, do some errands, and obtain some much-needed, strictly rationed, supplies for Munch. His friends knew—no one arrived unannounced at Edvard Munch's home.

Throughout his life he had sold his pictures with hesitation: he had a feeling that he needed his work around him constantly. There were paintings all over the place, inside and not least outside the house, irrespective of the long and cold Norwegian winters. He felt that it was good for the canvases. If they could not take that "horse cure" so generously supplied by inclement weather, there might be an inherent weakness in them which might tempt him to relegate them.

The Nazi spirit was of a different, destructive nature. A fire bomb could in no time streak through the atmosphere and annihilate his entire life's work.

This did not happen.

He died in that house. He died in his sleep.

The day was January 21, 1944.

The Nazi defeat in Norway came on May 9, 1945.

Thus died Hitler's claim to a Thousand Year's German Reich.

But Edvard Munch's canvases were alive.

The beneficiary of his estate was the city of Oslo, which in due time built the Edvard Munch Museum.

It includes the main part of his oeuvre: 1,100 paintings, 15,400 prints, 4,500 watercolors and drawings, 6 sculptures, and letters and manuscripts.

I have executed three bronzes of Edvard Munch.

One of them is entitled *Ambivalence*.

In this bust I have knowingly tried the impossible—that is, a psychiatric study of Edvard Munch in bronze.

There are valid counterarguments.

Visual art is proclaimed to be mainly a retinal art.

Still, a simple retinal impression, like a leaf of grass, requires a mysterious neurophysiologic activity of an alive brain to make it a meaningful observation.

In this bust of Munch I have, so to say, turned him inside out.

I see him in frontal view, in his mature years, full of wrinkles and energy.

The back of his head, however, is carved out. It is from this view that I see him from behind, like a schizophrenic, always aware of disturbing messages of alarming consequences coming in from all around in hidden images.

In this view from behind I have included figures from Munch's early works: his first self-portrait, the Madonna, a fetus, the giant sperms.

My friend Burnett, who does the photographing, asked me: "Could you do a better bust of him if Munch had posed for you?"

I said: "Absolutely not! If he had posed, I would have been limited by what I saw. Like Munch, I did the bust that way because I was aware of the picture on the reverse side of the eye."

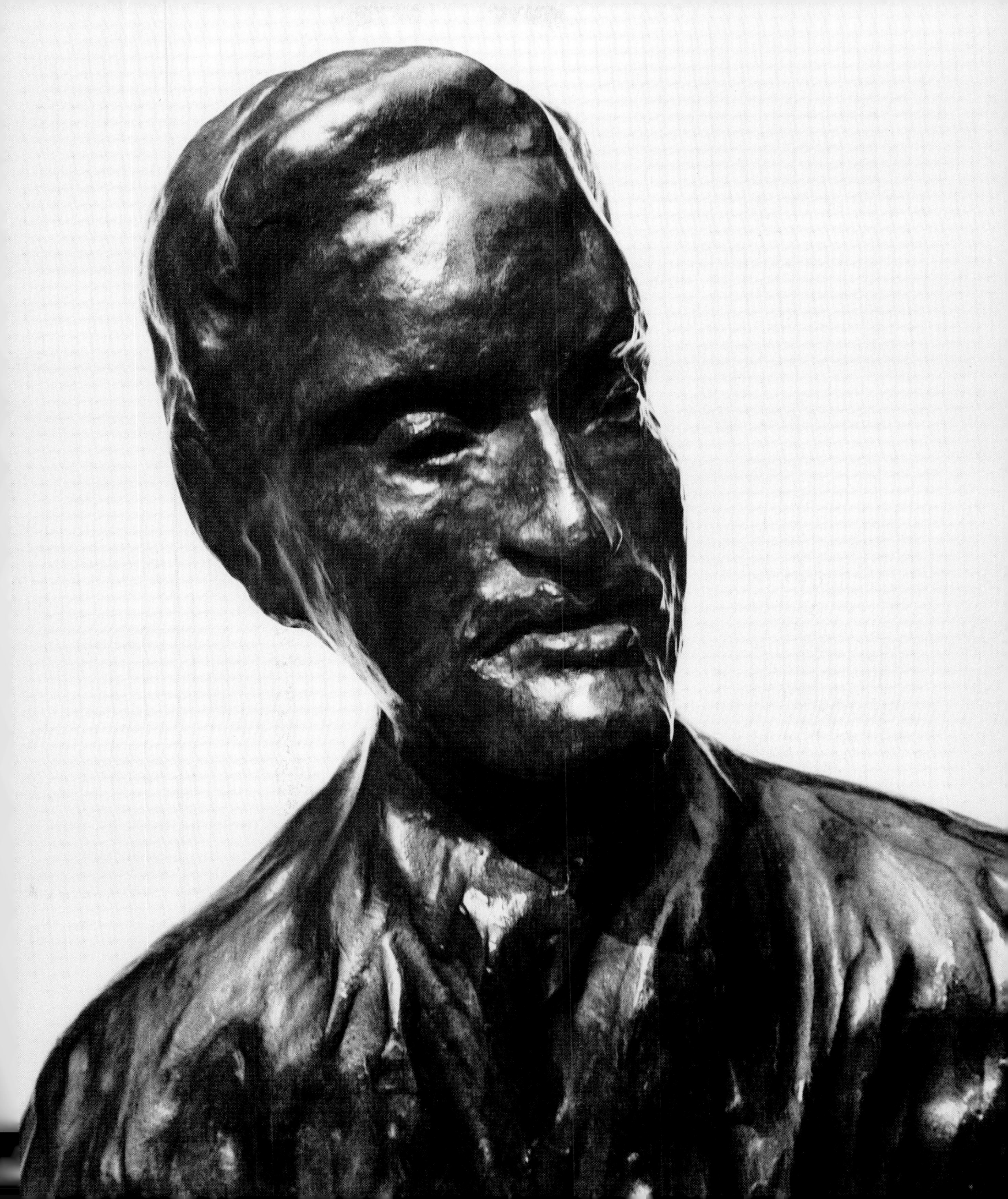

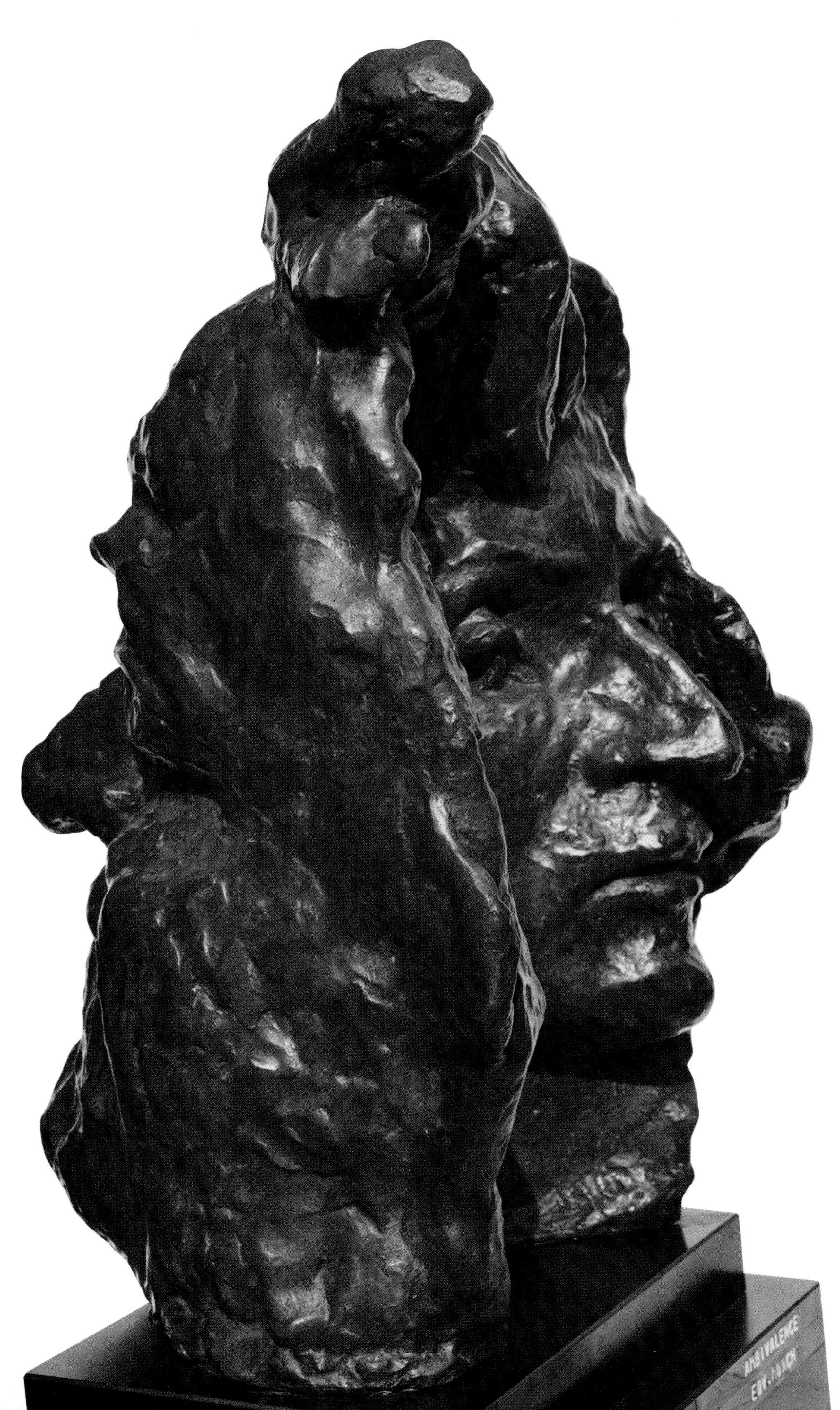
AMBIVALENCE

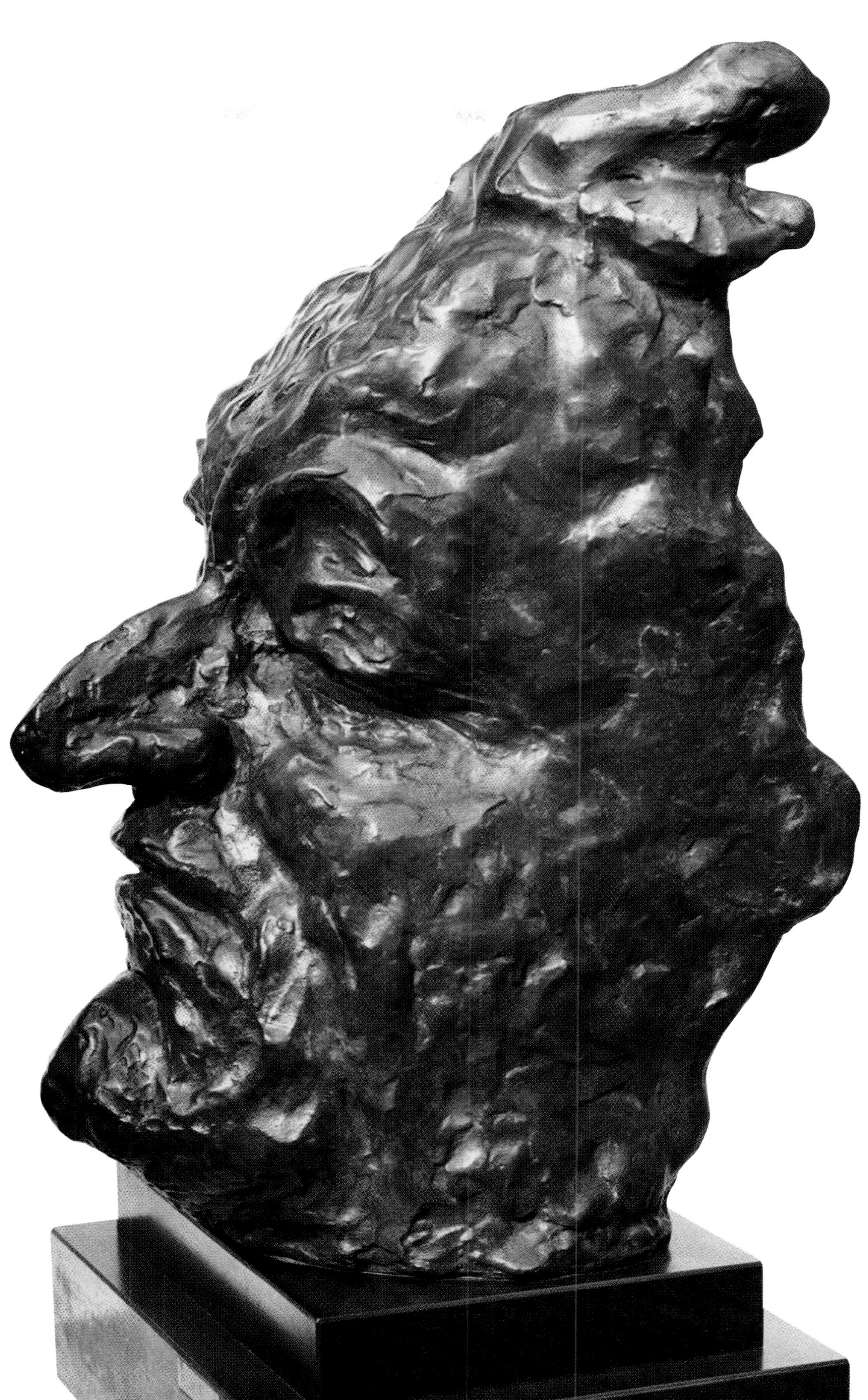

War Poem

During the night of April 9, 1940, Hitler's forces invaded Norway.

Due to the alertness and ingenuity of Carl J. Hambro, then President of the Parliament, King Haakon and the Royal family, together with the entire Cabinet and numerous members of the Parliament, were hurriedly brought out of Oslo by railroad express.

The first war meeting of the Cabinet and the Parliament took place the very next morning at a small town sixty miles north of the capital, with the king presiding.

During the night Hitler's emissaries had presented ultimata to the government: for the King to return to Oslo; for the government to abdicate immediately in favor of a Cabinet chosen by the Nazis.

The proposal had been augmented throughout the night and the following days by merciless bombings of the area where the legal Norwegian government had established its domain and legal status.

The Nazi proposals were refused.

It was unanimously determined by Parliamentary vote: Norway was at war with Germany.

All war activities by the Norwegians were under the direction of the King and his Cabinet.

These activities of war against Hitler were to be continued until the defeat of Hitler's forces even though the war situation might force the King and his Cabinet temporarily to establish headquarters outside the limits of Norway proper.

It proved to represent a unique and consequential document.

The war was fought in Norway and outside Norway, by the people in the underground and above the ground, on the high seas where 1,100 Norwegian merchant ships were, upon orders, steering to neutral ports during the next few days.

The war was waged in England and in Scotland. In Canada. In New York and Washington offices. It was raging intensely in the minds of people who were choked by the Nazi tyranny of turning might into right.

It took a long five years to bring Hitler to defeat.

On June 7, 1945, the King and that same legally elected cabinet returned to Oslo.

It took all those years. It took ultimate sacrifices. It took suffering and indignities all over the world. It took merciless dungeons.

It took seeming eternities to learn to regain freedom and liberty, and finally to learn to extend them to our own life where liberty is at stake every day, and freedom is daily to be ascertained by our own action and thinking.

We might learn from the past—even from a seemingly distant once. Words by Patrick Henry still ring in our ears. Words and sentences by Thomas Paine are not forgotten.

There must have been some similar urgent utterances pressing upon the population in Norway when the young poet Nordahl Grieg, only thirty-seven days after the invasion, wrote one of his famous works. He read it on the radio from an unoccupied part of Norway on May 17, 1940. The day is celebrated in commemoration of Norway's Constitution Day of 1814.

Nordahl Grieg uses the words, "It is to be sung and whispered with closed lips."

26″ × 12″ × 26″

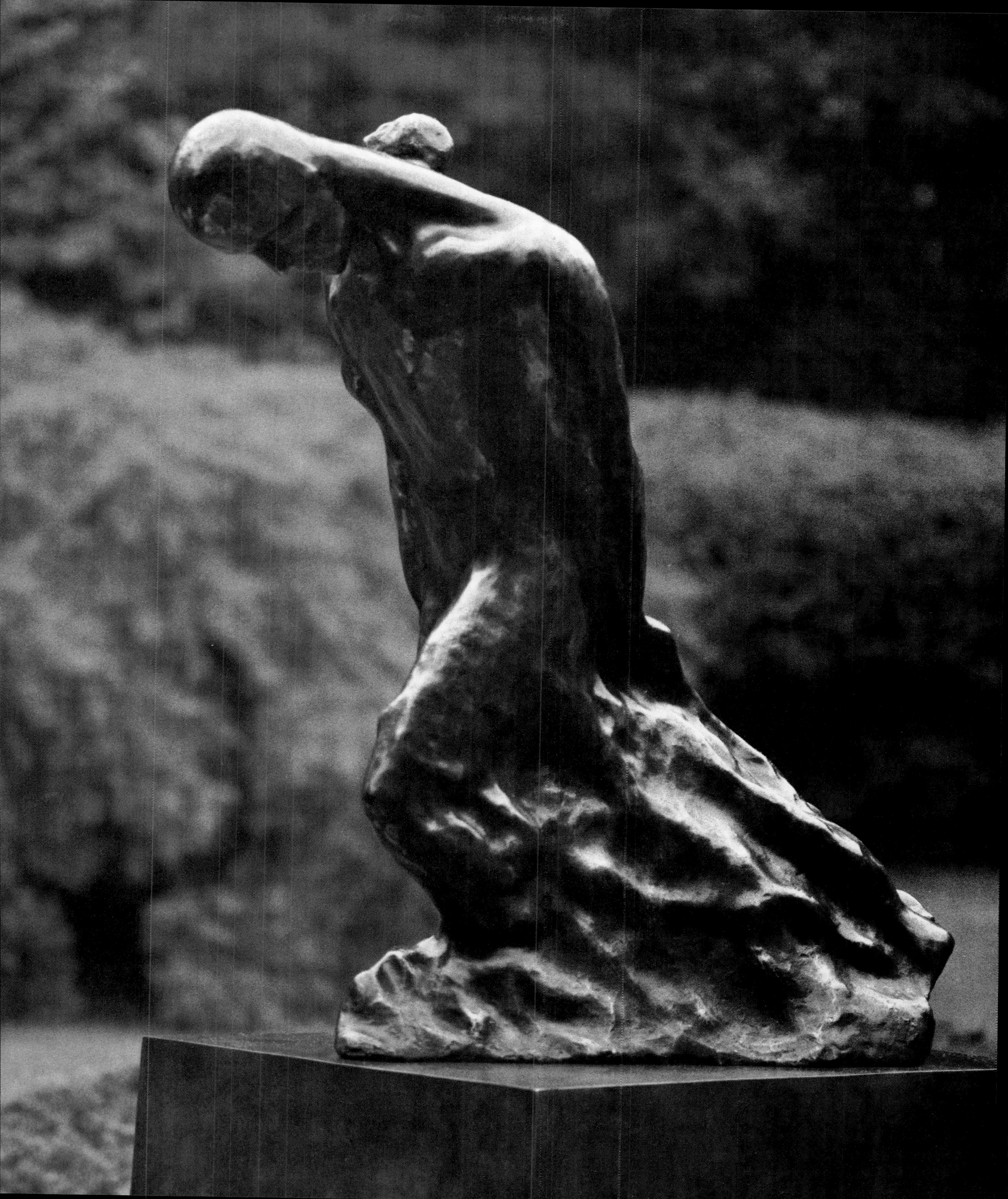

A whole country took this poem to heart. It was imprinted in their minds—and with the threat of death if sung.

The last stanza of the poem is the subject matter for this sculpture, which I executed many years later.

In translation it reads:

"We are so few here in Norway.
Each killed was a brother or friend.
We carry the dead with us
the day we see Norway again."

It should be added: Nordahl Grieg himself did not return to Norway with his fellow fighters. In December, 1943, he died in a raid over Berlin.

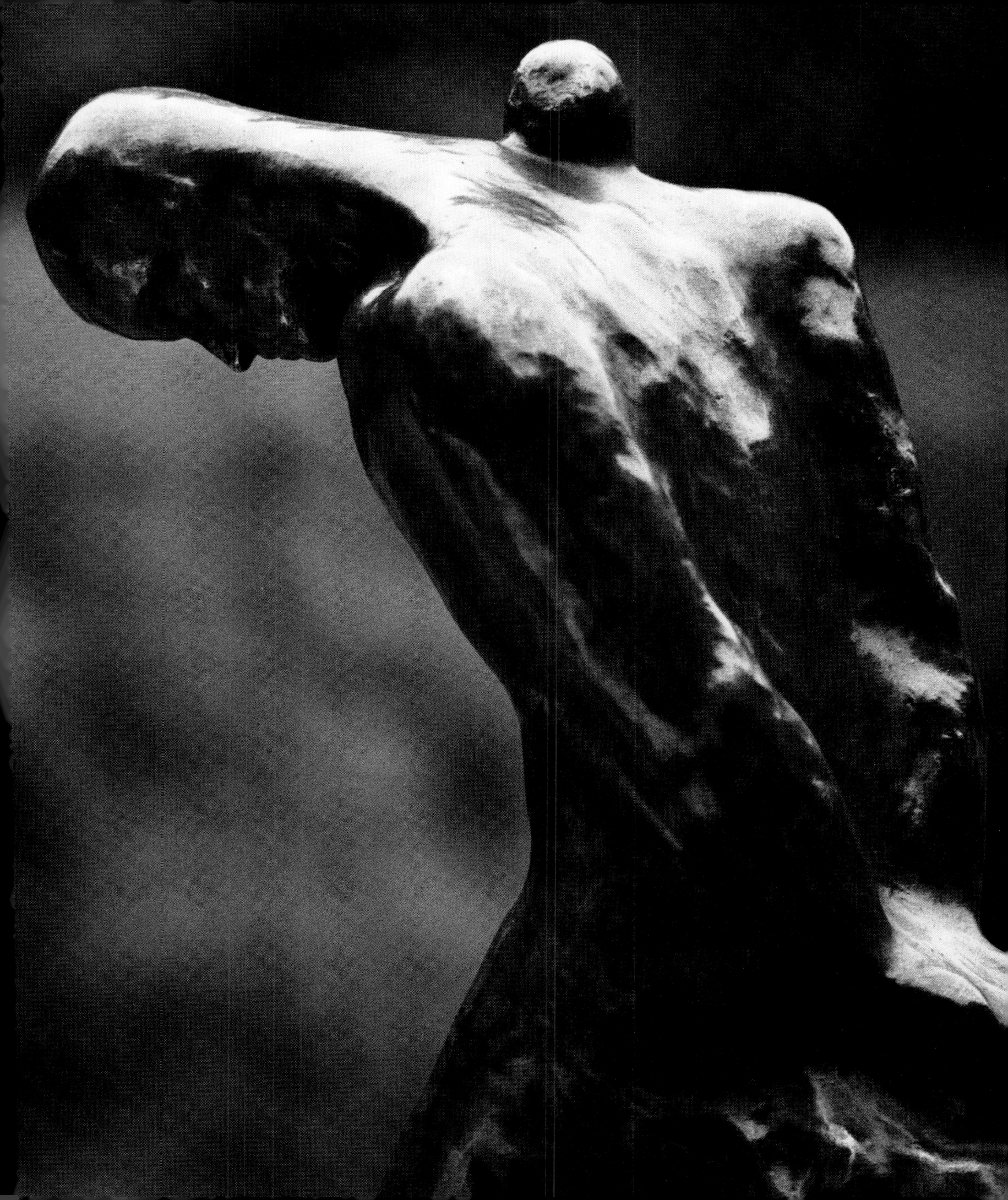

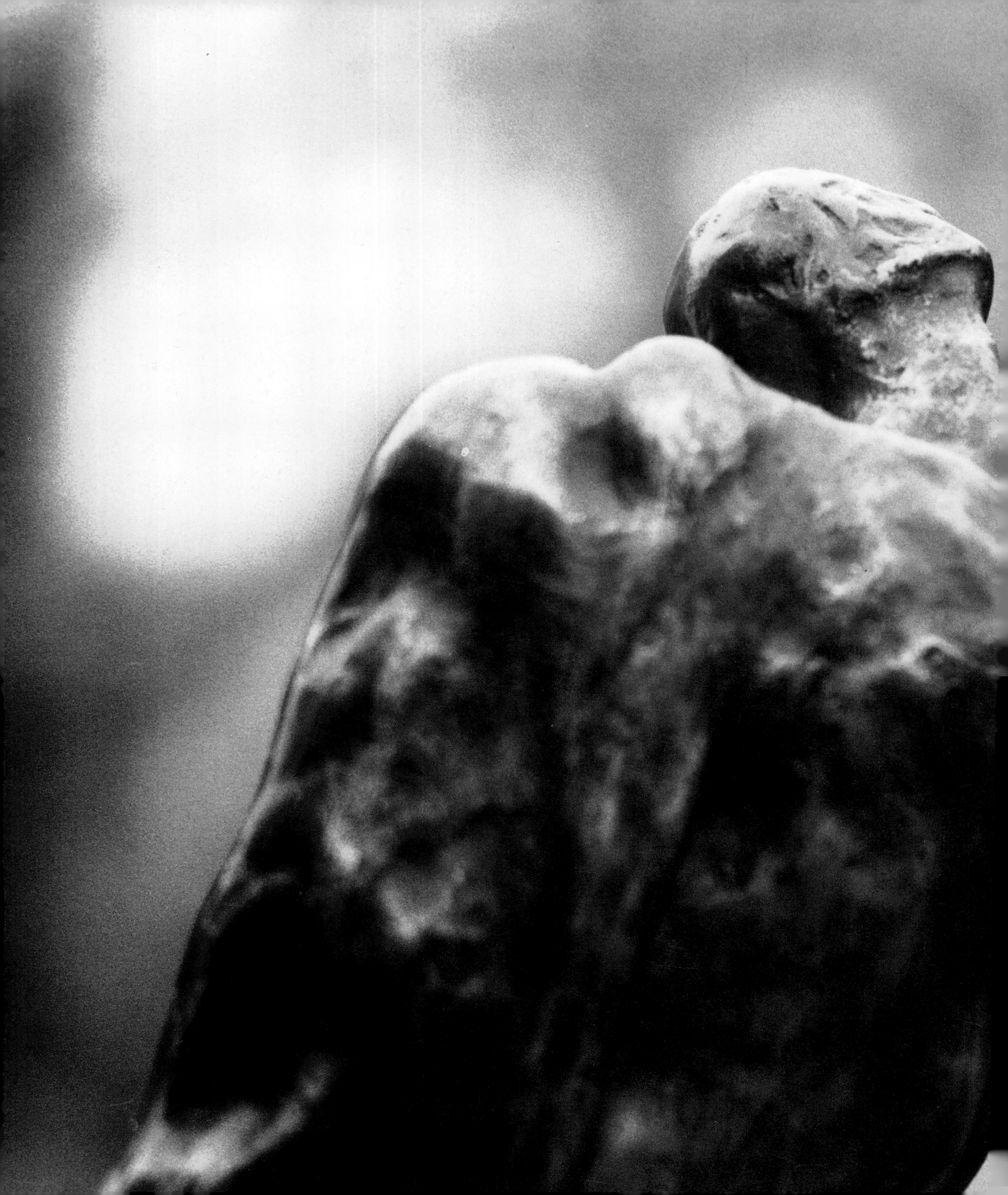

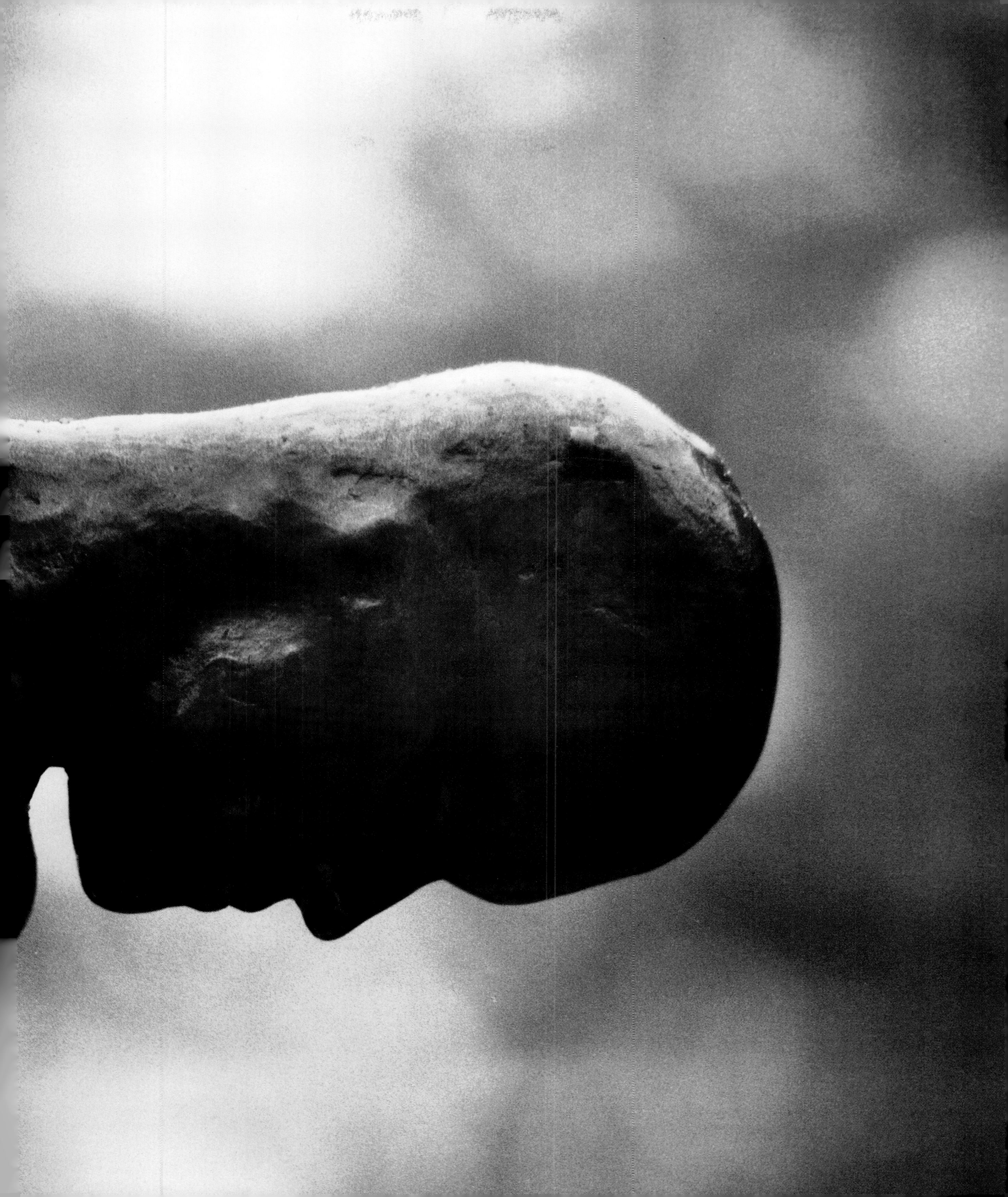

Ultimatum

I have committed a sculpture with that title. It is plastically a rough, but good, hand. I should be pleased by it. I am not.

I am frightened by it. I detest it.

It is the Caveman's hand. It is his hand in those seconds just before he is going to strike. He is up on his hind legs. His blood boils. He glares. Screams escape his howling throat. His hands form into viscious claws. In a moment his secret weapons, two catapulting strong arms, explode into the inners of his opponent.

Yes. In the beginning were the hunter and the fighter—the heroes of the herd.

Or to paraphrase Descartes: "We are here because they could fight and overcome."

But there comes a time!

The time is long overdue. We have to search for new heroes, new ideas, new ideals to lead us out of a frightening dilemma in which our destructive genius still seems to storm ahead, filled with the potential for sure self-destruction. A genius for the creation of life's continuity has not been granted a chance to accept a hero-ship in the minds of the world.

It would be futile to fall back upon the saying that only time will tell if homo sapiens is able to undergo the transformation from warmonger to peace-maker. It might be futile, since we seem to have been given very little time. A nuclear biologic annihilation might be imminent.

I have the sculpture on my desk. It is pointing straight at me—like the Nietzsche bust.

I confess that in the air about the fingers and in the hollow of the Caveman's hand I have tucked away these pessimistic qualms about his intentions.

A resolution of his essential enigma needs more than sculpture.

Bronzes can be very deaf and mute.

Still, let the air about the bronze commit you to a meaningful audience participation, where you take over when the artist had to throw in the sponge.

7″ × 6″ × 7″

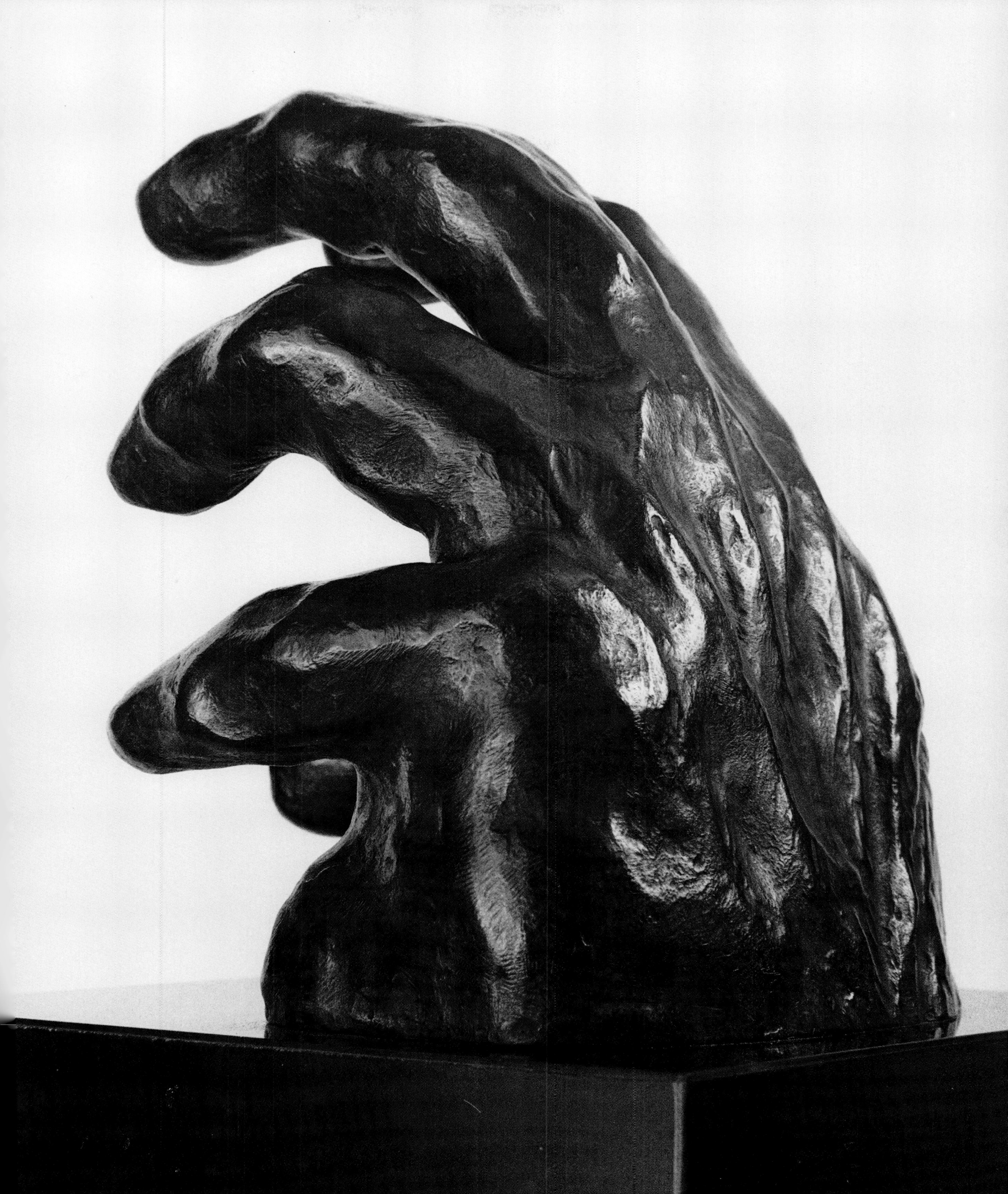

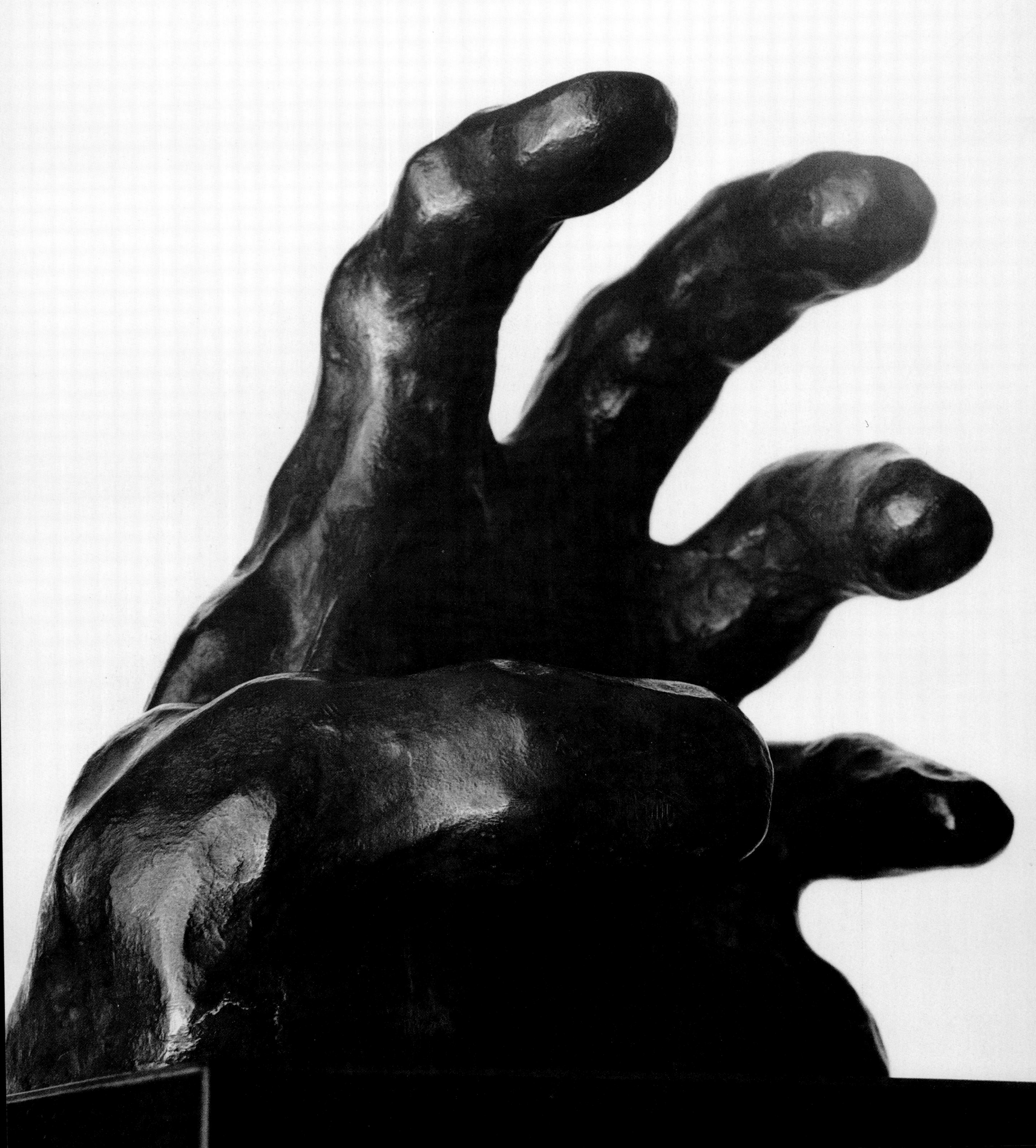

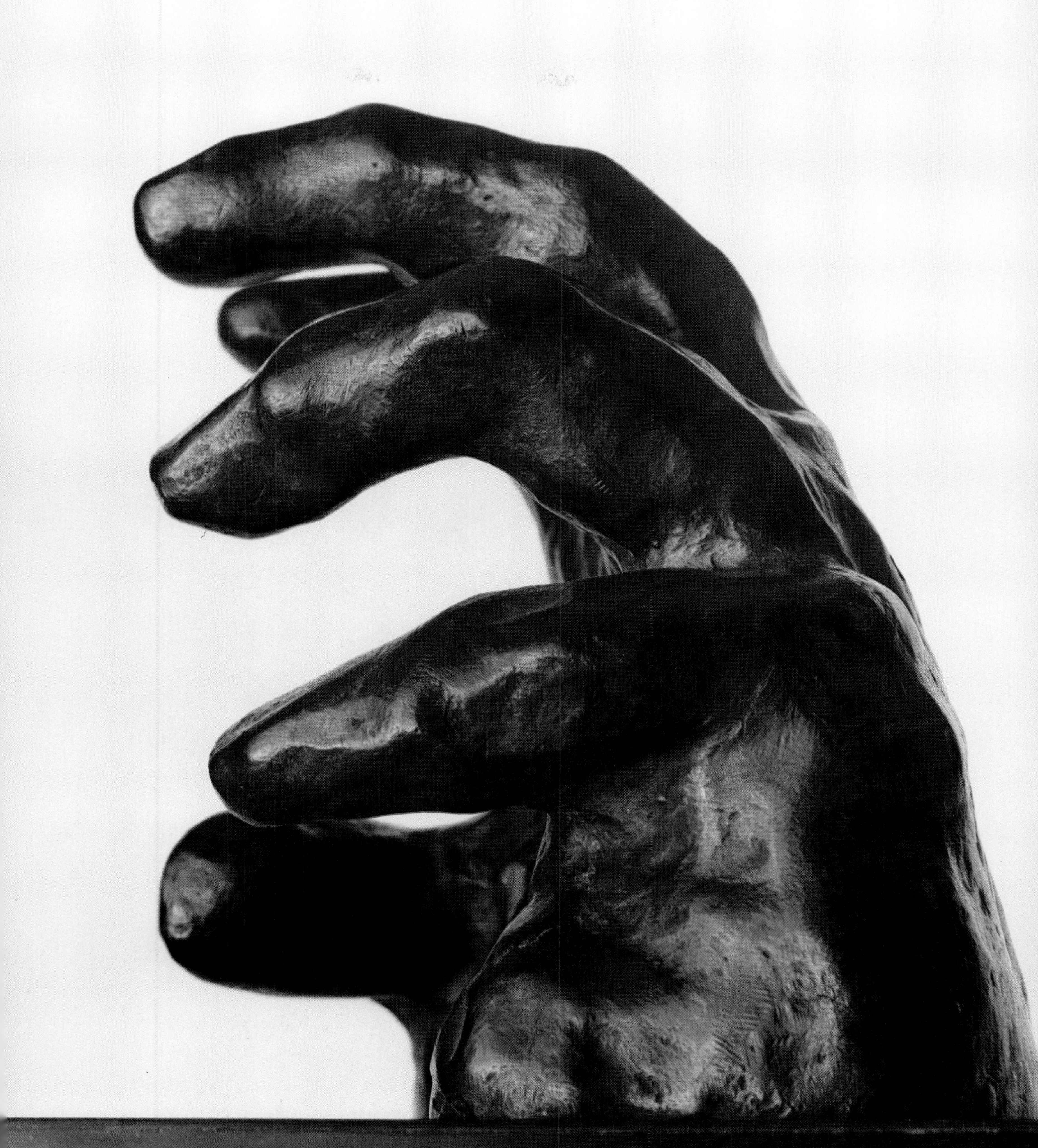

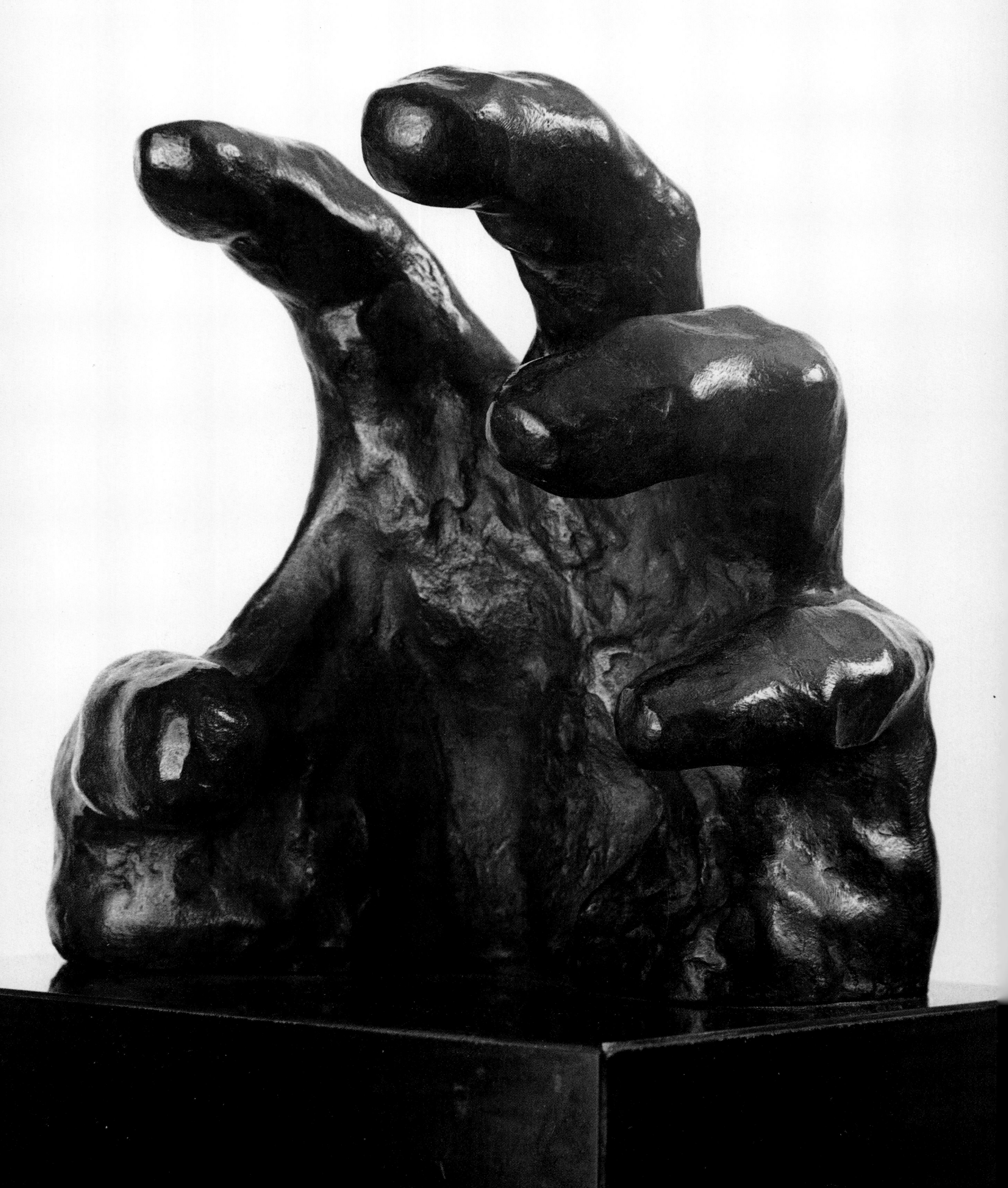

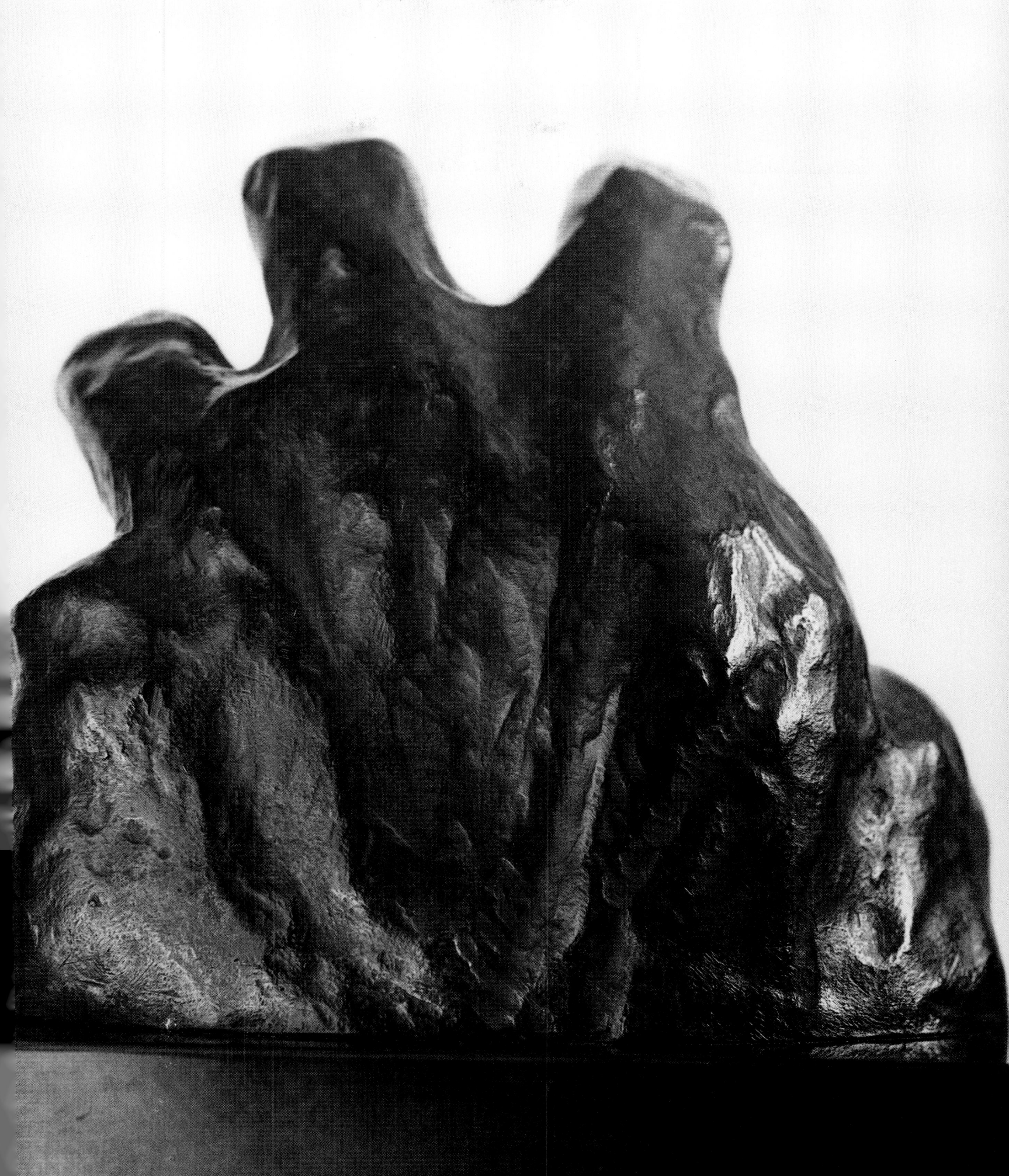

Viet Nam

What's in a name?

Bethlehem. Florence. Gettysburg. Omaha Beach.

Each one of them, in each of us, releases private, personal associations, ready to take off into realms of memories, emotions, and activities going in all directions.

The historical pages of Viet Nam do not linger with us. Those pages still burn in our conscience.

The conflict of arms during those years expanded a conflict in the soul of the nation carrying the sword.

The ever-recurring moral issues did not burn with the flaming villages.

Our honorable, purer human instincts have been left with an open sore slow to heal.

And it drove me to the clay.

16″ × 10″ × 10″

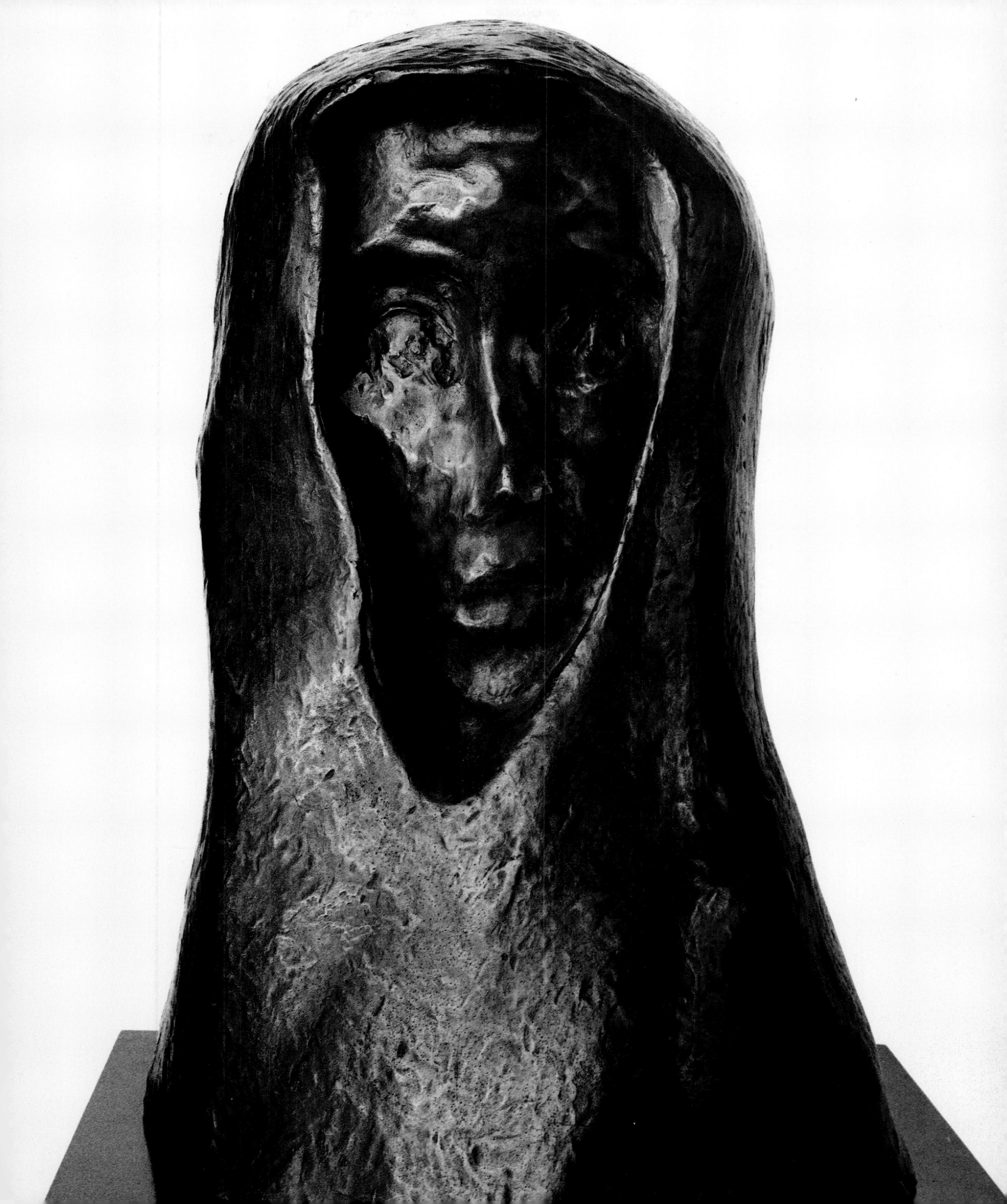

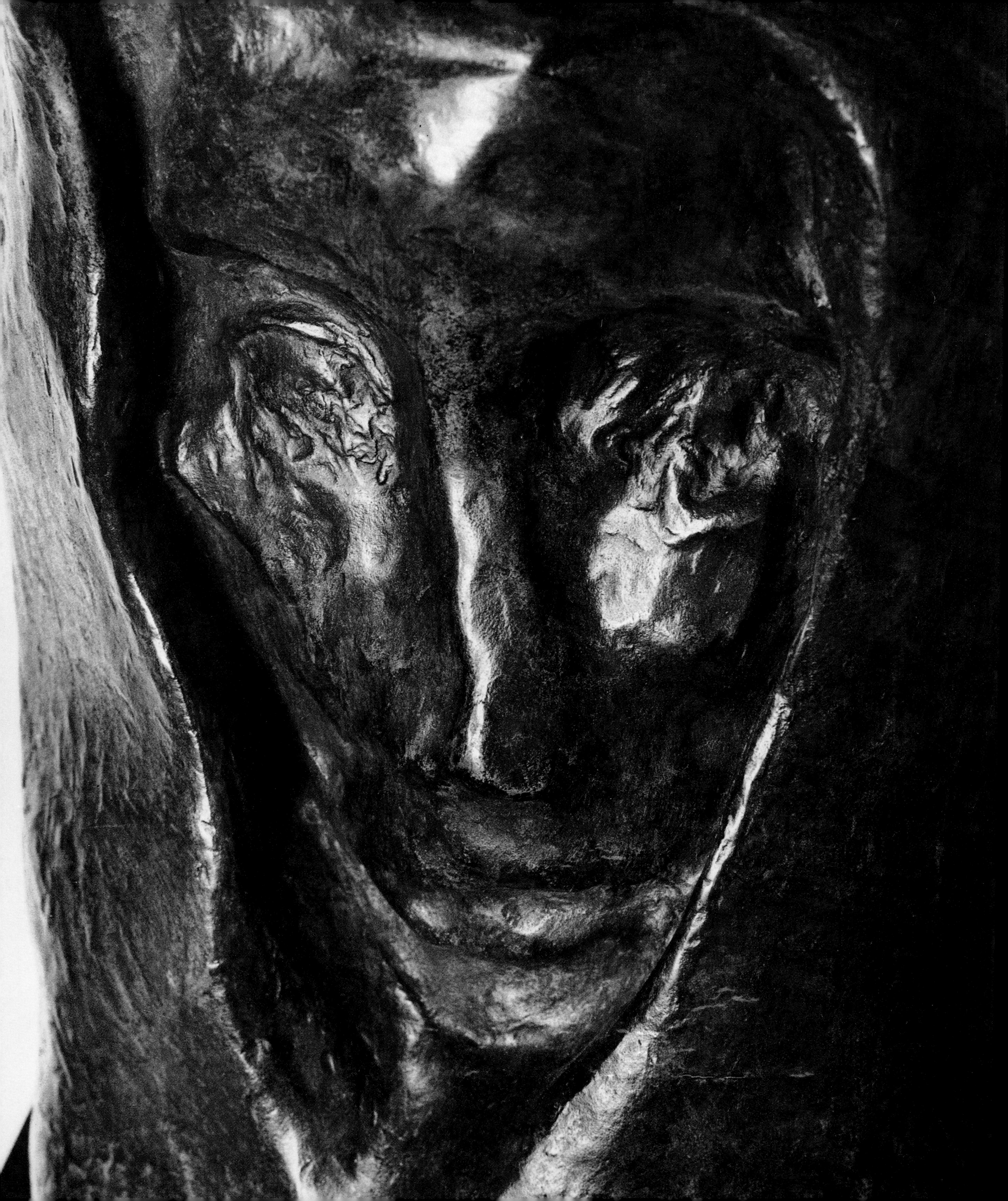

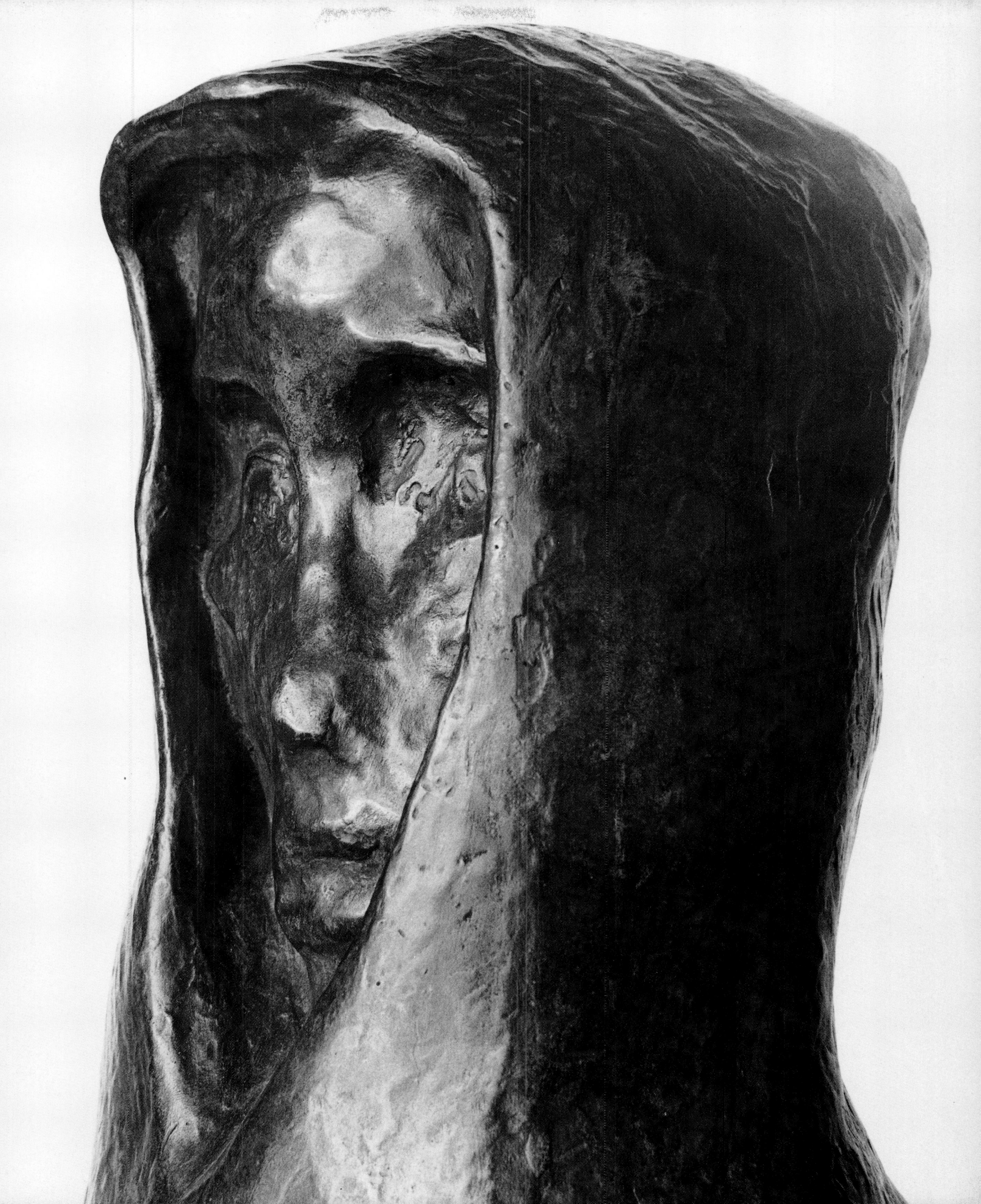

The Caveman

Let me confess: I am not at ease in the company of my Caveman. Strange. I am responsible for him. He sprang out of my brain. Still, I am frightened by him. I know him too well.

I knew him in the cave. I know him now. In some ways it is the same creature. In others not at all.

In the cave, he was protected. By his ingenuity, his strength, and by a sense that the herd within the cave was part of him. He thus also became its protector.

He learned to know the surroundings. Fruits were to be gathered. Intruders and ferocious animals were to be dealt with.

He ventured beyond those safe valleys into the unknown where he was no longer the sovereign.

He fought. He invented. He survived.

We are here. A testimony to his success.

He should be my hero. He is not.

He frightens me.

In my mind he is still the ferocious conqueror and inventor.

He split the atom.

He fused it.

He forgot that he is the protector of the herd. I do fear him. He will blow his flock into oblivion.

And there shall be no cave to return to!

12″ × 10″ × 11″

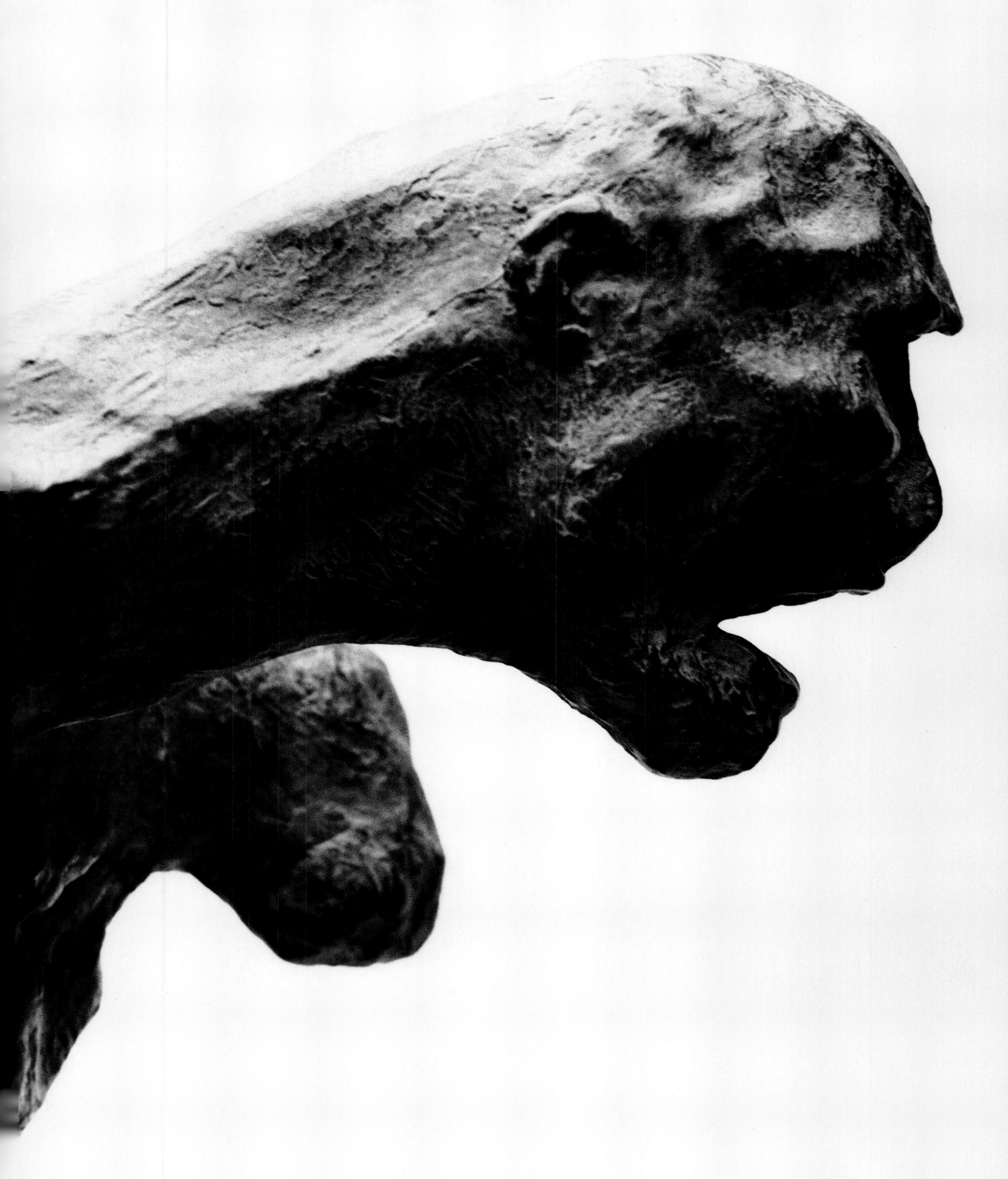

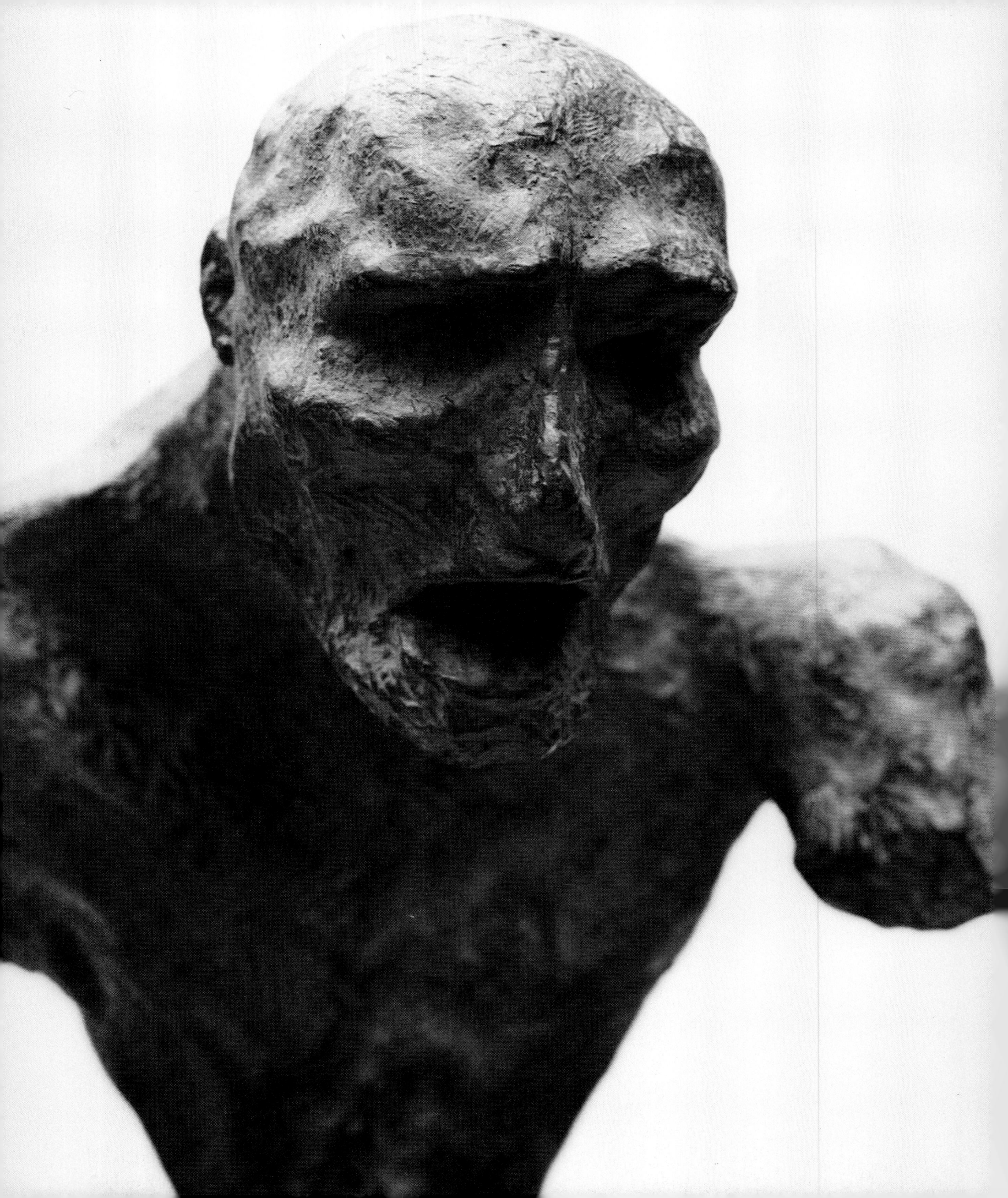

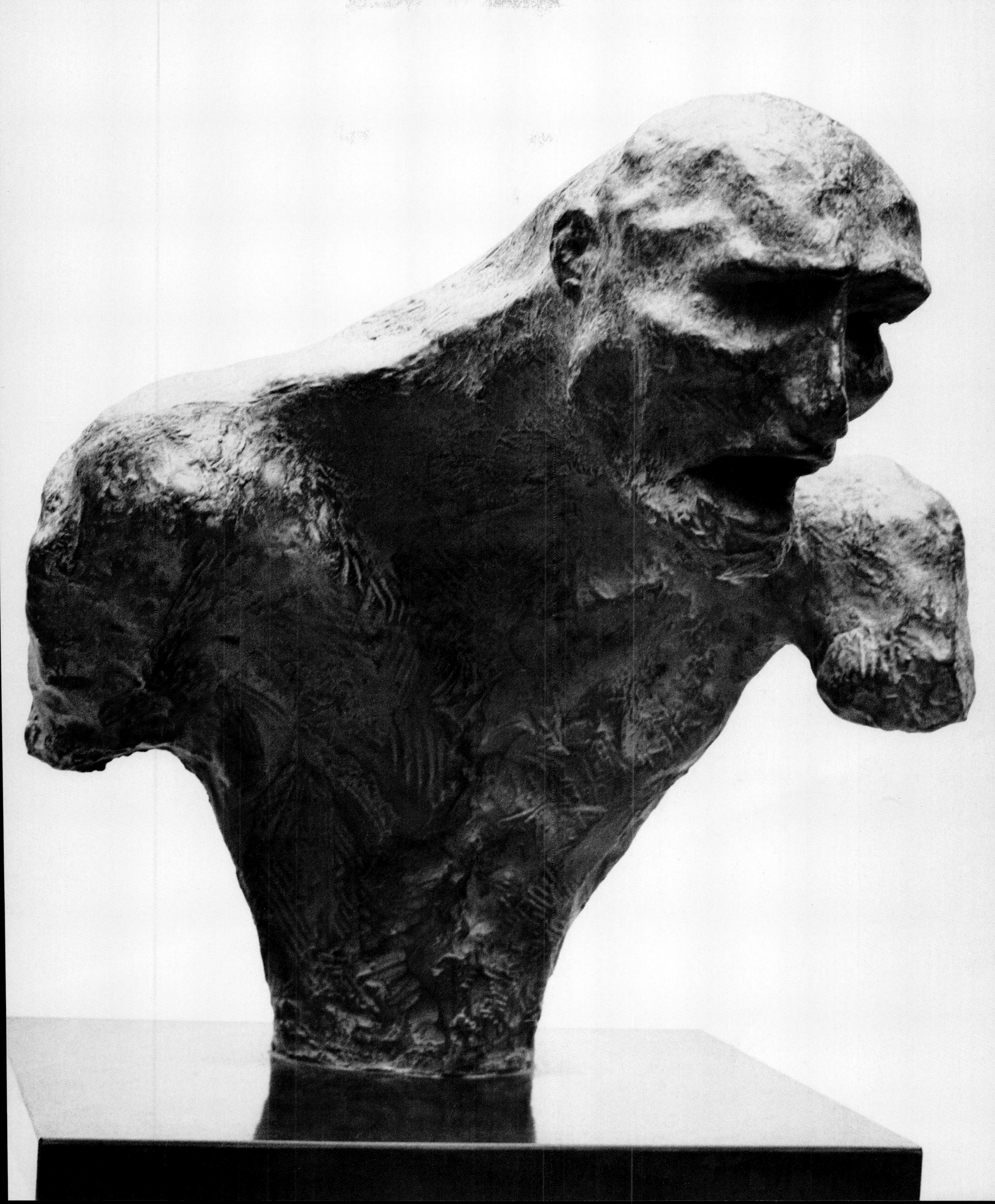

The Surgeon

What is the meaning of this simple sculpture? Many similar questions have been asked of me. It is not a self-portrait. It is not trying to depict one particular professional person.

I have been in surgery for fifty years. I recognize the stand. I must have been in that same position a few thousand times. I know I am on home ground. Sculpturally speaking, I am dealing with acts I do know. Still, while standing around with friends, looking and talking, I join with them in asking questions of myself.

No, I don't think he is right at the moment of going into the operating room. I think it is after the operation. Is he talking—or mumbling? Is he a bit downhearted? What is he trying to mean?

I sense that only a few surgeons are inclined to share with each other—or others—the emotional aspect of our work.

We are disciplined. Years and decades of strict training have honed us along those lines. We are disciplined. We have to be that way. Operations are not a question of courage, nor of emotions, although the surgeon can never be free—and he should never be free—of his personal and emotional involvement in the problems of the human being entrusted to his care.

In this statue, I sense that I have permitted myself to reveal the silent humility of a surgeon dressing in his daily operating room attire. He is somehow undressing himself in afterthought following a surgical procedure that is, like so many others, filled with technical road blocks which may be ingeniously overcome by experienced hands. Still, only months or years may finally prove whether the operation was a success.

Therefore, the word "jubilant" seems not to exist in the surgeon's vocabulary.

In that way there is a similarity between the surgeon and the sculptor. Their work, when finally judged by time, seems never completely to fulfill their hopes and their strivings.

This painful reality of two professional lives, I believe strongly, comes out in this statue of the surgeon.

His final composure implies a strong sense of humility, but a humility of that particular kind filled with responsibility and human resilience in face of disastrous sickness and accidents.

Or as William Osler translated it in 1892: "With humility comes not only reverence for the truth, but also a proper estimation of the difficulties encountered in the search for it."

POSTSCRIPT

Of course, you have to have brains to make it through medical school. And that goes for all academic enterprises.

More is required. A vigorous motivation. An ability and willingness to persevere through stormy weather and waters where maps are sparse and fog not unknown. If one possesses all that and much more, one eventually graduates and is awarded with the title M.D.

With added efforts you might obtain the license to practice medicine. This is not

70″ × 20″ × 20″

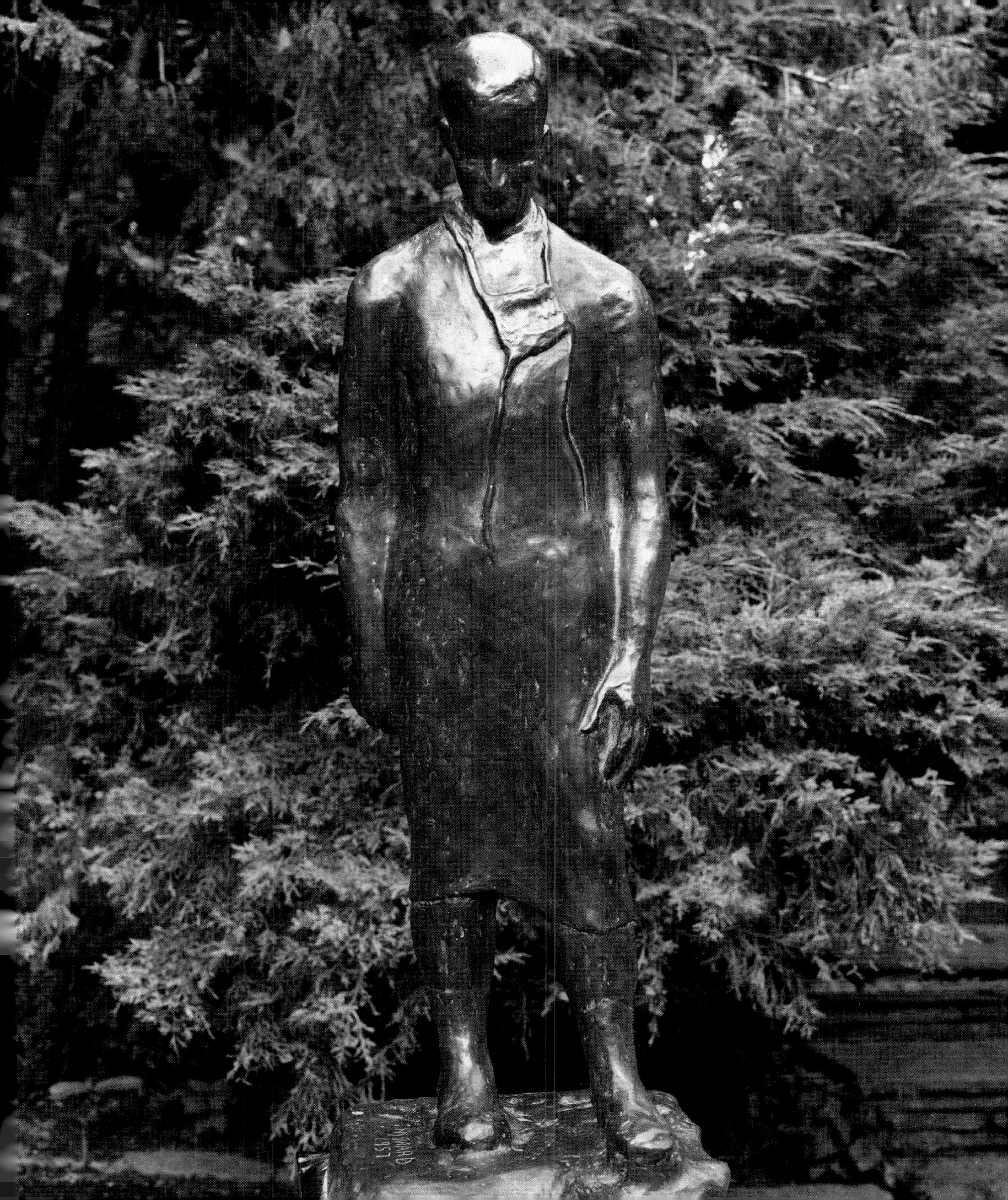

synonymous with the necessary ultimate goal in a physician's life: to practice the *art of medicine*.

To learn the mysteries and the miracles of medicine needs the lifetime of an audacious, willing, able, and persevering learner.

To translate and transform that volume of know-how into a meaningful, secure, and constructive aid to one's fellow man—all that transcendent activity needs more than a high I.Q.

What are those *more* qualities?

I shall not meet that question with stale platitudes.

We know those required qualities still exist.

If we are in doubt whether these qualities are with us, certainty and conviction might storm upon the physician when he is dragged into a burning building by courageous firemen trying to revive three kids trapped upstairs.

Or that morning in the emergency room when a child was brought in with his face, his trunk, his arms macerated into a bloody pulp by a vicious dog.

Or the mother in childbirth rapidly bleeding into oblivion till your trained mind and hands finally bring out the placenta.

The grave situations and incidences are multiplying.

There is no time left to flee in horror, disgust, and fear that so much responsibility should be weighing upon so few shoulders.

That is when you learn to know you are on the firing line.

You sense you must be there with all that is in you.

To do whatever has to be done.

To begin with, in no small fear.

Still prevailing is that just feeling that you are there with all the wits about you.

You are there at the right moment, in the right place, with all your brain working, with all the experience to back you up, and with the constructive intention to deliver the goods.

It is in those emergencies that the worker of God's medical vineyard feels the reward in the work.

It is in those moments that the medical student is transformed into a student of medicine and worthwhile life. It is in some of these seconds that a medical license is transposed into the meaningful arts of a physician.

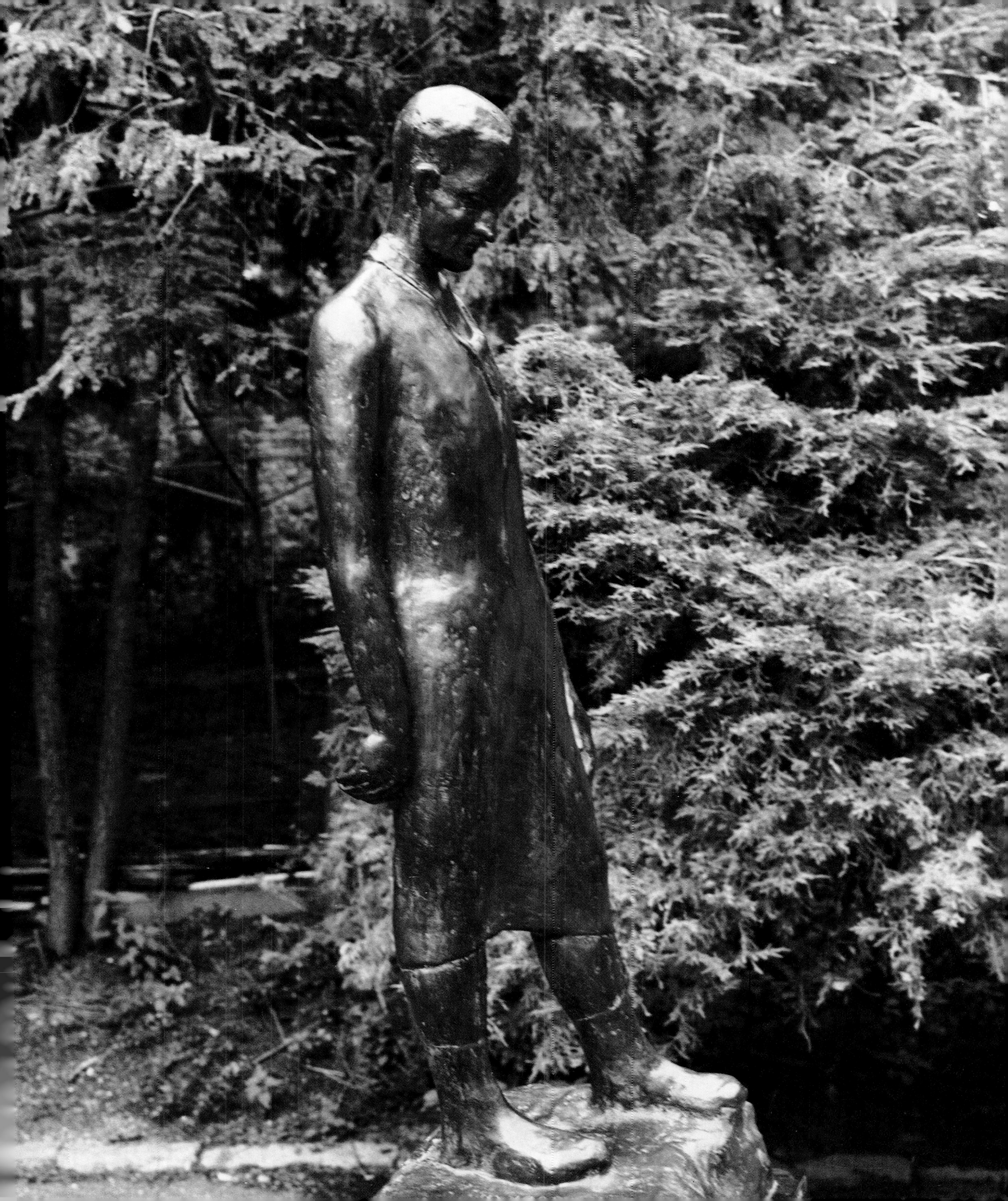

The Surgeon

The physician has dedicated his life to the art of medicine and to the benefit of his fellow man, although there are other rewards in the satisfaction of helping the patient, if help is humanly possible.

Not only does the encounter between doctor and patient affect the soma and soul of one, but also of the other. This profound effect can be seen not only in physical characteristics, but in expression, of feeling and state, of being.

All physicians are affected similarly, but the surgeon is exposed to the ups and downs more acutely because of his active and aggressive intervention in the illness of his patient. Not only has he participated in establishing the clinical diagnosis—others can give opinions—but he alone has to make the final decision for operation. His years of surgical training and his acquired technical ability are forged into the performance of an operation to treat the pathology encountered—most often with success, but sometimes without. The well-being of the patient weighs heavily on his mind as he leaves the operating room. Many thoughts race through his head: was the decision to operate right, was the operation appropriate, did it help, was it done well, will it offer the patient a chance of cure and life, does the patient need additive treatment, what to tell the patient and the relatives, and what decisions need to be made to ensure the patient's return to good health during the postoperative period.

Because of the cognitive processes and physical exertion, the surgeon may be physically and emotionally drained, both reflected in his appearance and mood.

To capture the state of the surgeon as he leaves the operating room takes an artist who has lived through these emotional and physical experiences, since only he knows their inner feelings.

In this sculpture, *The Surgeon*, K. K. Nygaard has created an image in precious metals for all to see the priceless ingredients affecting this physician as he leaves the operating room. His shoulders are stooped indicating physical fatigue and weight upon them, the face mask is about his neck—the operation is over—his hands are ungloved, his head is lowered in deep thought and compassion, reflecting his concern for the decisions and acts just completed, but his step is forward; he is thinking of the patient, the family, his associates, the young physicians and surgeons of the new generation, and how medicine can benefit society and mankind better. This is what surgery and the surgeon are all about.

OLIVER H. BEAHRS, M.D.
Mayo Clinic, Rochester, Minnesota

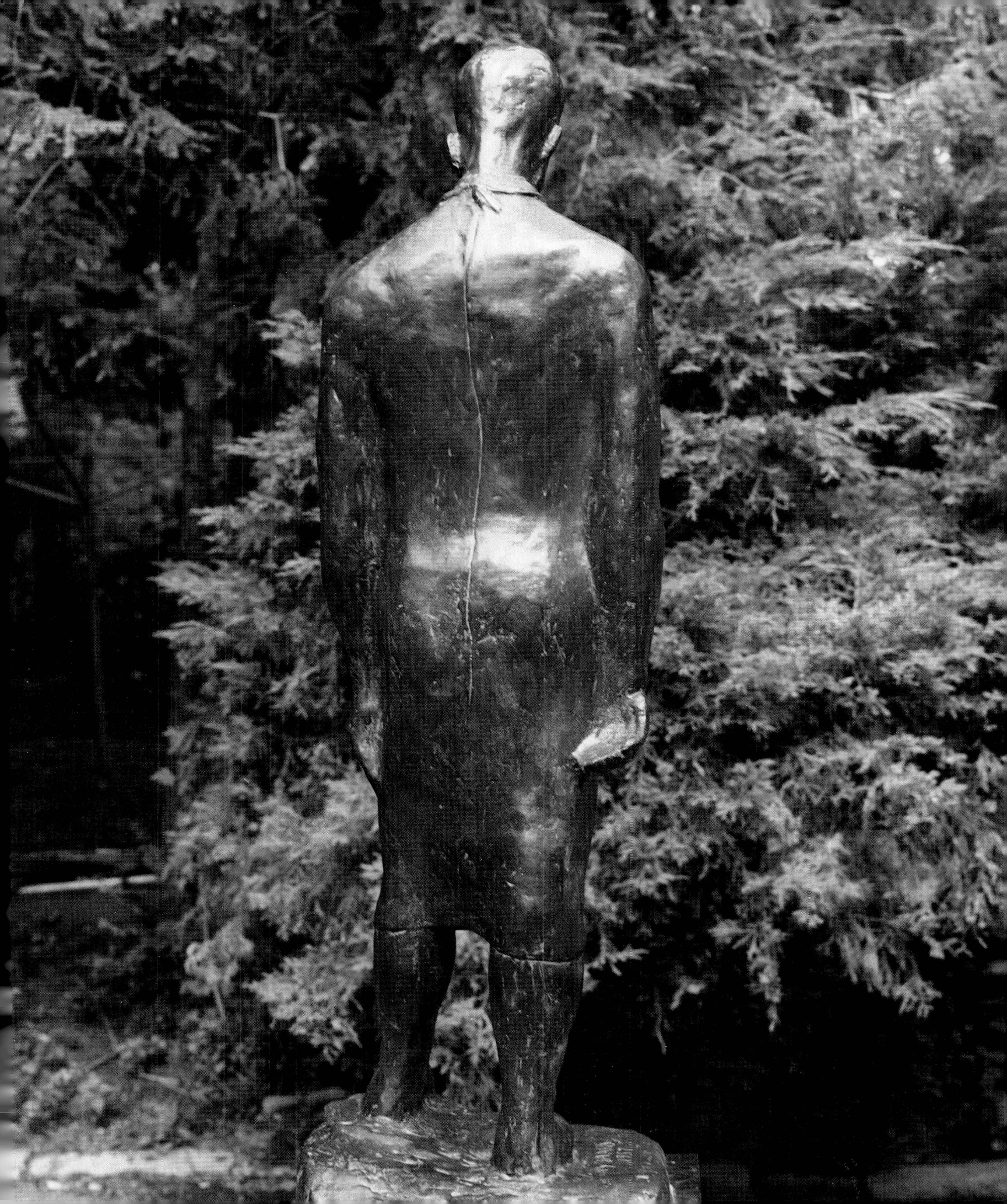

In Memoriam

17″ × 8½″ × 12″

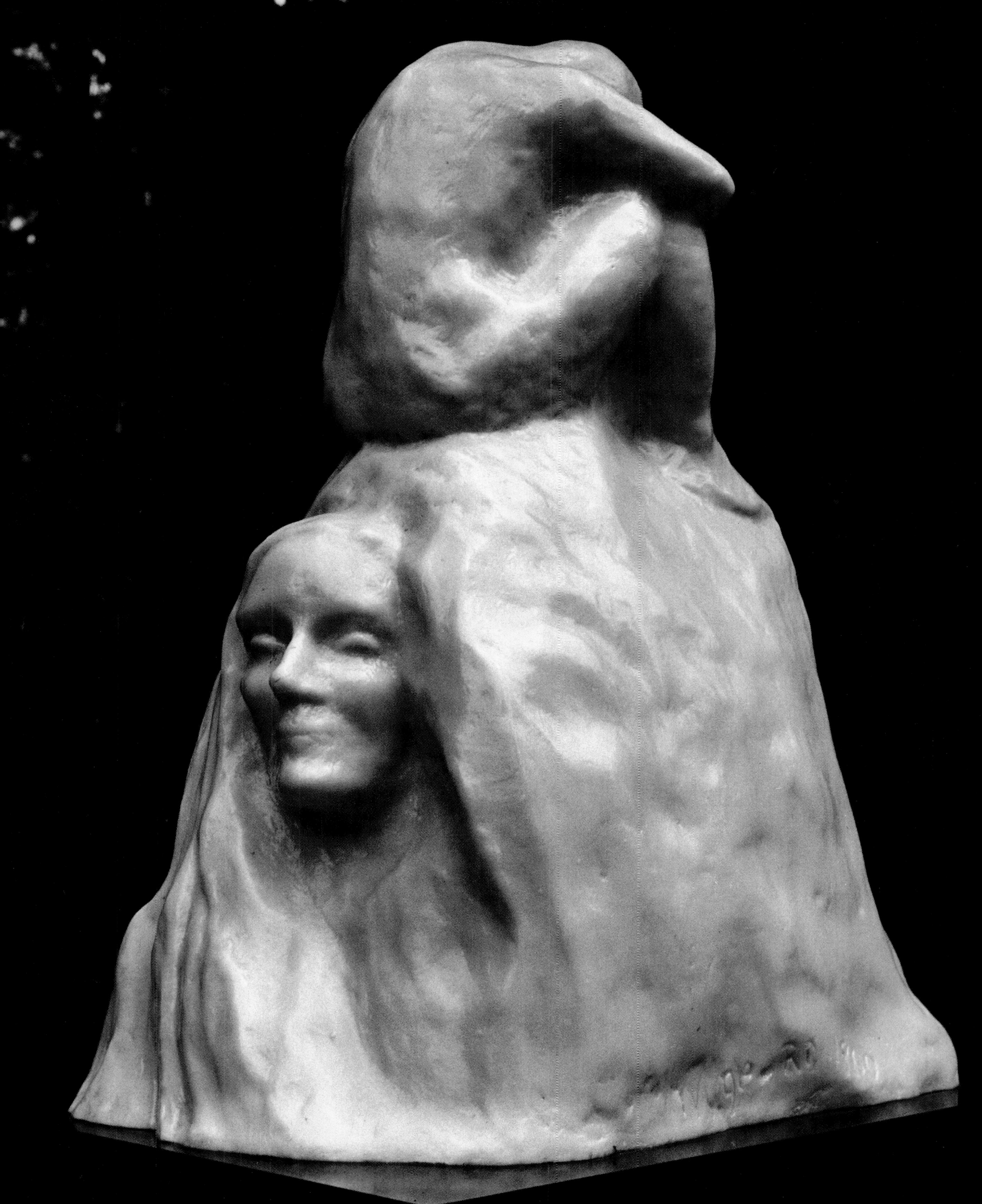

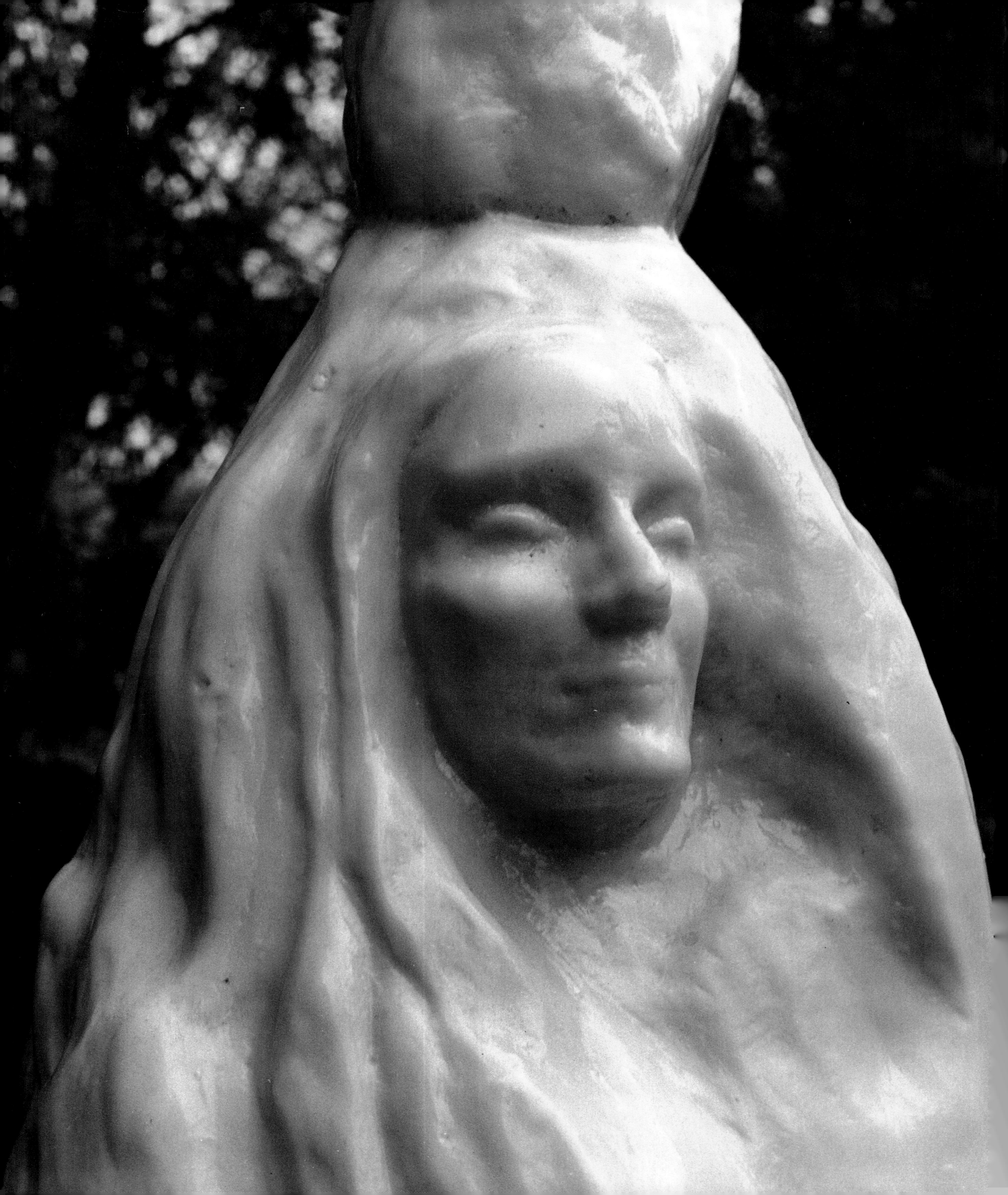

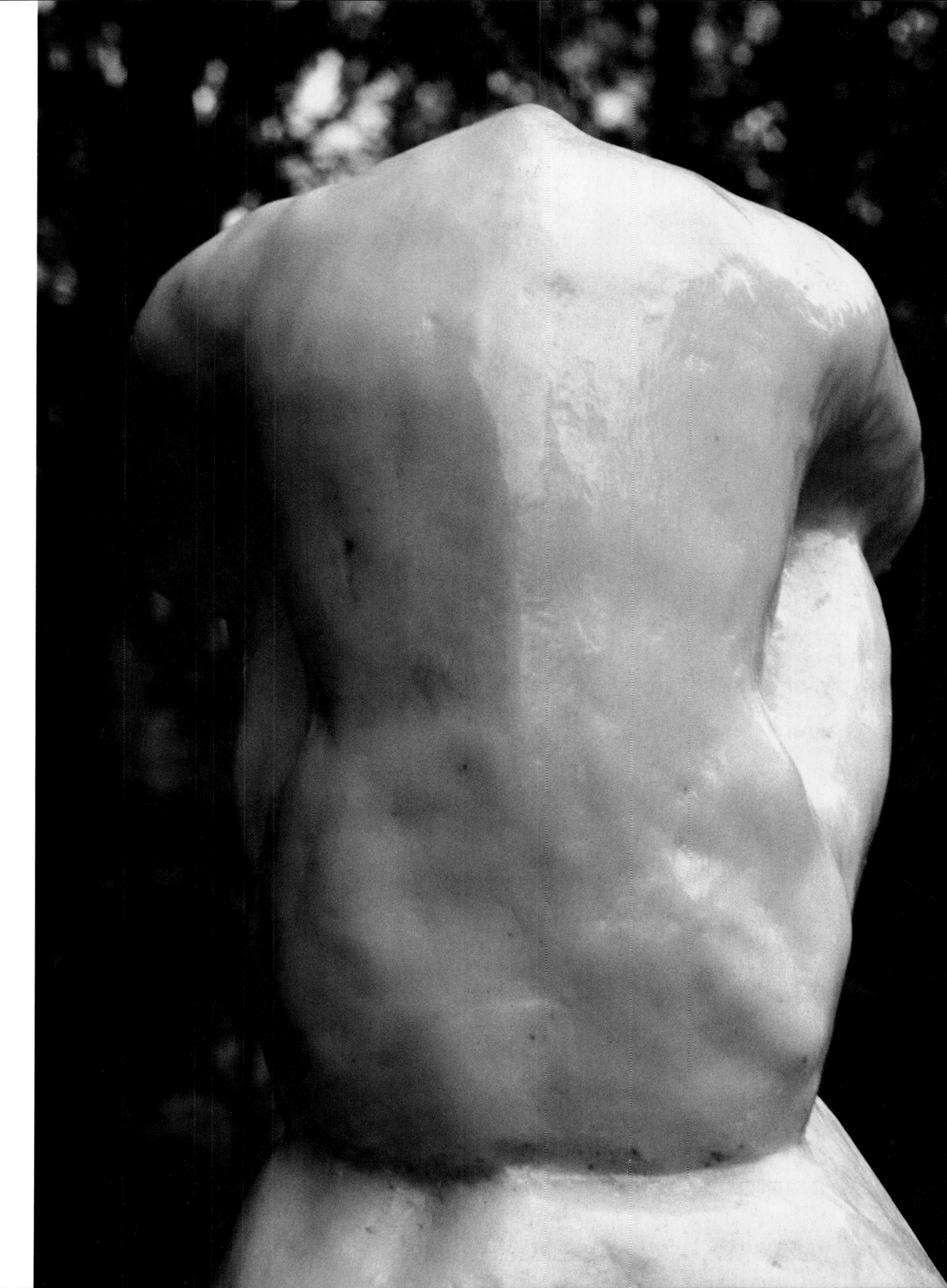

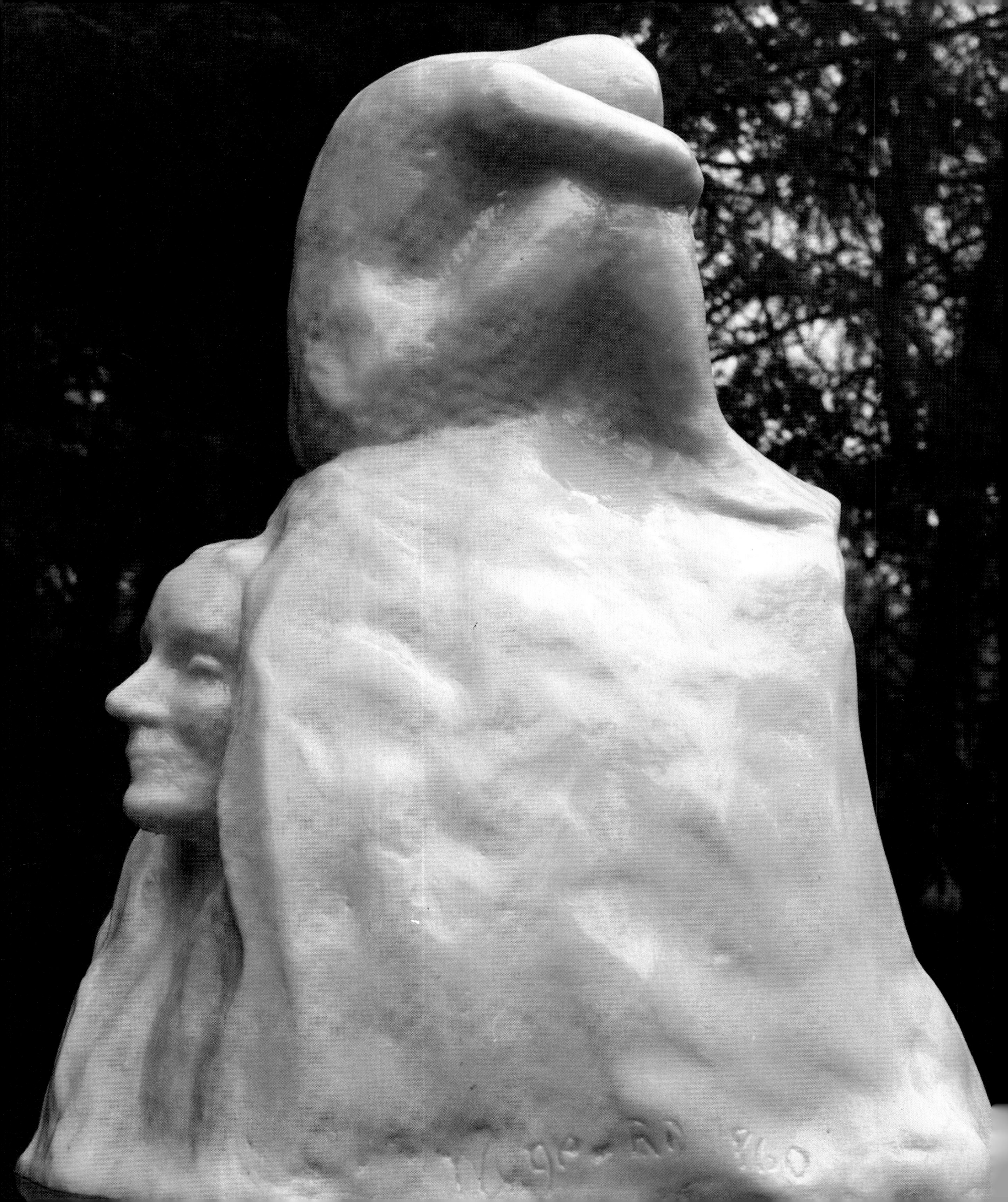

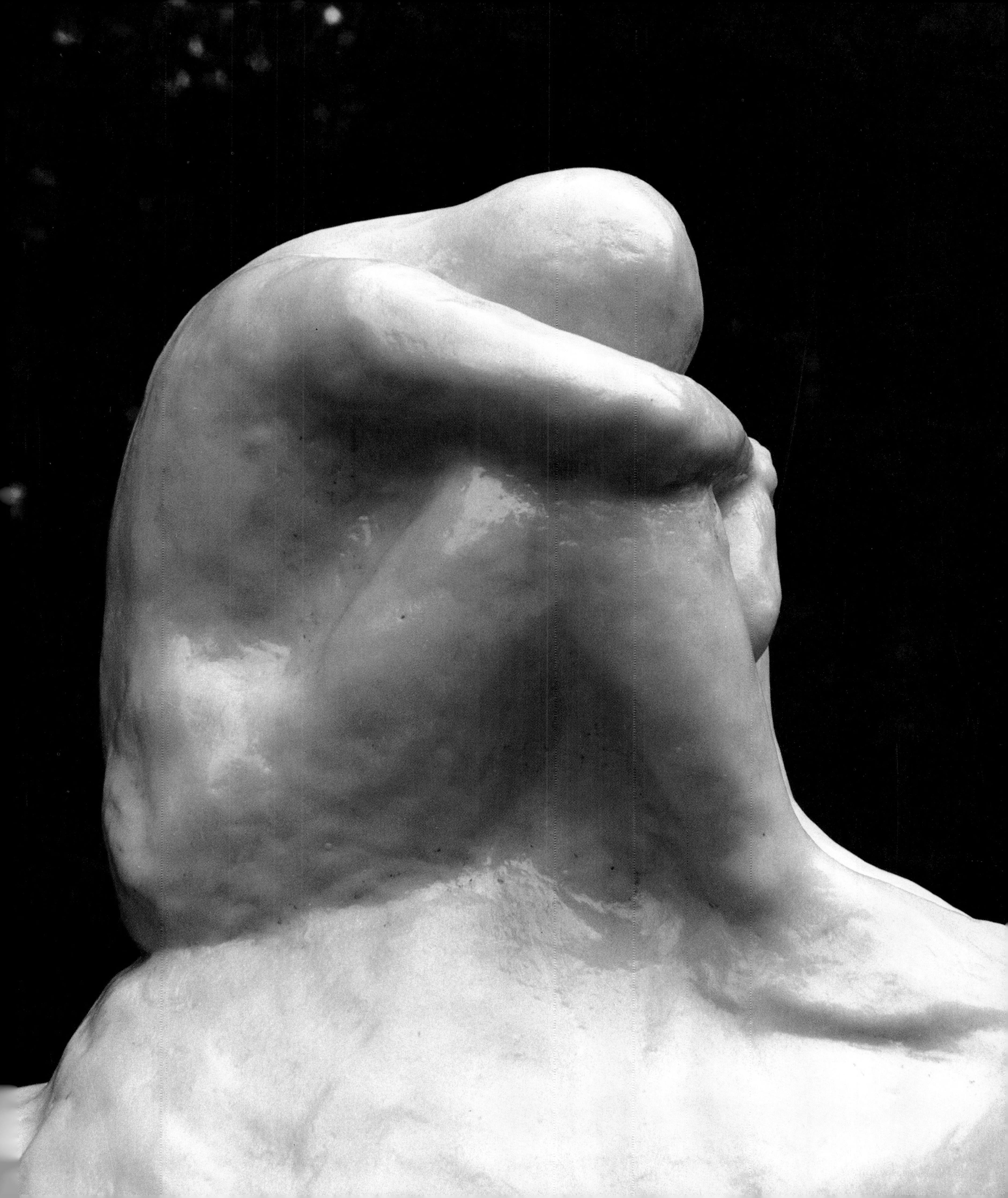

Hour of Meditation

My mother was a university-trained midwife, as was the custom in Norway at the beginning of this century. At the time of her legal retirement she could look back upon a challenging professional life, having brought close to four thousand babies into the world.

She knew the international statistics. The Scandinavian countries had the lowest infant mortality. She added with a smile: "Don't believe it is caused by the fact that the pregnant women of Scandinavia are all delivered by trained midwives, and not by M.D.s."

I learned more about it when I myself became a medical student.

Her thinking, in simplified outline, ran something like this: Since the last Ice Age, the people of this Scandinavian peninsula have lived a relatively isolated life, geographically remote from the central European countries, where, during the second millennium, multitudes of people from the east were pressing westward in massive waves of invasion.

This geographic nordic isolation or protection, aided by limited communication in a mountainous country, over the centuries might have biologically led to a not insignificant inbreeding with its negative as well as positive results. The unfortunate results might have created inferior types of people, who would not survive in near-polar living conditions. But the survivors would slowly develop into a fortified, uniform humanity, honed eventually into a biologically well-adapted society.

They were lighthaired and muscular.

The bony architecture of the women's birth canal fitted the comparable size of the head of the unborn creature. Thus our favorable statistics.

She added: do not expect an easy delivery in a country representing, by immigration, a conglomeration of biologically different races. There the obstetricians might be up against an entirely different problem, similar to the ever-recurring one of fitting a square head into a round hole.

Strange as it may seem, such convoluted thoughts raced through my mind at times, trying to find a sculptural form and a tombstone honoring a mother, who was vigorously alive for most of her ninety-two years.

At one point I was quite sure I had it: A monumental structure visually representing a naked bony pelvis. The clay protested—a ridiculous idea.

How about a narrative project, involving drama and triumph?

The challenge is still with me, and I have no valid solution. I have learned that some creations had better be left simmering, or better be left alone. The travel seemingly was coming to a halt.

No. It did not. At times, it seems, ideas get the notion of breaking away from the herd, like young calves making mysterious discoveries during their juvenile safaries.

Thus came about the *Hour of Meditation*.

It is the lamenting son in the outline of an abstraction of a bent-down human shape, spare in detail, heavy in expressive impact, and loaded with a weight pressing against the holy soil upon which it has come to rest.

33″ × 22″ × 19″

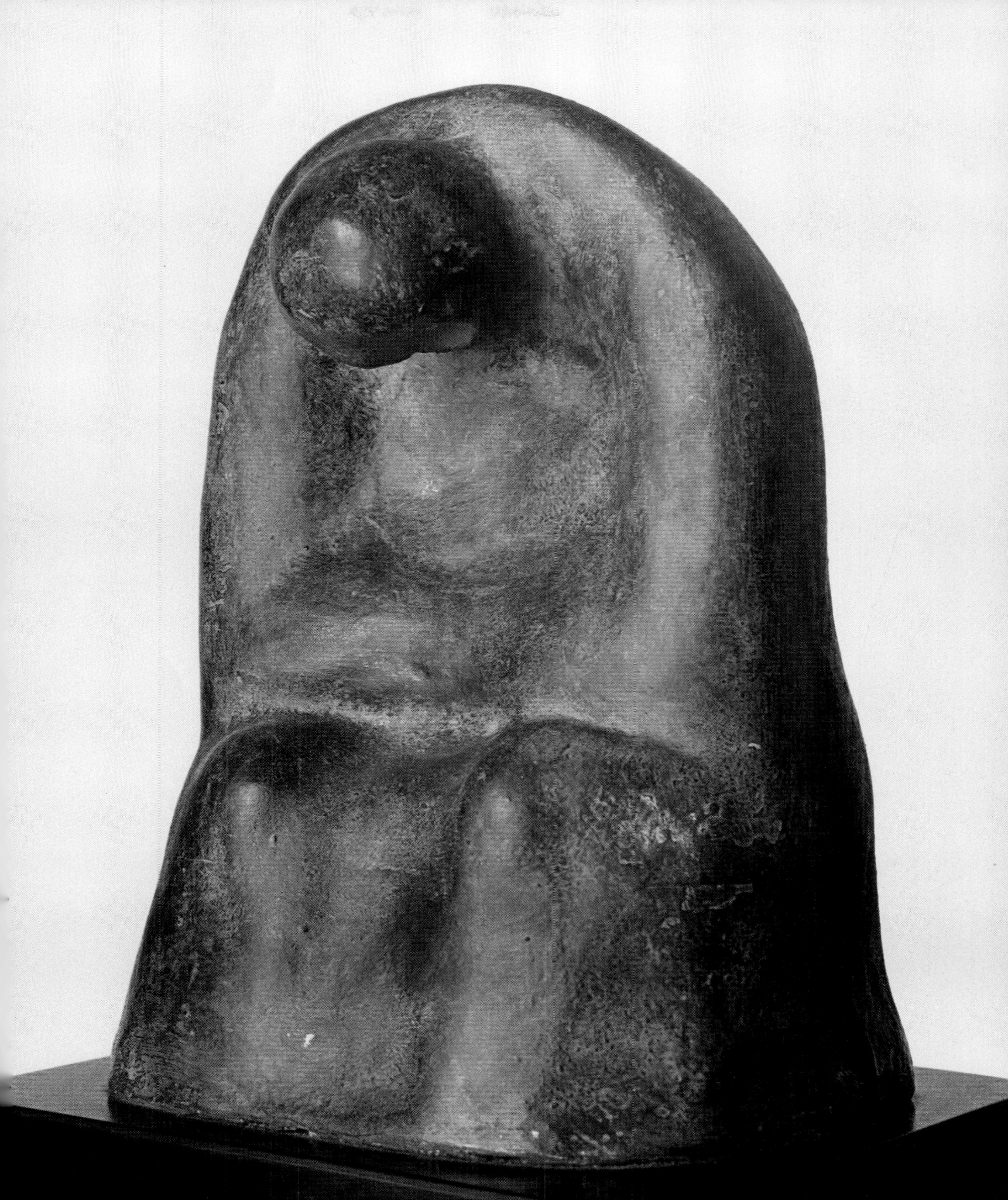

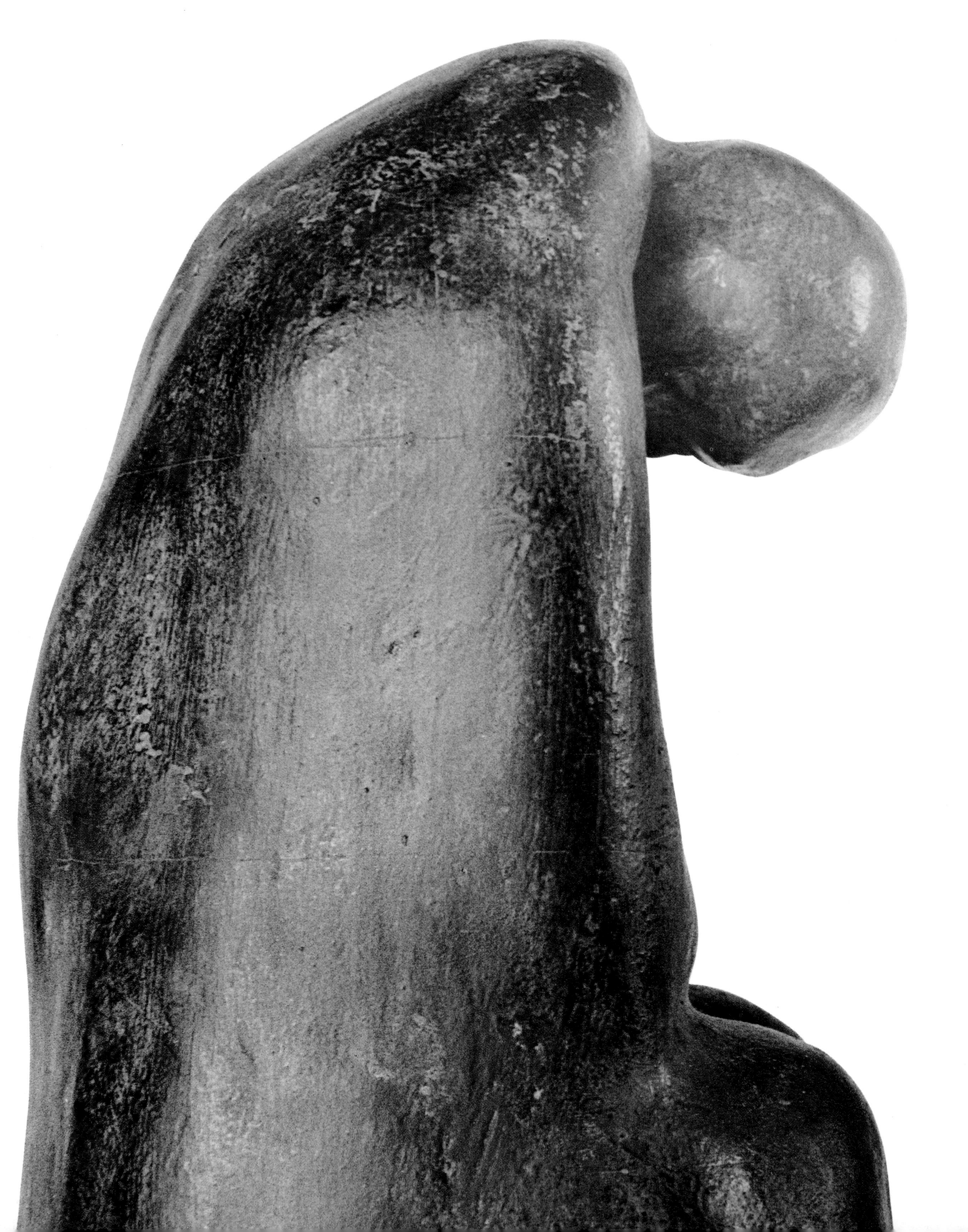

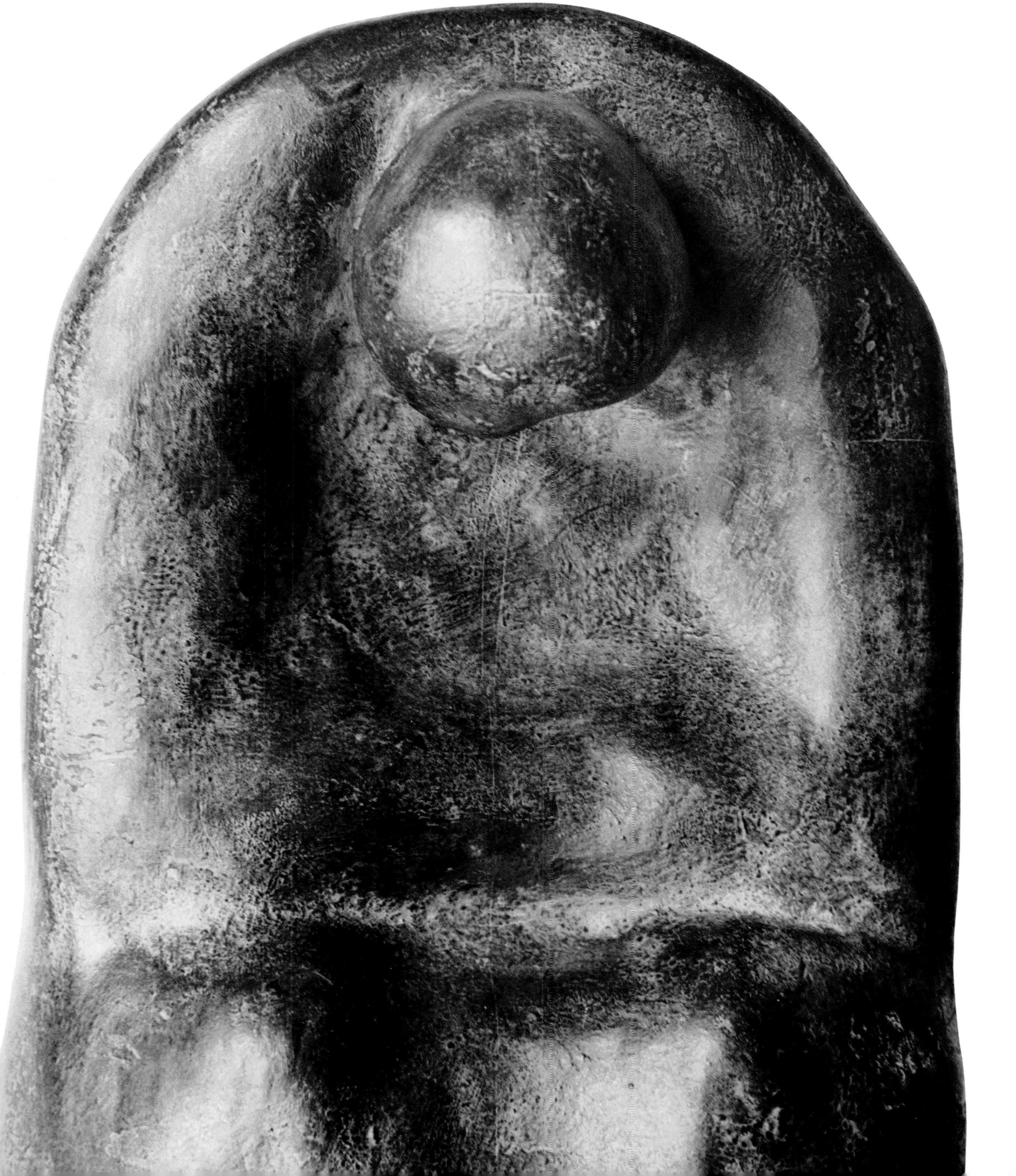

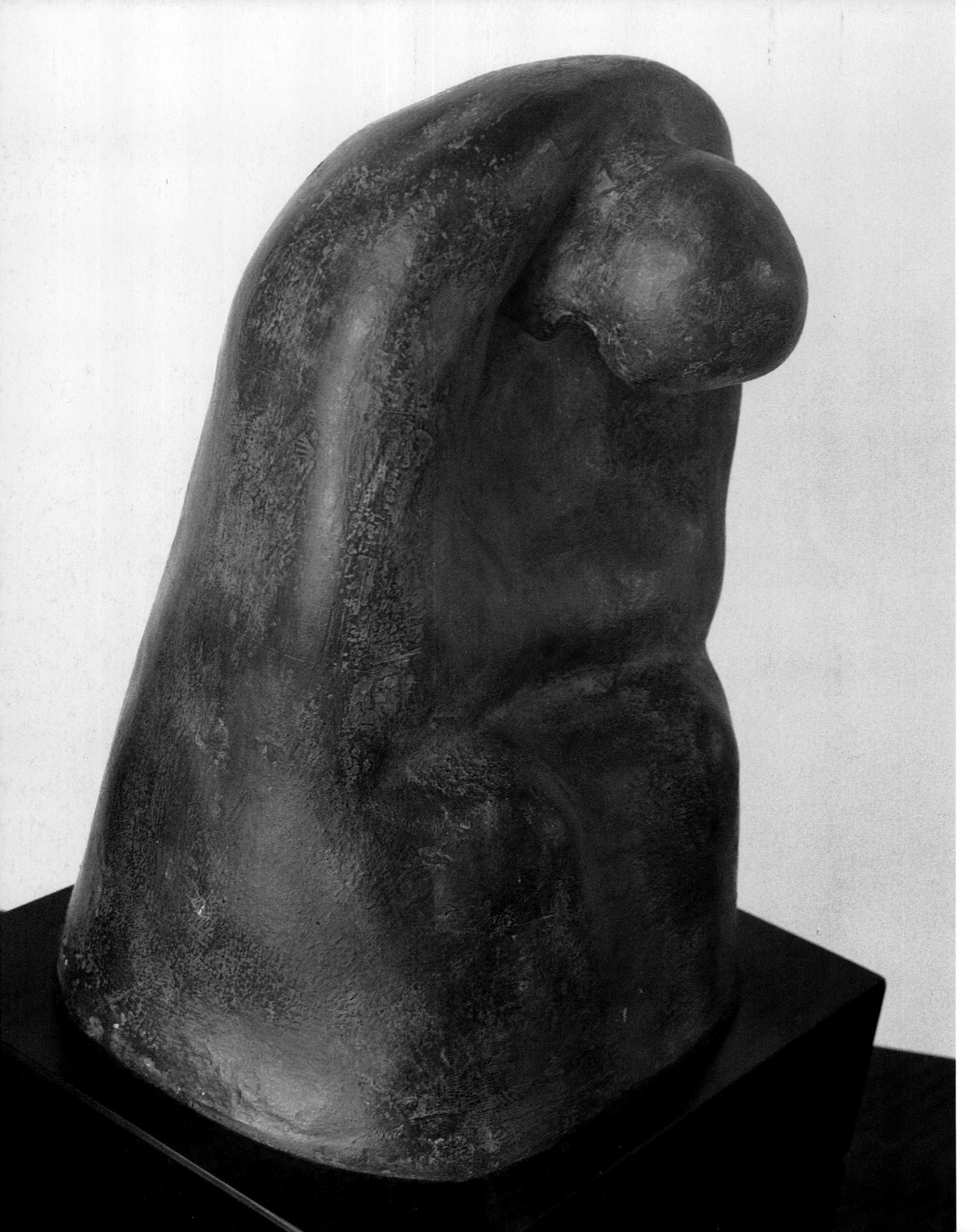

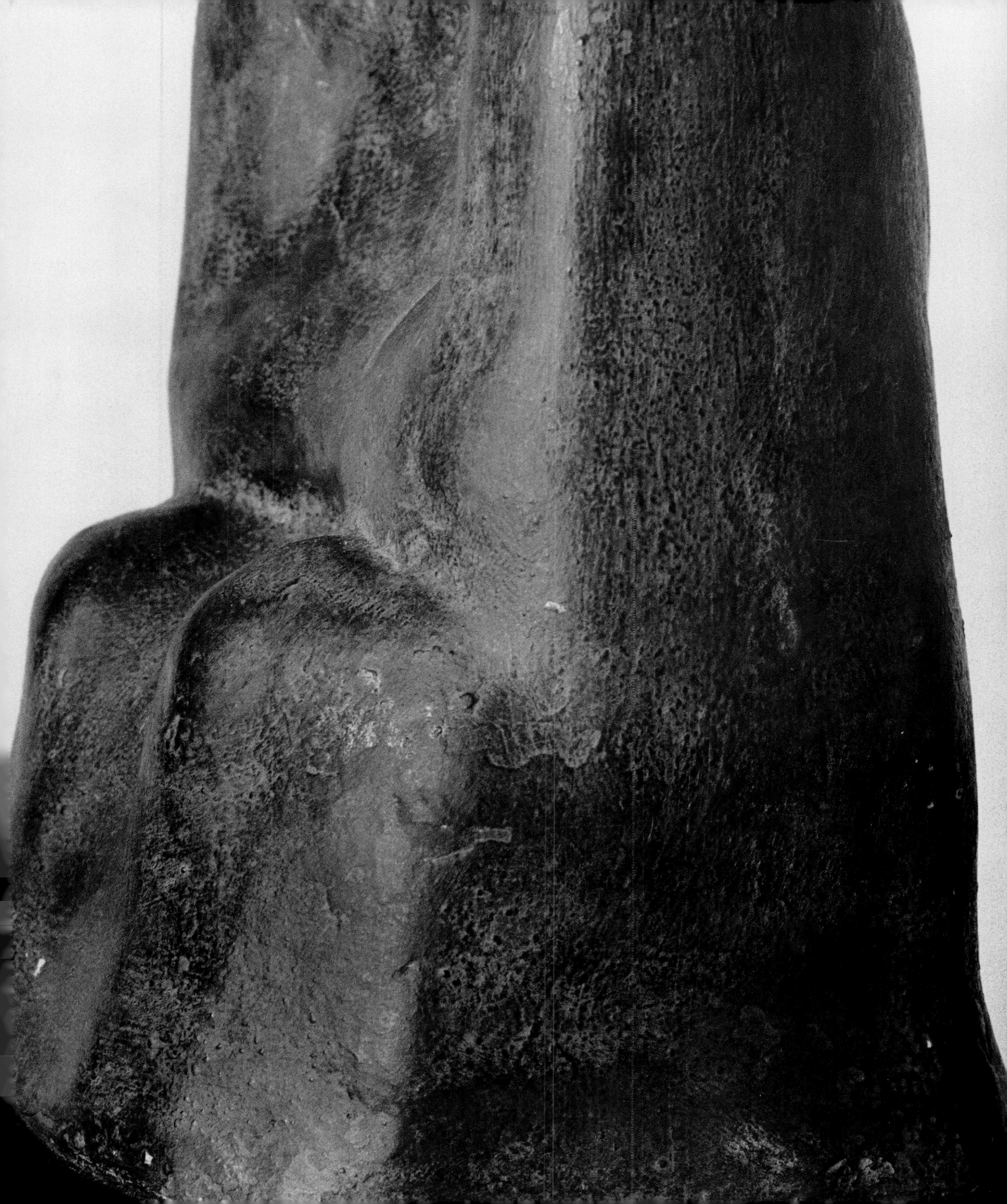

Cancer

A long time ago, soon after I had finished this work, it came to the attention of a good friend of mine who was an outstanding dean of the visual college of one of our universities.

"You must change the title! By retaining it you have significantly limited the scope of this sculpture and related it only to a disease." He stated that the large hand, striking out of nowhere and gripping mercilessly the naked body of a woman while her man valiantly struggled to loosen even one single finger of the combatant hand—this concept and constellation, he felt, eloquently spoke of the overall struggle of mankind trying to stay alive against myriads of antagonists.

His warning has stayed with me. Looking at the larger blueprint, I know he is right. Still, I have not hit upon a different title.

For once I know why I started to work at this group.

Decades of professional activity had brought me face to face with cancer: with those being inflicted by it and with the group of family members being affected by it in so many varied ways often bordering on catastrophe and tragedy.

Together with thousands of my surgical colleagues I could never declare myself unwilling or unable to accept this vital challenge on behalf of those coming to us for advice and assistance. We all knew that at times the surgical knife is the blessed antagonist that has cured cancer and that could, hopefully, do it again and again, while well realizing also the deviously destructive characteristics of the cancer cell.

On occasions we are granted rewards.

Carroll is now forty-three. She has three kids. When she was four years old I operated upon her by removing a rapidly growing cancer of the right kidney invading surrounding blood vessels.

Mrs. Johannesen still sings with the church choir every Sunday. It is thirty-six years after an extensive operation for cancer of the rectum. It could be added that aside from her choir activity she is still going to the bathroom in her own, good, private way.

We are the first to confess there may be a long and arduous road to travel. By enormous efforts and ingenuity, that roadbed seems studded with real advances now. We know that we are underway in the right direction. Still, we are all impatient, admittedly uncertain, and often scared.

It was in this spirit that I completed this sculptural group. It is a somber and helplessly struggling body of two human beings exposed to a universal catastrophe, symbolized by a giant crucifying hand.

A decade and a half after this group was completed cancer invaded our home in a manner more devastating than could ever be expressed by bronze. My wife died from that disease.

We had better hang on to the original title.

I better stick to the worse things I sorrowfully know best.

67″ × 27″ × 30″

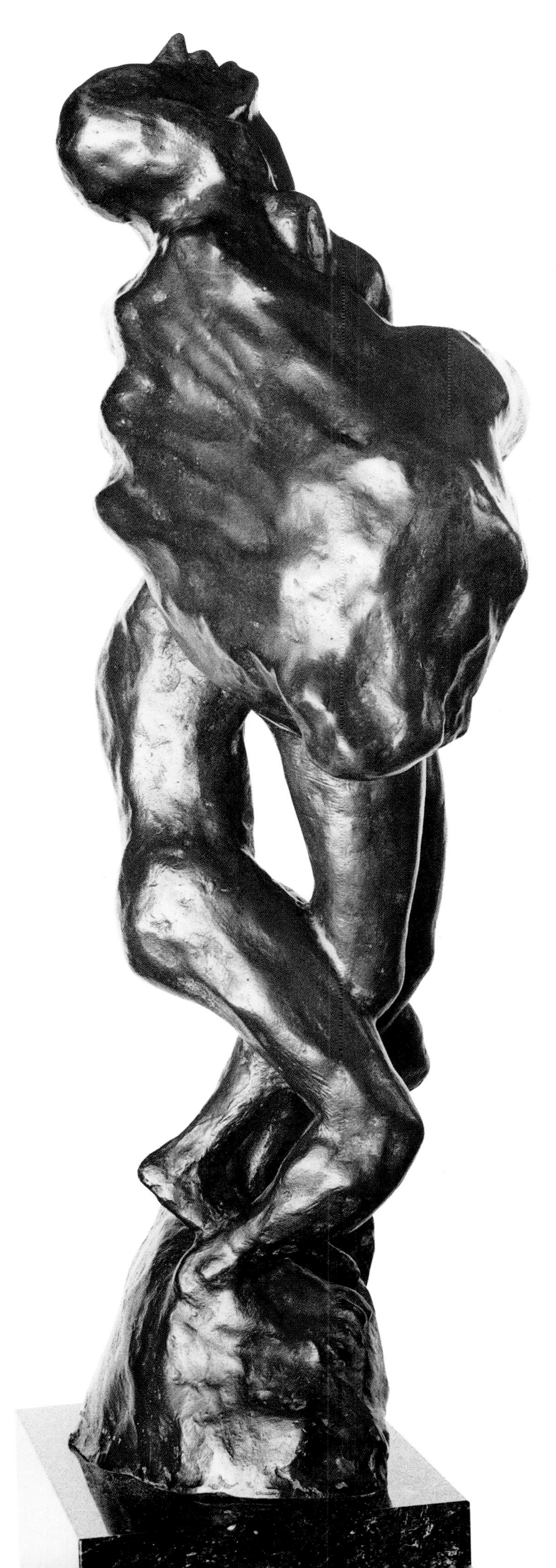

Prophecy

I am a cancer cell.
Of my earliest ancestry no relic remains.
When the earth's first creatures stirred the ancient seas,
When the Pharoahs wrought the pyramids,
When the mediaeval scribes laboriously recorded their dire philosophies,
I was there.

The ingenious Virchow, who recognized my stamp,
Marshalled the forces of science against me.
Malicious, relentless, insidious I am,
Full of hate, ripe for carnage,
Yet in my enduring frame I carry the secret of life.

Study me, Man,
And you will bring into the light of day
Precious urns of wisdom
Long buried in the tomb of ignorance.
For you I shall tell a wondrous tale
Of the beginning of things that are and are to be.

Study me, know me,
And you will hold the world in fief.
Neglect me, Man,
And as surely as the fingers of the dawn
Grasp first the temples of the East,
I will strike you dead.

R.W.C., *1950*

Printed with the permission of R. Lee Clark, M.D.
Anderson Hospital and Tumor Institute, Houston, Texas

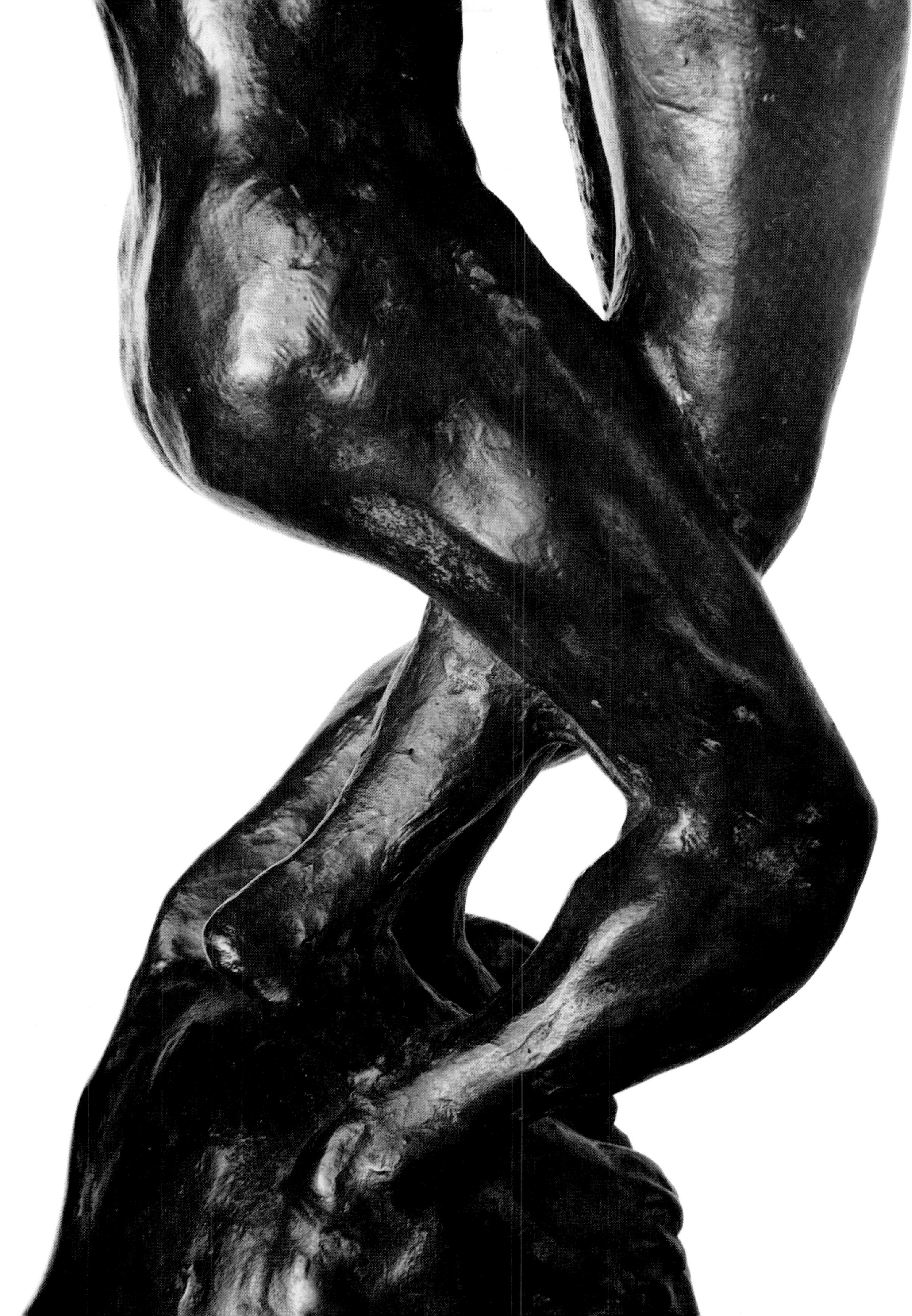

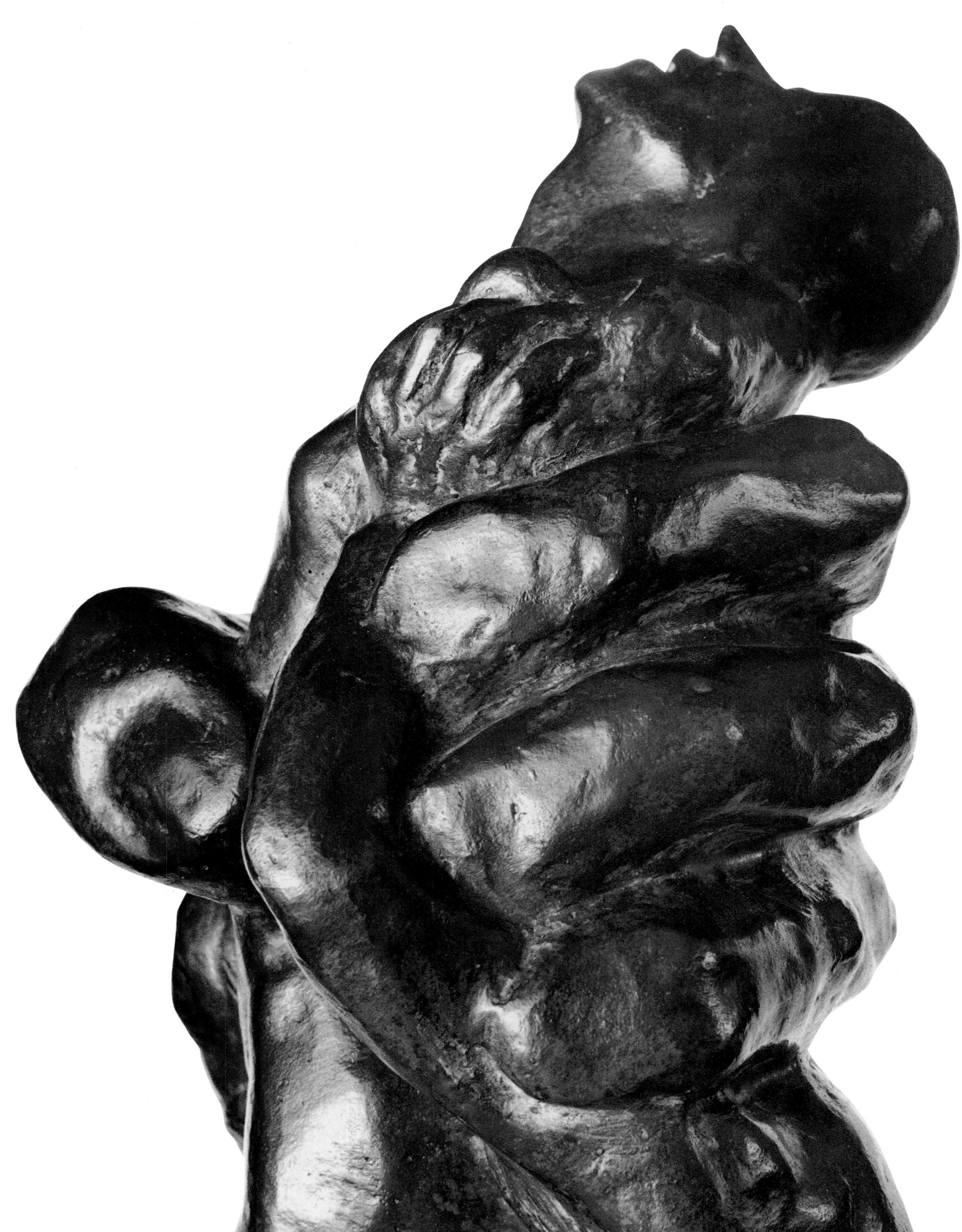

"I never weary of being useful.
I am not tired of serving others."

LEONARDO DA VINCI,
Aphorisms

Credo

At the end of the day
let me know I am free
of remorse and of guilt
for things I have missed
and never reached.

At the end of the year
let me pride in my work
which I charged with my all,
even this, at the end,
was not equal to all.

At the end of the day,
At the end of the year,
Stay firm in my will,
Stay clear in my mind,
Stay warm in my heart.

The things to be done,
even half way worthwhile,
are part of it all
and all is my life.

So serve and create.
So rise and stand tall.

K.K.N., *1986*

PHOTO CREDITS

Photographs by Amy Binder:

In the Sweat of Thy Face Shalt Thou Eat Bread,
Moses, Rodin, The Bifocal Marcel Duchamp,
Nietzche, The Museum Director, The Art Critic,
Homage to Vincent van Gogh, Homage to Paul Gauguin,
The English Barrister, The Poet and Pegasus,
Hamlet, Lamenting Hamlet, Knut Hamsun,
The Death of Savonarola, The Virgin Mary,
My Friend the Village Idiot, Father of the Village Idiot,
My Friend, Spirit of the Dance (*except page 99*),
Dance of the Spirit, Men Against Man (*except pages 108–111*),
The Refugees, The Drinking Horse, Girl With Cap,
Seated Lady with Cap, Dr. Ben Colcock,
Percy Grainger, Edvard Munch, Ultimatum, Viet Nam,
The Caveman, The Surgeon, In Memoriam,
Hour of Meditation, Cancer.

Photographs by Burnett Cross

Frontispiece, Walt Whitman, Pietà, Exodus,
Men Against Man (*pages 108–111*), The Little Horse,
War Poem.

Photograph by Erik Bergmark

Spirit of the Dance (*page 99*)